Cambridge Historical Series

OUTLINES

OF

ENGLISH INDUSTRIAL HISTORY

OUTLINES

OF

ENGLISH INDUSTRIAL HISTORY

BY

W. CUNNINGHAM, D.D., F.B.A.

AND

ELLEN A. MᶜARTHUR, Litt.D.

CAMBRIDGE:
AT THE UNIVERSITY PRESS
1928

CAMBRIDGE UNIVERSITY PRESS
Cambridge, New York, Melbourne, Madrid, Cape Town,
Singapore, São Paulo, Delhi, Mexico City

Cambridge University Press
The Edinburgh Building, Cambridge CB2 8RU, UK

Published in the United States of America by Cambridge University Press, New York

www.cambridge.org
Information on this title: www.cambridge.org/9781107666764

First Edition, 1895
Revised and reprinted 1898, 1904, 1910, 1913, 1920, 1928
First published 1910
First paperback edition 2013

A catalogue record for this publication is available from the British Library

ISBN 978-1-107-66676-4 Paperback

PREFACE.

THIS book, like the remainder of the series of which it is a part, is intended for the use of any persons who may be anxious to understand the nature of existing political conditions; but it differs from the other volumes, inasmuch as it fixes attention on English rather than on European history, and sketches, from one special point of view, the course of events over a very long period of time. It has also been thought unnecessary to give any bibliography of this wide subject, as students who desire to procure further guidance will be able to obtain it from the larger work, on the *Growth of English Industry and Commerce*, published by the Cambridge University Press.

No attempt has been made to depict the condition of English industry and trade with the assistance of maps, but a chronological table has been added, based on a suggestion for which the authors are indebted to Mr Graham Wallas; it is hoped that this may serve to give a conspectus of the subject, and to present in a graphic manner, in point of time and with some slight additions, the course of industrial development as treated in the following pages.

The book was planned before the General Editor undertook the supervision of the series, but the writers have to thank Dr Prothero cordially for many suggestions made during the course of their work.

W. C.
E. A. M.

November 1894.

PREFACE TO THE THIRD EDITION

The whole of the sheets have been carefully revised with a view to bringing this handbook into complete accord with the last (1903) edition of the *Growth of English Industry and Commerce.* Several recent works have also been included in the bibliography which was added in the second edition.

W. C.
E. A. M.

December 1903.

NOTE ON FOURTH EDITION.

In the present edition the text and bibliography have been revised and brought up to date as far as possible.

W. C.
E. A. M.

February 1910.

TABLE OF CONTENTS.

INTRODUCTION.

CHAPTER I.

IMMIGRANTS TO BRITAIN.

CHAPTER II.

PHYSICAL CONDITIONS.

Contents.

CHAPTER III.

The Manors.

CHAPTER IV.

The Towns.

CHAPTER V.

THE BEGINNINGS OF NATIONAL ECONOMIC LIFE.

CHAPTER VI.

THE VARIOUS SIDES OF NATIONAL ECONOMIC LIFE.

I. THE FOOD SUPPLY.

II. INDUSTRIAL LIFE.

III. COMMERCIAL DEVELOPMENT.

IV. ECONOMIC POLICY.

CHAPTER VII.

MONEY, CREDIT, AND FINANCE.

CHAPTER VIII.

AGRICULTURE.

Contents.

CHAPTER IX.

LABOUR AND CAPITAL.

CHAPTER X.

RESULTS OF INCREASED COMMERCIAL INTERCOURSE.

OUTLINES OF ENGLISH INDUS-
TRIAL HISTORY.

INTRODUCTION.

1. THE industrial history of England is a large subject it is the story of the material side of the life of a great nation. English agriculture—with its magnificent breeds of sheep, cattle and horses, and its ingenious implements—is the most enterprising in the world. English manufacturing skill—both in textile fabrics and in hardware—has a high repute in all parts of the globe. English ships traverse the most distant oceans and do the carrying trade for many of our neighbours. Yet all these great developments have come from such very small beginnings that it is not easy to trace the gradual steps by which primitive agriculture, industry and trade have attained their present proportions.

The scope of industrial history.

Industrial History deals with only one aspect of our national life, but the subject is most important. Material needs cannot be neglected or forgotten with impunity in this world. However high his ideals may be, a man must have bread to eat, if he is to enjoy health and strength and be able to devote himself to intellectual and artistic pursuits. Material prosperity too is necessary for a nation, if it is to be a power among other peoples and to exercise

a real influence in the world.   Material prosperity need
not be aimed at as an end in itself, and it has been and may
be misused both by individuals and by nations.   Still it is
well worth having, because it opens up the opportunity,
both to an individual and to a nation, of leading a noble
and influential life.   It does not, in itself, constitute greatness, but it is a condition without which national greatness is
impossible.   Hence the story of the material progress of
England gives us a means of surveying the opportunities
which Englishmen have enjoyed in the past, and are
enjoying to-day, and also of realising our responsibilities as
a nation.

2.   The subject is both vast and complicated.   No
Man and his part of it can be fully treated in a volume
surroundings. of *Outlines*, and some topics can hardly be
touched on at all.   It is well, therefore, to forewarn the
reader at once, as to the method of treating the subject
which has been adopted in the following pages.   In the
opening chapters (§§ 6—22) attention is called to two elements which are involved in all material progress.   There
is need, on the one hand, of the skill and energy of human
beings, and on the other of appropriate physical conditions
for the exercise of these rational powers.   We must think
of *man*, and also of his *environment*,—the active worker,
and the things with and upon which he works.   In tracing
English material progress we must go back to the time when
the English race was transplanted to this island, and note
the different elements which have since been grafted on
that stock.   It is curious to observe how often and how
effectively that race has been replenished with fresh blood
and alien elements.   (Chapter I.)

We must also turn our attention to the surroundings
in which and on which this much mingled race has worked.

Climate and soil have had much to do with our agricultural development. Easy internal communications and rich mineral products have been important factors in our industrial progress, while our maritime position and the mere character of the coast-line have favoured our advance as a naval power. (Chapter II.) Human energy and material conditions have co-operated together at every step of progress, and it is by their united working that the whole result has been attained.

3. These elements have not, however, worked casually and blindly. There has been *conscious and* Social groups *deliberate effort* throughout the whole story. and individuals. Men have set different objects before them; sometimes an advantage that lay but a little way a-head, sometimes a far-reaching scheme. With these different aims before them, they have seriously set themselves to apply human skill to available conditions, and many of their schemes have involved combined effort, and could not be accomplished by individuals singly and alone. If we are to follow out these conscious efforts, we must try to realise the different forms of social organisation which have been employed for economic purposes in the past. To understand earlier history, and to appreciate the interest of primitive or medieval institutions which survive in our own times, we must divest ourselves of many of our ordinary habits of thought and lay aside the assumptions we usually make in the present day. Not till comparatively recent times has there been complete economic unity in England, or the possibility of a free flow of labour and capital to different parts of the country. Neither the free play of individual enterprise nor of competition was possible in primitive society, while State interference was equally unthought of, when there was no effective central government. For centuries each little village was a more or less

isolated community which catered successfully for its own wants, and carried on infrequent and occasional intercourse with other places. In examining the history of the manors (Chapter III) we see that the ideal of the prudent man in the thirteenth century was to render his own estate self-sufficing, and thus to keep it apart from the rest of the realm. The towns, as they grew up (Chapter IV), pursued a somewhat similar policy. Under these circumstances it is difficult to say much of the condition or progress of England as a whole until the time of Richard II, when the growth of a national economic life (Chapter V) had so far advanced that we can describe it and trace its subsequent developments in different directions.

During the fourteenth and preceding centuries we have to deal chiefly with the condition and progress of different manors, or of towns, each of which was then economically distinct from the rest. From the fourteenth century onwards these local organisations have come to be of less economic importance; they have long since ceased to be more than subsidiary elements in English economic life. From the time of Richard II we can follow the gradual growth of national organisation until it exercised effective control over all the various developments of industrial life throughout the country (Chapter VI); and we can examine the aims which came to be more clearly recognised. In the time of Elizabeth, the period of transition was over. Laws and institutions were devised for the regulation of grazing and tillage, of industry and commerce, and a definite scheme of economic policy was carefully thought out and deliberately pursued. The efforts to modify and maintain it under changing circumstances eventually proved impracticable. Adam Smith showed that such efforts at regulating industry in the national interest were no longer beneficial, and during the first half of the present century attempts of the kind were deliberately discarded.

4. The description of the types of organisation which have existed in England, and which have been Direction of superseded in turn, serves to bring out the change. economic structure of society at different periods. It is also desirable to notice the direction and the nature of the changes which have occurred in the great departments of economic life; in the use of money and in finance (Chapter VII), in agriculture (Chapter VIII), and in manufacture (Chapter IX). The subject of money and the medium of exchange comes in the forefront, and dominates the whole for a very simple reason. The general course of economic change of every kind in England may be most easily summarised by saying that the use of money and of bargaining has gradually permeated every department of life; each has been reconstituted under this influence. The changes from natural to money economy are most obviously exemplified in the affairs of state; but the increased prevalence of money bargaining has been a most powerful factor in the change from customary to competition prices; in the introduction first of capitalist pasture farming and then of capitalist tillage (Chapter VIII); and in that intervention of capital in industry which made more minute division of labour possible and led the way for the industrial revolution (Chapter IX). In the concluding chapter an attempt is made to show how this thorough-going money economy, exemplified in the freedom of commercial intercourse, has reacted on social institutions and brought into being the anxious problems of the present day.

5. The story of the past is full of varied interest, but there is one aspect in which it appeals with special force. It gives us a clue to unravel much that is strange and

difficult in the present day.   Our existing society is the
outcome of the life of preceding ages.   Much
The Present of its evil, as well as much of what is best
and the Past. in it, is a heritage from our forefathers.
Hence we are forced to turn to the past if we wish to
understand how present conditions have arisen.   We may
often have to go back a long distance in time if we would
trace out the factors which have combined to produce
the economic *régime* under which we live.   It has been a
constant aim, in compiling the following pages, to explain
to some extent the genesis of the present by a study of the
past.   The story has been carried on to a point at which
some of the great problems of our own day loom into sight;
and occasionally an opinion on matters in dispute has been
hazarded with a view to indicating how closely the experience of the past is connected with the struggles that lie
before us.   Whether the future shall confirm the opinions
here expressed or not, they will at least serve to illustrate
the importance of trying to view our new difficulties in the
light of experience drawn from bygone times.   We may
see how the new problems have arisen, and how similar
difficulties have been met, while we may also be saved the
disappointment of trying a road which has been already
proved impracticable.

It may be hoped, however, that some readers will not
be satisfied with these brief outlines, but will feel the
fascination of trying to understand the past so strongly, as
to wish to advance to a fuller knowledge of the industrial
and commercial life of our forefathers.   There are many books
easily procurable in which they can find additional information on every one of the subjects touched upon.   Professor
Ashley's *Economic History* contains most interesting chapters
on the Middle Ages.   The *Discourse of the Common Weal*

gives a vivid picture of the transition in Tudor times, and this, as the work of a contemporary author, is of peculiar interest. Mr Rowland Prothero's *Pioneers and Progress of English Farming* and Mr and Mrs Sidney Webb's *History of Trade Unionism* deal with aspects of the recent history of rural and of manufacturing industry.

Others may perhaps wish, not so much to extend their reading on particular points as to know the grounds for the various statements made in this volume. Authorities have been rarely mentioned in these pages, because it is easy for anyone to find them by referring to the same topics as treated in the *Growth of English Industry and Commerce.* This larger book gives fuller information on many points, and will, at any rate, serve as a guide to those who are anxious to get to the solid rock, and to base their knowledge on a study of original authorities.

CHAPTER I.

IMMIGRANTS TO BRITAIN.

6. ENGLISH HISTORY may be said to begin with the
The English invasion of the Roman province of Britain by
Conquest. Teutonic bands about 449 A.D. The progress
of the English invaders was slow; nearly one hundred and
thirty years elapsed before they had cleared the Western
Midlands, before, in fact, the land of the English took a
definite and, to some extent, a permanent shape. The
Romanised Britons, or Welsh, were confined in Wales and
Cornwall or were driven back towards the northern part of
the island. It is a great question how far the English conquest was complete, or how far elements of Roman civilisation survived through the period of the barbarian invasions,
as was the case in some other parts of Europe. But though
some few names and terms were embodied in the new
speech, and some groups of inhabitants continued to exist
as elements in the new social order, the evidence drawn
from language, religion and law combines to show that
hardly anything of Roman civilisation survived. This conclusion is confirmed by other considerations, for archæo-
logical evidence seems to show that the towns were either
deserted or destroyed. Where so much was swept away it

seems unlikely that agriculture as practised in the Roman *vills* would survive. We have no sufficient evidence that these vills were the direct ancestors of our English villages, or that there was continuity in rural life from the period of Roman domination to subsequent times.

On the whole it appears that the conquest of England was so far complete, that the basis of our civilisation may be said to be Teutonic. Whatever elements of an earlier civilisation were absorbed by the English invaders were very few. There were of course some. In the Forest of Dean and near the Peak of Derbyshire the old inhabitants probably continued to pursue their avocations under new masters. In many households there might be domestic slaves, who maintained some tradition of the old arts, language, and religion, but these elements appear to have been comparatively slight, and to have had little effect on the growth of the newly transplanted English stock.

The completeness of the change from the civilisation of the Roman province to the simple life of the English tribes does not, however, seem so surprising, if we remember that society in the province of Britain was much disintegrated before the English invasion began. Besides this, the conquest of the invaders was so gradual that the Romanised Britons were able to withdraw before the foe, and were thus saved from the necessity of submitting to the alternatives of slavery or death.

7. Although the English settlers seemed to absorb so little from their precursors in Britain, they did   The Roman not long remain unaffected by outside in-   missionaries. fluence. The British Christians, who had been ousted or driven to the West, appear to have held aloof from their conquerors; but the missionary zeal of the Columban monasteries in the North and of the Bishop of Rome himself, was soon

brought to bear upon the heathen English. It is one of the
most striking instances of the manner in which religious
and economic progress have been connected. The communication, which was opened with much searching of heart
as a dangerous religious duty, came to be of the first importance for trading and other purposes. England, when con-
verted to Christianity, though insular was no longer isolated.
The monastic houses were centres of learning as well as
of religion; and the legal conceptions of the later Roman
Empire, introduced under ecclesiastical influence, affected
the charters and wills. The frequent communication of
churchmen with Rome was combined with opportunities
for trade, and did something for the improvement of the
arts of life. The very remains which survived from the
Roman occupation of Britain were now turned to better
purpose; the ruins of Roman ramparts and towns afforded
building materials, while their military roads and bridges
were available for internal communication. Under Christian
influence the English tribes came to be more definitely
organised under kingly rule, while frequent and friendly
communication with more civilised neighbours became
possible.

8. Very different in character was the next influence
which was brought to bear upon the English.
They were attacked by their kinsfolk, the
Danes and Northmen, and at first it appeared
as if their settled life and new organisation had unfitted them
to hold the land which their fathers had conquered. The
Northmen came at first as plunderers to ravage. The
coasts were defenceless, for Englishmen seemed to have lost
their old skill in seamanship, and the Northmen were even
able to sail up the rivers, and to carry on their depredations
in the very heart of the country. The English rallied under

The Danes and North-men.

Alfred (871—901), and after a struggle peace was made with the new invaders. Nearly half the country was treated as Danelagh, since it was occupied by Danish rather than by English inhabitants, and was ruled by Danish rather than by English law.

Peace was soon followed by a practical amalgamation, and then it became apparent how much the English gained by the infusion of this new element. The English were satisfied with rural life; they were little attracted by the towns which the Romans had built, and they did not devote themselves to commercial pursuits or to the manufacture of goods for sale. The Danes, though so closely allied in race, appear to have been men of a different type. They were great as traders and also as seamen. We may learn how great their prowess was from the records of their voyages to Iceland, Greenland, and America, from the accounts of their expeditions to the White Sea and the Baltic, and from their commerce with such distant places as the Crimea and Arabia. Their settlements in this country were among the earliest of the English towns to exhibit signs of activity. Not only were the Danes traders; they were also skilled in metal-work and other industrial pursuits. England has attained a character for her shipping and has won the supremacy of the world in manufacturing; it almost seems as if she were indebted on those sides of life, on which she is most successful, to the fresh energy and enterprise en-grafted by Danish settlers and conquerors. By the efforts of Roman missionaries she had been brought into contact with remains of Roman civilisation, but by the infusion of the Danish element she was drawn into close connexion with the most energetic of the Northern races.

9. The next great immigration into England was due to men who were closely allied to the Danes, but who had,

for some time, been settled on the Southern side of the
English Channel. With the accession of
Norman soldiers and immigrants.
Edward the Confessor, Norman influence
began to make itself felt in England. Norman
fashions were in vogue at court, and Norman or Burgundian
artisans apparently settled in considerable numbers on English
soil, but after Duke William had established his position
as English king, this immigration seems to have taken place
on a much larger scale. Domesday Book shows that many
English estates were held by Continental barons, and in
their households or on their lands there would be employment for many of their followers. We know that a number of
Flemings were attracted to the land whither Queen Matilda
had gone, and there can be little doubt that the same sort
of tie would lead many to settle on the new estates of the
Norman tenants-in-chief.

But though this incursion of foreign artisans was important, it was not the most striking economic result of the
Norman Conquest. The Continental possessions of the
English kings were so wide that the kingdom came to be
one province of a large realm. Her destinies were inextricably
involved with European politics, and even when she regained
her insular character, by the loss of Anjou and Normandy,
she still continued to be a part of the European system.
The ecclesiastical connexion with Rome had come to be
far closer in regard to many matters of church government
and ecclesiastical taxation. The intellectual and religious
movements of Europe were felt in our island ; the rate of
progress varied considerably in different lands, but the course
of economic development was similar in many ways. The
rise of the religious orders, the influence of the Crusades,
the growth of municipalities, the devastations of pestilence,
the revival of learning, the discovery of the New World, the

growth of nationalities, were events which affected the whole of Christendom, and produced similar economic results in many lands. And it was with the Norman Conquest that England entered for the first time into the common life of Christian Europe.

10. If the first two centuries of Norman and Plantagenet rule were important because of the new relations with the rest of Christendom, they were also marked by great changes within the realm. Before the reign of Edward I the new *The consolidation of the English nation.* elements introduced subsequently to the Battle of Hastings (1066) had practically coalesced with the English and the Danish immigrants to form one people. This united race had common institutions; there was one Parliament in which the different parts of the country and the different classes of the community were at last represented, and the broad lines of national life and development were clearly defined. This consolidation of national life had its counterpart in the consolidation of municipal life as well, for during the twelfth and thirteenth centuries the various elements which had existed side by side in different towns combined, and old internal jealousies gave way to popular municipal government. The towns, like the nation, thus came to have an organic life and free institutions.

11. The national and town life of Englishmen was thus constituted and organised under Edward I, and there has never been since then a large incursion of foreign conquerors, or of aliens who came in the train of a conqueror. But for *Influx of weavers under Edward III, Elizabeth, and later.* all that the immigration of foreigners has continued time after time. Definite political or economic reasons have attracted settlers to this country, and they have sometimes

been gladly welcomed by the government as useful, though extraneous, elements.

(*a*)   The first of these immigrations was that of the Flemings, who were invited to this country by Edward III. The fact that England was a wool-producing country, and supplied the raw material for the Flemish manufacturers brought England at an early time into close relations with the Low Countries.   Edward III, who was keenly alive to commercial considerations in all his political undertakings, appears to have seen that it would be possible, and ultimately profitable, to transplant the manufacture from Flanders to England, while local disturbances rendered many of the artisans willing to come. Though there had, doubtless, been much weaving in this country in the twelfth and thirteenth centuries, the trade appears to have received an impetus in consequence of this new immigration and to have grown rapidly, so that a very large proportion of the English wool-clip was subsequently retained for manufacture at home.

(*b*)   There is some reason to believe that a considerable number of Italians and other aliens were naturalised in this country towards the end of the fifteenth century, but the next great immigration occurred during the Reformation period. In the time of Edward VI some foreign Protestants were established at Glastonbury, and though England ceased to be a refuge for them in the succeeding reign, large numbers came over during the reign of Elizabeth.   They were settled chiefly in Colchester, Norwich, and in Kent.   As the victims of the Duke of Alva they were warmly welcomed by the government. In the towns, where they were allowed to settle, and where they competed effectively with less skilled native workmen, they were regarded with somewhat different feelings.   Their influence on the trade of these places was however soon found to be sufficiently beneficial to allay the

apprehensions with which the new comers had been originally regarded.

(*c*)   The Revocation of the Edict of Nantes in 1685
caused a considerable wave of emigration from France.
Many of the Southern silk-workers and of the Northern linen-
weavers were Huguenots, and the popular indignation at
their expulsion prepared a warmer welcome for them in
England than they might otherwise have received.   The
silk-weavers settled chiefly at Spitalfields, at Coventry and
at Macclesfield, and as the trade they practised was but
little known in England they do not seem to have given
rise to so much local jealousy.   The linen-weavers were
diffused more widely, and they too found few English com-
petitors; their numbers were increased by a similar immigration in 1709, when many families from the Palatinate,
some of them in the direst distress, found their way to our
shores.   Some of these destitute aliens were passed on to
the colonies, while others were planted as linen-weavers in
Ireland and in Scotland, the two parts of the United Kingdom where flax was most readily obtained.

12. It is easy to see that English civilisation has gained
much from the extraneous elements which   Effects   on
have at various times been absorbed in it. It   industrial life.
has gained in disposition and character.   The curiously
mixed race has been able to take advantage of new opportunities and to utilise new physical conditions, but it has
also gained in manual skill.   Before the age of machinery,
success in manufacturing depended on the dexterity, often
the inherited dexterity, of artisans.   However much Edward
III might have desired to improve English workmanship,
he could not have done it except by importing more skilful
workmen.

With each of these successive waves of immigration some

trade was introduced, or was at all events so much developed that it seemed to be a new thing.   From the time of Edward III we have the manufacture of heavy English broadcloth, known as the 'old drapery.'   In Elizabeth's reign we find the introduction of the 'new drapery'—serges and other light goods, or mixed goods like poplins—while, in the seventeenth century, the silk trade and the linen trade took a fresh start.   All these were industries which offered employment to large numbers, and gave rise to elaborate organisation; there were also many minor manufactures, such as the making of paper and of earthenware, and im provements in cutlery, which were introduced by Flemish or Huguenot refugees.   Thus it is hardly too much to say that these immigrants laid the foundations of England's industrial greatness in more than one department.

There is also some reason to believe that they exercised an important influence on our industrial institutions.   It is in the Danish towns, with their artisan population, that the first germs of municipal self-government occur; and shortly after the Norman Conquest we find the first traces of those craft gilds, which were, in various shapes, such important industrial authorities for many centuries. The germs of banking and insurance appear to have come from Italian merchants settled in this country.   If we turn to other spheres we see that conscious and deliberate imitation of the Dutch affected English finance in the seventeenth century; while Dutch engineers and drainers had a large hand in recovering the Fens.   If England has attained to industrial and commercial supremacy, it is, in some measure, because she has succeeded in attracting to herself the most energetic and enterprising, as well as the most highly skilled, portions of the population of neighbouring lands.

CHAPTER II.

PHYSICAL CONDITIONS.

13. IT might seem easy enough to describe the physical features of any portion of the globe, and especially of a little island like ours, but it is not quite easy to point out their precise economic importance. The precise economic

The relative character of natural resources.

value of physical advantages depends on the skill and energy which characterise the inhabitants of any particular country. Natural resources are relative to human capabilities. There may be much mineral wealth, which is worthless, either because it has never been discovered, or because the inhabitants have not metallurgical skill to work it. In the same way the opportunities offered by good harbours, or a fertile soil, are thrown away on any race that does not profit by them. It has been the good fortune of Britain that her various conquerors and settlers, as well as the various immigrants who have reinforced them at different times, should have brought together different and fresh kinds of skill, which could find new advantage in the physical conditions of the country. Physical conditions afford opportunities to those who can use them. Physical barriers are obstacles to men who have not the skill and patience to

overcome them.   In this country they have served rather to
affect the lines on which English civilisation has developed
than to call forth its original vigour, or to give it additional
impetus.

14.   Long before the time of the English settlement,
Britain was visited by Phœnician or Carthaginian traders, who came to the Scilly
Isles and Cornwall to procure tin.   Of all
the mineral products of England this seems
to have been the one which was first worked for purposes of
trade, and all through the Middle Ages tin, together with
lead, was one of the chief articles of the export trade.   The
lead of Derbyshire was undoubtedly worked by the Romans.
They also carried on iron-mining and smelting in the Forest
of Dean, and the mineral wealth, thus discovered and utilised
before the English invasion, continued to be utilised throughout the history of the conquering race.

More important for English trade than any metals, have
been the large beds of coal found in many parts of the
country.   The Romans used this fuel in the camps on the
line of Hadrian's wall, and the Northumberland and Durham
seams have been worked time out of mind.   The coal was
so near the coast that it could be readily shipped, and in
the sixteenth and seventeenth centuries it came to be the
source upon which London relied for a supply of fuel.
In the eighteenth century the invention of the blast furnace
rendered it possible to use coal for smelting iron, and this
led to an enormous expansion of the coal and iron trades.
Steam power was first utilised for industrial and commercial
purposes about the same time, and the possession of an
enormous coal supply gave England an opportunity of taking
the lead in the application of machinery to manufacture and
to shipping.

Marginal note: Mineral wealth. Tin, lead, coal and iron.

15. While these mineral products have been of importance, English prosperity has been largely due to the products of the soil. Britain was a fertile province, which served as one of the granaries of the Roman Empire. There have been times when the art of agriculture has progressed but slowly, and when there has been some temporary exhaustion of the soil. On the whole, however, the skill of the farmer has advanced along with the new demands made on it by succeeding ages; and the produce per acre of land under crop is probably larger now than it has ever been in bygone times. Here and there land has gone out of cultivation, but considerable additions have been made to the cultivable area by embanking the sea and draining the fens, while the nineteenth century system of thorough drainage has greatly increased the facilities for working the land profitably.

Suitability for tillage and forestry.

Much of the land that is now cultivated was at one time occupied by woods and forests. These had a high economic value while they lasted. They provided a fuel which was easier to work and pleasanter to burn than coal can ever be. In many places wood was the only fuel procurable, until the construction of canals rendered the midland coalfields generally available. The forests also gave a wealth of materials for building the old-fashioned houses, which are so fast passing away, as well as for constructing ships. Though substitutes of various kinds have been found for these materials, it may still be a matter of regret that the forests were so recklessly used up. The chief blame for this extravagance probably rests with the iron manufacturers in the seventeenth and eighteenth centuries. The exhaustion of the soil is an evil from which recovery is possible within a comparatively brief period, but the waste or destruction of natural woods and forests cannot be so rapidly replaced.

16.   England has also been a great wool-growing country.

Pasture-
farming and
grazing.   This was the case, to some extent, during the period before the Norman Conquest, but it was not until the twelfth century that English sheep-farming became important. This development occurred chiefly in the North of England, where land, unoccupied since the devastations of the Conqueror's days (1069), could be easily and profitably used for the breeding of large flocks. The Cistercians, for whom many houses were founded in the twelfth century, devoted themselves more especially to this avocation, and merchants from Lucca and other Italian towns, as well as from the Low Countries, soon afterwards engaged in trafficking for their wool. Pasture-farming continued to increase, and in the sixteenth century such a high price could be obtained for wool, that it led to a great development of sheep-farming at the expense of tillage. With the development of the arts of manufacture, a time came when but little wool was exported in its raw state. English breeds of sheep were highly prized from early times, and the quality of their wool was considered to give England a practical monopoly in certain branches of the clothing trades. The importance of the wool was so great that it has overshadowed and obscured the great advantages which England derived from her pastures by the breeding and rearing of cattle. They were a considerable source of food, and served for the victualling of ships; but, besides this, the leather trades have been an important element in English prosperity from medieval times. Hides, wool, woolfells and lead were staple commodities in the time of Edward III, but cattle farming contributed to our wealth before that period, for butter and cheese appear to have been ordinary exports soon after the Norman Conquest.

17.   Even more important, in some aspects, than the

products of the land, has been the harvest of the sea. Fish abounds on all the English coasts, but the herring fishery off the Norfolk coast has been of special value. The take of the herring fleet was in early times disposed of on the beach at Yarmouth, where the town grew up as an adjunct to the fishery. In Tudor times, when serious efforts were made to develop English shipping, special attention was devoted to the fishing trades as a school for seamanship. The aptitude thus fostered was, doubtless, of service in distant expeditions, and may help to account for the acknowledged superiority, which England obtained, from the first, among the fishing fleets off Newfoundland.

Fisheries and seamanship.

18. While England has these various advantages for industries of different kinds, she is also well provided with natural facilities for commerce. Throughout the Southern, Eastern, and Midland Counties, where the wealth of the country was concentrated in earlier times, there are no great mountain ranges to offer serious obstacles to intercommunication. Engineering difficulties in the making of roads have, therefore, not been formidable, and the main lines of communication were well served by the great Roman roads, which formed the most important part of the English inheritance from Roman Britain. The maintenance of roads and bridges was one of the strictest obligations, which fell upon all landowners in feudal times, and from this not even the most favoured tenants were exempted. But much was also done by the monastic houses, and by private individuals as acts of piety. In the fifteenth century when there was much local disorganisation, the roads fell into a worse condition than had been the case in earlier days. So far as we can judge there was little improvement, despite some occasional efforts, till

Roads, rivers, and canals.

the eighteenth century, when the matter was seriously taken
in hand. A general Highway Act was passed (1741) and
so successfully enforced that the first twenty years of George
III's reign showed a remarkable change in the possibilities
for intercommunication, not only in good weather, but in
bad. The progress then made has been maintained, while
the invention of Macadam (1816) and the skill of Telford
and other English engineers brought the roads, in coaching
days, to a very high standard of excellence.

The physical conditions which rendered road-making
comparatively easy have given a character to English rivers.
They are not rapid torrents, but streams working their way
along level plains or in broad valleys towards the sea.
Many of them are tidal to a considerable distance inland,
thus affording sufficient depth of water for sea-going ships,
and providing a current which diminishes the labour of
working up the stream. Water traffic gives the easiest facilities for the carrying of heavy goods, and more than one of
the great fairs of England, like those of Stourbridge and
St Ives, were held near a convenient water-way.

Communication with Holland in the seventeenth century caused Englishmen to turn their attention, especially
in the period succeeding the Restoration, to the improvement of their water-ways; but not until a hundred years
later was much done to improve the rivers or to use them
as feeders for canals. The success of the Manchester and
Worsley canal was, however, a great encouragement to this
kind of enterprise. The chief towns of England were
brought into connexion with one another by canals, and
communication by water was established between the principal river-basins. The new facilities for traffic gave opportunity for the profitable working of coal in many districts,
from which it could not previously have been conveyed to

market; and the development of the South Yorkshire and Derbyshire fields followed as the result of these improved methods of transit.

19.   In the latter part of the eighteenth century water came to be of new importance, not only in   Water connexion with internal commerce, but for   power. manufacture as well.   Water power had been used from time immemorial for corn-mills, and it was also employed in the fulling and dressing of cloth.   But during the last century, with the progress of invention, it came to be rendered available for various manufactures, so that there was a migration of industrial enterprise to those districts where abundant water power was obtainable.   Both the hardware and the textile trades were susceptible to this attraction.   For iron smelting, water power was needed to produce a sufficient blast for the furnaces.   It was also found that the power for driving the machinery employed in the processes of preparing the wool and also in finishing and dressing the cloth, gave a fresh advantage to the clothing trades of Gloucestershire and Yorkshire; business migrated to these districts, and the old-established industries of the Eastern Counties were completely ruined.   When power spinning and power weaving came to supersede hand-labour, water was the agent which was first employed to drive the new machines.   Steam eventually superseded water power; for it could be easily increased at will, and the constancy of the supply could be reckoned on with certainty.   But, though this was the case in later times, the physical distribution of water power did not a little, in the first instance, to determine the localisation of the principal English industries.

20.   If the course of English history has   Insular cha- been affected by the nature of her soil and pro-   racter and ducts, and by the facilities for internal communi-   royal power.

cation, it is none the less true that her insular position
has been of great, though perhaps of indirect, economic
importance. The sea has, on the whole, served as a defence
against external invasion, and no part of England has been
the scene of frequent conflicts such as were but too common
in France and Italy for centuries. Security from attack is
one of the first essentials for industrial progress; the greatest
commercial centres of the old world, Tyre, Rhodes, and
Venice, relied on their maritime position for protection. It
has been the good fortune of England to have an unexampled
history of industrial and commercial development carried on,
for several centuries, with entire immunity from successful
invasion by, or subjection to, foreign powers.

Political security, the result of her insular position, has
reacted favourably upon her industrial life; and a similar
indirect influence has been exerted by some other features to
which allusion has already been made. The remains of the
Roman roads and the navigable rivers of England offered,
from very early times, comparatively easy facilities for internal communication and afforded the material conditions
which favoured the eventual growth of a strong internal
government. It is at all events noticeable that in Norman
times the royal power made itself felt in maintaining the
king's peace, to the advantage of agriculturists and of traders
alike, while private war was still rampant across the Channel.
The town life of England grew up in subordination to, and
under the patronage of, the central power; while the cities
of Germany and Italy were almost independent powers, and
those of France were engaged in frequent quarrels with
their wealthy neighbours. There was a gradual and har-
monious development of constitutional and municipal life
in this country, which could not but be favourable to wise
fiscal administration and commercial regulation.

21. Geographical situation has also been highly favourable to English commerce, and the coasts of   Facilities for
England afford a number of excellent harbours.   maritime
From a very early period, London has not only   commerce.
had a part in the export and import trade of this country,
but has served as an important commercial depot.   The
great routes of trade in the early Middle Ages formed a sort
of parallelogram, of which Constantinople, Marseilles,
Wisby and London may be regarded as the corners.   When
the discovery of the New World revolutionised the commerce of the Old, England had facilities for access to the
new region where her great Dominion still stretches, even
though the most flourishing of her colonies have thrown
off her sway.   It was only after contending with many
rivals that Englishmen forced their way to the East, and
founded and maintained a commercial empire there.   Commerce with the New World, however, seemed to lie ready
to their hands, and they not only monopolised the trade
with their own colonies (1651), but also undertook a large
part of the carrying trade for Spain (1713).

22. The most cursory review of the physical advantages
which England has enjoyed cannot but raise   Physical
a question as to the stability of her present   bases of our
prosperity.   Commerce depends in many   prosperity.
ways on agriculture or on manufacture.   Unless we have
wealth to sell, we cannot buy wealth from others.   In early
times England exported corn to supply some other parts of
the Roman Empire, and even as late as the end of the
eighteenth century she produced corn in sufficient quantities
to be able to export a surplus.   With the vast growth of our
population, we no longer have corn to sell when we enter
the market of the world; we need to buy it from abroad.

The same has been the case with wool.   In the thir-

teenth and fourteenth centuries wool was our chief article
of export and the mainstay of English commerce.   When
the manufacture, in all its various branches, was successfully
planted here, our clothing trade held a specially strong
position.   Abundance of material was supplied at home,
and there were many markets abroad where our cloth was
in eager demand.   But, since the wool famine at the close
of the last century, English manufacturers have been forced
to look elsewhere for materials to work.   The development
of sheep-farming in Australia has destroyed the preeminence
of England as a wool-producing country, and has struck a
blow at her practical monopoly in the manufacture of cloth.

It is still more obvious that her mineral wealth cannot
afford a permanent basis for her commerce.   The fuel supplied by her woods was often recklessly wasted, and there is
little sign of any practical attention being paid to the ap-
proaching exhaustion of our coal.   The immense accession
of wealth which came from these mineral resources enabled
us to bear the brunt of the struggle with Napoleon, but our
financiers could only do it by mortgaging the future and
adding largely to the national debt.   It is not easy to see
how that burden of indebtedness could be defrayed, without
intolerable pressure, if the coal and iron trades were seriously
crippled.

The industrial foundations on which English commerce
has been built up hardly seem sound enough to inspire great
confidence in the maintenance of our position, but other
commercial realms have prospered as depots, even when
their industry was not of first-rate importance.   Tyre was a
commercial depot; so too was Venice.   Their failure came
not through a blow to their industry, but through the opening
up of better commercial routes, which left them on a siding.
England still holds her own in the carrying trade of the world,

and London is still preeminent as a commercial centre.
How far the development of new areas or the opening up
of new routes may affect her position we cannot guess;
it is, at least, not impossible that history may repeat itself
and that, with new political combinations, the centre of
gravity of the commerce of the world may be shifted once
more.

CHAPTER III.

THE MANORS.

23. IN modern social life we find that every citizen

Parochial, municipal and national life. may easily recognise a number of distinct interests in which he has a personal part. He is anxious for the maintenance of the power and prosperity of the country as a whole, even though he may not be able to specify the precise way in which any great national disaster would press upon him personally. He is interested in the good government—in the lighting, paving and sanitation,—of the town with which he is most closely connected. He probably has a friendly feeling towards one or more country districts, and is glad if the crops are good, and the people comfortable. We have here three distinct types of social life, in each one of which most of us have some sort of interest. But whereas, at the present day, national disaster or national well-being—the ebb or flow of trade—is generally and widely felt, while local politics and parochial interests seem to be comparatively trivial, it has not always been so. There was a time when a vast number of Englishmen hardly had reason to look beyond their village or their town, and only came occasionally into conscious contact with the world outside. The prosperity of their own village or their own town was all that concerned them then; whereas all of us now, for the very bread we eat, are affected by the state of trade between England and other lands. National life has developed apace, so as to outgrow and overshadow the interests and politics of the village or the town. In the twelfth century, for almost all the purposes of life, the village or the *manor* was by far the most important of these social organisms, when few towns existed and when national ties were of the slightest. As in course of time *towns* grew up, they became the important centres of trade and of industry; the stream of progress, instead of flowing along the narrow channels of village life, can be most readily observed in the larger life of the towns. They, in their turn, fell into the background, as *national* regulation and national institutions became more powerful to watch over and to promote common national interests.

Each of these different forms of social organisation has been required to serve different purposes. Their powers have been brought into play (*a*) to secure the subsistence, (*b*) to provide for the defence, and (*c*) to regulate the activities, of the persons who compose them; and in the discharge of each of these functions, they have had to deal with questions that are really economic. This is obvious in regard to the means of human life, whether they are procured by agriculture, by industry or by trade. It is also clear that the necessities of defence involve military obligations or taxation, and that the military system must be taken account of in its fiscal aspects. Similarly, legislative and judicial administration control the conditions under which industry is carried on, and lay down the rules by which it is regulated. All these sides of social life have some economic bearing, and each of them must be at least alluded to in an industrial history which deals with these various groups in turn.

24.   When we go back to the earliest times, from which
Manorial   we have full and clear information about the
organisation.   social condition of this country, we find a
state of affairs when there were few great towns engaged
in industry and commerce, while by far the larger part
of the population were directly interested in rural pursuits.
Throughout the length and breadth of England there were
manors, which we may think of as villages inhabited by
men, who differed considerably in status, but all of whom,
in a greater or less degree, were responsible or subject to the
lord of that manor.   Despite the infinite variety of local
usages, which prevailed among these manors, it is yet possible
to describe a common type to which they approximately
conformed.

(*a*)   So far as the means of subsistence are concerned,
Subsist-   we have no difficulty in understanding the
ence and   nature of the policy that was pursued.   This
household
management.   is clearly brought out in the books on estate
management, which were written by Walter of Henley
and Robert Grosseteste in the thirteenth century.   Each
group had an independent life economically.   The authorities in each manor aimed, so far as possible, at rendering
it *self-sufficing*, although they did not disapprove of the
disposal of surplus commodities to outsiders.   To supply
all the wants of the inhabitants from the resources of the
manor was a sign of good management, though it was of
course occasionally necessary to buy some articles at
markets or fairs, or from travelling chapmen.   It is hardly
possible to conceive a greater contrast than there is with
the present day, when rural districts sell the largest part, if
not the whole, of their produce in markets, and depend for
their supply of the comforts and some of the necessaries of
life on their power of purchasing from the towns.

We can best see how completely this was true of the
poorer classes, when we notice the system adopted, even in
great households, by men who could most easily procure
the means of transport. The king and the great magnates
who were the owners of many estates, found it simpler to
transport the *personnel* of their establishments from place to
place than to gather the produce from their estates at any
single palace. The great landowner was frequently on the
move from one manor to another; and the practice of
making but a brief sojourn on each estate continued,
long after the commutation of food rents for money
payments had rendered such a course unnecessary. This
may, to some extent, account for the curious lack of
comfort to which the rich men of Norman and Angevin
times submitted. They and their retinues would be shel-
tered in a large hall, with one private chamber—the solar—
at the end. There was little or no furniture, as the rough
tables on tressels and benches brought out for meals were
cleared away, when the company settled themselves to sleep
on the straw, with which the unboarded floor was littered.
A lack of knives and forks, of glass and china, rendered
inevitable habits of eating and drinking which are inconsistent with our notions of refinement; while the *débris* of the
banquet was discussed by the dogs on the floor, and was
finally removed when a great occasion required that the
hall should be strewn with fresh straw. When the food
which could be conveniently stored at one centre began to
give out, the cavalcade would move on to another estate,
each of which was separately managed, and each of which
could afford subsistence for a longer or shorter period of
residence.

(*b*) Though these manors were thus independent and
self-sufficing in this aspect, we may yet see that for

purposes of defence they were closely linked together.

Defence and fiscal obligations.

From the time of the Norman Conquest, at all events, each shared in the obligation to contribute to the royal treasury for military purposes. The fiscal obligation of each manorial lord to the Crown was a very real tie with the central authority, and bound these isolated self-dependent groups into one whole for defence against external foes. Such is the picture of England put before us with great detail in the wonderful record known as *Domesday Book*. This book embodies the results of a survey taken by William the Conqueror in 1086. He desired to know, not only the rent obtainable from the Crown estates, but also the amount at which each separate landowner throughout the country was assessed for the payment of Danegeld. This tax, originally levied for the purpose of buying off the Danes, had come to be employed as a means of raising money for military purposes. In the earlier Norman reigns it was levied occasionally, and not as a regular and annual tax. The sheriffs—officials who acted as the king's representatives in the counties—were charged with collecting the royal rents and the royal taxes. They made their payments to the Exchequer, and in the records of that court, which exist from the times of Henry II onwards, we get an immense amount of information, in regard to all parts of the country, reflected in the entries of payments, or of remissions of payments, to the central Exchequer.

The aspect of the manor which is thus brought under our notice is fiscal. The lord of the manor was responsible for the payment of a certain sum to the sheriff, and he may, therefore, be looked upon as the officer by whom the smaller contributions of taxes were actually collected. On almost every manor some of the tenants seem to have been

practically independent of the lord in various ways, and free
to deal with their own land as they liked, while yet they were
not directly responsible to the king for the payment of taxes,
since they paid through the lord of the manor.   By far the
larger number of the inhabitants, however, were bound to the
lord by stricter bonds.   The lord's chief means of defraying
the Danegeld came from the produce of his own estate.
This consisted partly of his demesne lands, and partly of the
holdings, which were granted to villeins on condition that
they should render regular and specified service on the
lord's demesne.   In this way the villeins were an integral
part of the estate, for without them no cultivation was
possible and fiscal obligations could not be discharged.
Their relation to the lord can hardly be expressed with
accuracy in modern terms.   It might be said that they were
the lord's tenants, who paid their rent not so much in money
or kind as in service.   Or it might be said that they were
the lord's labourers, who received for their work not wages,
but a ready stocked allotment, which they could work in
their free time.   But the precise nature of their obligations
at different dates must be more fully considered below.

(*c*)   The third aspect of the manor as a judicial or administrative centre need not be dwelt on at   Manorial
length, though much of the business that   jurisdiction.
came before the courts had an industrial bearing.   There
are many records of manorial courts which show us how
constant and how varied was the work they had to do.
They were much concerned about the weight of bread
and the quality of ale.   The manorial court was also
the place where important business connected with the
estate took place.   There the tenant took up his holding,
and there the villein formally entered on his obligations as
a tenant.   There too formal complaint was made if any

C. & M.   3

villein deserted the village, and thus left the estate short-
handed.   And since the majority of the labourers were
practically *astricted* or bound to some particular estate, there
was no opportunity of hiring labour or of seeking employment such as we are familiar with to-day.   Hence, in
matters of internal regulation, as in regard to internal
economy, the manors were singularly independent.   The
mutual obligations of the landholder and of the peasantry
were settled, less by a general law which held good for the
realm, than by the custom of each particular manor.   Many
small cases, connected with buying and selling or with
ordinary police administration, were adjudicated on in the
manorial court according to local customs, since there was
little statute law on such topics for the whole realm.

25.   We can trace these manorial groups as far back as
the time of the Norman Conquest, for Domesday Book gives us very clear indications of
the existence of this social type with all its
different functions.   In the forefront of each entry we get a
statement of the rate at which each place was assessed for the
Danegeld ; while at the close of each entry, in most counties,
we have estimates of the value of each estate, and these help
us to see where taxation pressed most heavily.   We also get
details of the condition of each estate for subsistence—of
the stock with which it was worked, of the villeins on whose
labour the lord could depend, of its resources in the way of
meadow and pasturage, and of any special sources of wealth,
such as a market, a fishery, or a mill.   Besides these details,
there are some indications of the judicial rights, criminal or
civil, which the lord of the manor could exercise.   The
whole is put clearly before us, as it existed eight hundred
years ago; but when we try to look behind the Domesday
record, and to see how this complex rural institution grew

The early history of the Manor.

up, we find ourselves brought face to face, not so much
with positive evidence, as with various conflicting theories,
which would trace the development of the manorial organisation to royal influence, or derive it from changes in voluntary associations.

Each of these social factors may have contributed some
elements to the growth of the whole. In the fiscal and
judicial functions of the manorial lord, the influence of royal
authority is tolerably clear. There is also much to be said for
tracing the organisation of manorial households to a similar
source, and for supposing that other households were regulated and organised on the model of the royal establishments, as if the manor were organised from above.

But in Domesday Book and in later sources there are
various traces of communal life, and of communal rights
against the lord, which seem to show that the first English
settlers were men who voluntarily associated themselves together for combined tillage, and for sharing common
responsibilities. This associated and collective organisation
of labour is certainly found among the serfs in medieval
manors, and though some writers seem to think that it was
imposed by masters from above, it seems more likely that it
arose, at all events in some cases, from voluntary association.

The whole question of the origin and early history of the
manors is still in dispute among scholars, and in the mean
time it may suffice to put forward two negative conclusions.

i. There is no reason to suppose that every centre of
rural employment grew up in the same way; some may have
originated in a body of serfs and some in a voluntary association. There is no reason why the origin of one should
not have differed from the origin of another. Instead of
disputing whether they were all free or all servile, we might
do well to recognise the third alternative that they had, as

agricultural communities, no special political character at all;
but, as soon as any rural group came to have a political
character and to be used by the Crown for judicial and fiscal
purposes, its main features would resemble those of other
social groups which had had a different previous history.

ii. There is a temptation to regard the manors or centres
of rural employment as survivals from Roman times.   This
suggestion is at least unproved; in the face of the evidence already adduced as to the complete destruction of
Roman society in Britain in the fifth century, it does not
even seem very probable.   There are of course many striking
similarities between the vills, of which the remains are
found in so many parts of Britain, and the manors described
in Domesday Book.   There are many points of likeness
between a great estate at one time and a great estate at the
other, but there are also great differences; while some of
the similarities are directly connected with natural conditions and give no evidence of historical derivation.   Resem-
blances must necessarily be found in the cultivation of
similar crops on similar land, with similar ploughs and
similar oxen; and when we also take account of the manner
in which Continental customs and Roman terminology were
introduced, subsequently to the conversion of the English,
there is but little ground for supposing that Roman vills
survived as centres of rural employment.   The continued
existence of the Roman vill is the last line of defence
maintained by those who hold that our English civilisation
is directly derived from that which existed in Roman
Britain; but it is at present an unproved hypothesis.

26.   Though the origin and early history of the manor

Manors in
the thirteenth
century. Re-
cords.

are so obscure, we may get a full and detailed
description of its working as a centre of rural
employment in the thirteenth century.   At

that time, a careful system of administration and the rendering of written accounts had become common on all well-managed estates. We have several handbooks on English estate management, dating from the reign of Henry III; the most celebrated of these treatises continued to be the standard book on the subject for nearly three hundred years. It was written by a Dominican friar named Walter of Henley, who probably had some practical experience in connexion with the estates of the great monastery of Christ Church, Canterbury. We are, besides, able to refer to three different forms of records which were kept on well-managed estates. The *extent* or *rental* gives us the list of the tenants with a statement of their obligations, whether they were discharged in kind, in services, or in money. It was a sort of survey of the manor, which was made at intervals, and required little modification between times. It gave a statement of the resources of the estate and the legitimate expectations of its owner. The *accounts*, which were made up each year, not only showed the produce of the demesne farm and the purposes to which it was applied, but enumerated the live stock on the estate, and showed how far the obligations of the villeins and other tenants, as recorded in the *extent*, were actually discharged in any particular year. Again, we have the *Court Rolls*, or records of the manor on its judicial side, which tell us of the changes in the *personnel* of the tenants, and occasionally of modifications in the character of their obligations. From these sources it is possible to reproduce, in considerable detail, a picture of the life on manorial estates.

27. We may think of the manor in the early years of Edward I as an estate, managed by a bailiff on behalf of the lord. If the latter were a wealthy man with many estates, he would

The officials and the villeins.

appoint a higher official or *steward* to represent him, and to supervise the details of management in his behalf. The *bailiff* was the responsible official on each estate, who had to account in detail for the stores and the stock each year, and who also had to see that the villeins did the work, and made the payments, required from the holdings they enjoyed. There was also a foreman (*praepositus*) elected by the men; it was his business to represent them in all transactions with the lord, while a *hayward* superintended the actual work and saw to the contributions of seed-corn.

The arable land of the lord and of the villeins would often be intermixed (cf. below, § 112), but the portion which was directly managed by the bailiff was known as the *demesne*. The lord himself possessed a good many oxen for working this land, but the villeins were called upon to contribute the labour of their stock, as well as their personal services, on the lord's land. The demands of the lord appear in earlier times to have been somewhat indefinite and therefore arbitrary, but by the time of Edward I they were, generally speaking, perfectly certain and precise. The typical villein's holding consisted of a *yardland* or *virgate*, which would, approximately, be thirty acres of arable land. When the villein entered upon the holding at Michaelmas he would find part of his land ready sown, and he would have a couple of oxen assigned to him as the necessary stock for working it. When the holding was delivered up to the lord, as for example at the villein's death, the full stock with which it had been let was returned. For the maintenance of this stock the villein would have a right to the produce of a strip of meadow-land, while he might pasture his cattle, and perhaps some sheep in addition, on the common waste of the village. In course of time additional portions of land were separated from the waste, to be

used either as separate crofts or for additional tillage, but the
lord was always bound to see that there was no such reduction of the common waste, as to encroach on the fodder
available for the cattle of the village. This acknowledgment of
common rights was enforced by one of the earliest Acts found
in our Statute Book, the Statute of Merton passed in 1236.

The villein who held a yard-land would be subject to
such obligations as the following. He would have to render
three days' work a week on the lord's land from Michaelmas
till St. Peter ad Vincula (Aug. 1), but he was allowed holidays
at Christmas, Easter, and Whitsuntide. He had to plough
with his own team four acres of the lord's land. He had to
carry manure, to weed and mow the lord's meadow, as well
as to cut and make and carry the hay. From St. Peter ad
Vincula to Michaelmas he was to put in twenty-four days'
work, so that he might be kept consecutively busy in the
lord's harvest operations. It was clearly defined whether
he should have his meat and drink from the lord, at each of
these times of obligatory service, or not. The harvest work
must have been regarded as specially long and heavy, since
he had to pay a penny to be free from one day's labour at
that time, whereas a halfpenny was regarded as the equivalent
of the day's work at other times of the year. He had, moreover, to pay 1s. 8d. at Easter and a similar sum at Michaelmas-
Day, and to present a hen at Christmas time. These were
the chief obligations of a tenant in villeinage at Borley in
Essex, early in Edward III's reign, but they may be taken as
typical of the obligations of villeins generally, although the
custom of each manor might vary in some details.

On these estates there were groups of men who were of
similar status, and liable to similar obligation, and who thus
formed a sort of community on the estate. They appear to
have been collectively responsible for the work, so that if

one failed, the others had to make up for his deficiencies. The *praepositus* was their own elected officer, who ruled them in their own interest, and was their spokesman with the lord or his steward. Though they were, in some ways, in a servile position and astricted to the land, they yet had a definite social status, which they may well have valued. Outsiders, who were dependent on casual employment, and who had little, if any, land to work, were in a certain sense free, as the villeins were not, but it hardly seems that the free labourers were a superior class till after the agricultural revolution which followed the ravages of the Black Death in 1349.

There was one change which seems to have been going on with more or less rapidity in the fourteenth century. The landlord, apparently, was at liberty to choose whether he would have the actual services rendered, or receive the recognised money equivalent. In some years the accounts of an estate would show a large entry for *opera vendita*, i.e. for payments made by the villeins in lieu of service. On the whole it was to the interest of the landlords, in the early part of the fourteenth century, to take money instead of reluctant service, and to get the necessary work done by hiring free labourers, or others when they wanted them, instead of finding work for the men at stated times. In some cases there was a formal agreement that money payments should be regularly taken in lieu of actual service. In an agreement of this kind, made in 1343 at Granborough in Buckinghamshire, the tenants became collectively responsible for deficiencies in money payments, as they had been, in all probability, in earlier days with respect to service. Even where there was no formal agreement, the practice, if not the binding custom, of taking rents in money and not in service, came more and more into vogue during this period.

28. The terrible plague known as the Black Death, which swept over England in 1349, had many results on English society. In the rural districts it rendered the old system of bailiff-farming impracticable, and thus brought about a revolution in the management of manorial estates.

Immediate effects of the Black Death. Stock and land leases. Sheep-farming.

The immediate effect of the pestilence, which killed off, roughly speaking, about half the population, was to make labour very scarce. On those estates where the money-system had come into vogue, labour could not be hired on the old terms. In some cases there was reason to fear that the crops would be utterly lost, because the labourers stood out for unprecedented wages; and a statute was passed, which was several times re-enacted, to compel them to work at the old rates. This *Statute of Labourers* (1351), could, probably, not be permanently enforced, and the money-system of estate management, which had been coming in before the Black Death, proved unremunerative. The lord had the necessary stock and the necessary land, but he could not afford to pay for the requisite labour at the new rates. Under these circumstances the simplest expedient was to give up the attempt to farm through his bailiff, and to break up his demesne farm into holdings which could be let, together with the stock necessary to work them, at a regular money-rent. This was the beginning of leasehold farming, and, ere long, it came to assume the modern type. The *stock and land lease* appears to have been a transitional form, which gradually gave way to an arrangement by which the tenant supplied the stock, while the landlord was responsible for the land and buildings. These leaseholders were probably drawn, not from the villeins who already had holdings, but from the class of free labourers; the new holdings would not, however, differ much from those of the villeins. As the leaseholder could not hire extra labour, his holding would be such as could be worked by a man and his family. It would correspond with the virgate, though as the lease-holder would have all his time for himself, he would be able to till a somewhat larger area, or to work a smaller area more thoroughly.

In the case of other estates, where this expedient was not open, the landlord found it profitable to take to pasture-farming. Sometimes he might be able to do this without encroaching on the arable holdings of any of his humbler neighbours, or interfering with their pasture. As the change went on, however, there were many landlords, who showed little scruple in this matter; bitter complaints were made of their conduct, but the early history of the large sheep-farms is little known. It need only be pointed out that pasture-farming was a possible expedient which landowners might adopt, when it proved hopeless to carry on bailiff-farming on the money-system, either because so many villeins were dead, or because the estate had been *depopulated*.

29. The problem was somewhat different on those

The Peasants' Revolt.

estates where the performance of actual services was still habitual, or was, at least, a recognised alternative. On these lands bailiff-farming could be continued. It would be distinctly to the advantage of the lords to obtain services, and not money; and in so far as they could procure servile labour, the land could be worked to great advantage. But, apparently, they were only able to enforce their claims by putting great pressure on the villeins. Those who had been in the habit of buying their freedom from a good deal of work, would resent a refusal to take their money. If, as a consequence of the plague, very few villeins were left alive on an estate, it might be difficult to enforce their collective and communal responsibility without serious oppression. The comparative freedom and prosperity of the new leaseholders would also render the villeins dissatisfied with their position, and thus social discontent, coupled with political unrest, brought about the wide-spread and organised rising of the peasants in 1381.

30. This rising was very wide-spread, and yet, in some ways, was very local. Norfolk, Cambridge, St. Alban's, and Kent are the districts about which we hear most. The precise cause of complaint at each of these centres of disturbance was different. The insurrection was, in the main, directed against the manorial lords and their demands. As the rising took a local colour in different districts, so too it seems that some districts were entirely exempt from its influence. On the manor of Littleport, near Ely, the accounts of the year show no trace of any irregularity, and the services of the villeins appear to have been rendered according to the old routine. Still the villages which felt no effects of the movement must surely have been exceptional; for the rising assumed such proportions, that its leaders were able to obtain considerable success. Charters of manumission were granted; but these were subsequently set aside, on the ground, apparently that they had been extorted by force. The forces at work were too strong to be arbitrarily checked. Commutation continued until the changes in estate management had gone so far that villein service was no longer demanded.

It seems very probable, however, that the discontent of the villeins, which had broken out so violently, put increasing difficulties in the way of working the land on the old system of bailiff-farming with obligatory labour. The break-up of the demesne farms into leasehold tenancies, or the conversion of the land into sheep-walks, became increasingly convenient.

In particular, a growing demand for wool rendered sheep-farming highly profitable. The temptation to get rid of the inhabitants and to use the land for pasture only, was strong. In 1459, serious complaints were made at Coventry of the manner in which tenancies had been destroyed, teams broken up, and parishes laid desolate in parts of Warwickshire; while the current sneer of foreigners about our reliance on sheep, instead of on ships, shows that the change was not confined to a single Midland county. The tendency continued to operate with varying force till the close of the sixteenth century; depopulation was regarded as a serious political danger, and seems to have been carried out in some cases, at least, in a ruthless fashion. Whether the dispossession of the inhabitants was effected with due regard to their legal rights, and how far they were illegally evicted, are questions of much difficulty, but it is not of much importance with respect to the economic effects of the change.

As this rural revolution advanced, the manor ceased to be an important centre of employment, while owing to changes in the levying and collection of taxation, it was no longer a unit for fiscal purposes. In many cases its judicial functions had also come to be of subordinate importance, as they were being superseded by other agencies. From the time of Richard II onwards we find that the importance of justices of the peace increases; and in the Tudor period the overseers of the poor came to exercise some of the duties of local administration. In these ways it appears that before the Reformation the manor had ceased to occupy a prominent position either as a centre of rural employment or of local administration. The formalities of this jurisdiction still survive in many places, where manorial courts are held and copyhold tenures exist; but they seem now

to be mere anachronisms, not effective instruments of local
government.   This gradual decay of the manorial organisation on all its sides resulted in the disappearance of serfdom.
Such a change is not easy to date, but there is evidence to
show that some of the disabilities of the state of villeinage
remained, and were felt to be serious grievances as late as
the time of Elizabeth.

CHAPTER IV.

THE TOWNS.

31. A GREAT many of the towns grew up under manorial patronage so that their earlier history is really the story of a prosperous manor. Some, indeed, of the most important—such as Sheffield—grew up and flourished under this system, and Manchester had very little of the constitutional character of a town until 1846. A town, in this constitutional sense, was a place where the inhabitants were collectively responsible for the king's taxes, and came, in consequence, to have considerable authority for local self-government, and for the assessment of the quota which each householder had to pay for the royal taxes. A group which had attained this fiscal character is easily distinguishable from the manors, in each of which the lord was personally responsible for taxation. During the period of the Crusades a very large number of English towns had so far advanced in wealth and importance that they were able to obtain charters, which granted them this direct responsibility and freed them from the interference of the sheriff, as the king's representative, in their internal affairs. It was not until they had attained a considerable amount of prosperity

Manors and towns. Fiscal responsibility.

that they could be trusted in this fashion, and the history of English municipal life before the era of the Crusades, although very interesting, is very obscure. One of the chief difficulties about it is, that the occasions of progress and the manner of progress have varied so much in different towns. The story of each one ought to be traced separately and individually, but here, it is only possible to indicate some of the varied influences that have been at work, and to illustrate the manner in which they have operated in different places.

32. It scarcely admits of doubt that the Angles and Saxons, when they invaded the deserted Province of Britain, were little attracted by the remains of the Roman towns. Some of them they burned. Others they allowed to fall into decay, while they themselves settled in rural districts and in small self-sufficing groups, which, under these circumstances, offered scant opportunity for internal trade, and few attractions to foreign merchants. A few pedlars may have gone about the country, and occasional fairs may have been held, but there was little regular commerce to favour the maintenance or lead to the revival of town life. Of the fifty-six cities of Roman Britain, there is not one in regard to which it is perfectly clear that it held its ground as an organised centre of social life through the period of English conquest and English settlement.

Early England. Monastic and Danish influence in favour of town life.

The manor has been spoken of as a centre of rural employment. Towns must be regarded as centres of trade and commerce, and any social gathering or settlement, affording opportunities for trade, supplied a nucleus, which might sooner or later develop into a town. The introduction of Christianity, and the struggle with the Danes, each brought about social conditions which favoured their growth. Opportunities of trade were offered in Christian times at places of pilgrimage, especially on the days when the patron saint was commemorated, while the great Benedictine monasteries formed large establishments, which were often partially dependent on goods brought from a distance. Norwich and Canterbury, Bury, Reading, and Worcester are among the towns which have thus come into being under the shadow of a great abbey.

On the other hand the forts, built by the Danes or erected by Edward the Elder and his sister, the Lady of Mercia, to hold the country against the Danes, were also centres of trade; and the growth of such towns as Leicester and Tamworth may perhaps be traced to these causes. But so soon as active contest with the Danes had abated, and they were adopted as a constituent element on English soil, the progress of the towns was rapid. The Danes were given to seamanship and trade as the English had ceased to be. They brought England into intercourse with their own settlements on the Baltic, in Iceland, and in Ireland. They seem to have devoted themselves to industrial pursuits and to have furnished some common articles of trade. The importance of the Danish contribution to town life is seen in several ways. Besides the boroughs which had Danish *Lawmen* to govern them—Lincoln, Stamford, and Cambridge—there were others, like London itself, which reflect the Danish influence in their constitutions. The Husting Court is a Danish term. We can trace them more widely by their religious associations. Just as the origin of different Greek or Phœnician settlements is evidenced by the worship in their temples, so the Danish element in English towns may sometimes be detected from the dedication of a church to a Northern saint. There is a St. Olaf's not only at York, but also at Southwark and in Exeter. When we take these various and apparently trivial indications into account, we

can realise how deeply the progress of English towns
has been affected by the influence of these later settlers.

33. While these influences made it possible for town
life to arise, there were various physical conditions which rendered one point or another
especially favourable for the new development.
The English rivers offer facilities for carriage

Domesday
towns. Rural
character.
'Conflicting
jurisdiction.

far into the country, and more than one town has arisen at
the point where the tide served to bring the small seagoing
vessels of early days. Perth and Stirling in Scotland,
Ipswich, Norwich, and Chester may all be regarded as illustrations in point. In other cases the great Roman roads
remained to offer facilities of communication; and new towns
took their rise in the immediate neighbourhood, or on the
very sites, of the Roman ruins. Where social and physical
conditions were alike favourable, there was, doubtless, considerable opportunity for regular trade. This had led to an
increase of settled population, at the time of Domesday Book,
in many of the places, which were, even then, called
boroughs or towns, though they had but few of the charac-
teristics which we associate with urban life. Even in mere
external appearances they must have been very different
from the towns we know. We are accustomed to streets of
shops, in which stores of finished goods are exposed for sale,
but of shops in this sense there were probably few, if any,
outside London. Stocks of goods were only exposed for
sale at the annual fairs, which were arising in different parts
of the country, and the artisan who lived in a town would
expect his customers to provide the materials for his work.
It is still more strange, according to our ideas, to find that
householders in towns were engaged in rural occupations.
Thus the sheriff of Cambridge, at the time of the Domesday
Survey, was guilty of extortion in requiring too frequent

C. & M.   4

use of the townsmen's teams; while the inventory of Colchester in 1296 gives us a picture of a distinctly rural community.

A still more curious feature of town life is revealed by the entries in Domesday Book, for even the principal towns show little, if any, trace of common municipal life. We find, instead, abundant evidence of conflicting jurisdictions. In some, it is clear, that there was a large Norman or Flemish population—such as the *francigenæ* of Shrewsbury and Norwich—who did not always pay the same taxes as other townsmen or conform to the same customs. In many places, two or more houses in a town appear to have been attached to and taxed with a neighbouring estate. These conflicting responsibilities and jurisdictions in one thickly inhabited area seem to us very strange; but it may be well to remember that even the City of London was a curiously composite body, in which each ward had a singular independence as late as the time of Edward I.; while it was only in 1856 that the separate jurisdictions of the boroughs of Canongate, Portsborow and Broughton were merged in the City of Edinburgh. It would be most interesting, if it were possible here, to trace in detail the growth of that common town-life, which gradually found expression in common municipal institutions.

34. In so far as we find traces of its growth, first in one

The struggle for chartered liberties. Inter-municipal commerce.

place and then in another, it is marked by the obstacles which the townsmen had to encounter, and from which they endeavoured to procure their freedom. Where the town was a populous centre on the lands of a single manorial lord, the inhabitants had a common interest in purchasing their freedom from the interference of his officers. They might desire to be free from the obligation to contribute for

the ploughing of his lands, and the men of Leicester
obtained this freedom by a charter from Earl Robert in
1190. Many might desire to be free from such a restriction
as that of grinding their corn at the lord's mill; the men of
St Alban's had not obtained freedom to use hand-mills of
their own in 1381, and the right was still in dispute at
Manchester during the last century. There were all sorts
of minor matters of police jurisdiction and of sanitary regulation, about which the townsmen preferred to be free to
legislate for themselves. On all these points they won their
freedom, bit by bit, as various rights were conceded to them
in different charters by the manorial lords.

There were other rights which they desired to have, and
for which it was necessary that they should approach the
king himself. One such privilege was the right of being
collectively responsible for the payment of the royal taxes.
This freed them from the interference of the sheriff, and
enabled them to assess the quota which each inhabitant
should pay, as a house-rate, towards the common burdens.
They were also glad to exercise powers of jurisdiction
among themselves according to their own customs, and
thus to be free from judicial interference from without,
in the ordinary business of life. And, besides this, they
were desirous of being allowed to associate themselves
for certain trade matters, and to have their own *gild
merchant.* These various rights were highly coveted;
and they were secured sometimes in larger, sometimes
in smaller, degree by royal charters, for which a substantial
contribution to the royal exchequer had generally to be
paid. The era of the Crusades, when the king and the
great lords were eagerly endeavouring to raise money, was
a period when very many charters were procured, and when
some populous places attained the status of self-govern-

4—2

ing towns presided over by their own elected officer, the
Mayor.

Similar causes were at work over a great part of Christendom in the twelfth century, and gave rise in all lands to
a new and vigorous urban life. The institutions which grew
up at this time are so much alike that instructive comparisons
can often be drawn in regard to the details of their administration. This resemblance was so close that intercourse
between towns for business purposes was possible. The
mercantile customs and the methods of recovering debt in
one town were much the same as those in vogue in another.
But though similar in type, each separate borough had well-
defined privileges of its own, and heavy burdens which its
own inhabitants were called upon to bear. Each had its
own documentary history, consisting of a series of charters,
by which its special privileges were conceded or confirmed.
Each was a self-centred independent body, though it might
have frequent relations with other similar bodies. And as
these towns were trading centres, the commerce of the day
took something of the character of the social groups in
which it was carried on, and may be fitly described as
municipal or *inter-municipal* trade.

35. The towns, like the manors, were called upon to
pay for the defence of the realm, and many
Fiscal con-
tributions and
internal ad-
ministration.
of them obtained the dignity of this fiscal
responsibility about the end of the twelfth
century. The inhabitants were collectively
responsible for the *ferm* of the town; besides incurring
a large fine to procure the charter which secured them
this right, they were under an obligation to make an
annual payment to the Exchequer. The various burgesses
contributed a house-rate, and they obtained immunity for
their travelling merchants from the exactions which were

often levied by local authorities in the places they visited. They were very strict in the exaction of their own rates, and very jealous of admitting any one to the advantages of their town, who did not share, as an inhabitant, in its burdens. The earliest town laws are directed against *up-land* men and other outsiders, and against any inhabitant who under the guise of a partnership shared the advantages of his position with them and *coloured their goods*. This jealousy is a striking and rather unpleasant feature in the life of these communities, but the danger against which they endeavoured to guard themselves was not imaginary. In the time of Edward I we find that the pressure of municipal burdens was sufficiently heavy to cause the migration of some of the inhabitants of Northampton to more favoured districts. In the fifteenth century it was found necessary to grant remission of taxation to many places, and it is generally admitted that the pressure of their taxes had a good deal to do with the distress of the older towns in the Tudor period, when new commercial centres were rising into prominence. The exclusiveness then, though apparently harsh, was exercised in self-defence ; and it must also be remembered that townsmen were willing to welcome strangers as *tensers*, if they were willing to take a definite footing in the town, and to contribute to its expenses in a fashion that should correspond to the partial privileges to which such non-residents were admitted. But those who tried surreptitiously to evade these obligations aroused keen animosity, and this feeling was extended to such bodies as the Hansards, or the Jews, who lived in a town under royal protection, but were not of it, since they were not at *scot and lot* with the other inhabitants. These settlements of aliens, entirely exempt from local authority and responsible to the king directly, are among the last indications of conflicting privileges among the

residents within the City of London; comparatively little is
heard of difficulties affecting them after the time of Edward I.

In his reign the internal government of the more advanced
boroughs was in the hands of elected officials; the character of
their business, the rules they enforced, and the penalties they
imposed, may be most clearly seen from the printed records
of such towns as London, Ipswich, or Nottingham. But there
were also many cases where this internal jurisdiction had not
passed out of the hands of the original manorial authorities,
and where the desire of the townsmen for a fuller measure of
internal self-government gave rise to bitter and sanguinary
struggles. These occurred very frequently in the towns
which had grown up under the patronage of some great
abbey. There is an interesting agreement which closed the
era of frequent riot at Reading in 1254. The disturbances
at Bury in 1327 seem to have been more serious, but those
at Norwich in 1272 were worst of all, and resulted in the
burning of the Cathedral and the siege and storm of the city.

36. The town, like other social groups, had not only
a fiscal and administrative side, it was also

Gilds
merchant and
weavers'
gilds.
concerned with the maintenance of its own
prosperity. It was as centres of commerce that
the towns grew, and there is no doubt that
the inhabitants especially prized the right, which we find
in many Norman and Plantagenet charters, of obtaining
freedom to associate themselves for the purpose of regulating their commerce. The grant of a *Hanse* or gild
merchant gave them the character of an important commercial unit, which could enjoy a share of trade, both
local and distant. At the same time it is not easy,
despite Dr Gross's unwearied investigations, to determine
the exact functions of these bodies. Though the gilds
were so closely connected with the town authorities, that

their precise spheres are difficult to discriminate, they do
not appear to have had a judicial character in English
towns, or to have been in a position to settle disputes
between merchants.   They were certainly eager to guard
against any encroachment on their privileges, but it is not
quite clear what these valued privileges were.   It seems
that they exercised a general regulation over the manner in
which trade was conducted.   The conditions of buying and
selling, and to some extent the quality of goods, as well as
the nature of weights and measures, came within their purview.   They were doubtless able to enforce the methods of
dealing, which they believed to be for the interest of the town,
upon all their members, and they were also able to prevent
persons who were not members from carrying on regular
dealing there, although the latter might probably visit the
town on market-days and at fairs.   But it seems probable
that these gilds had also another side, and that they were
found useful for the purpose of collective trading.   When
foreign ships visited a town, it was advantageous for the inhabitants to refrain from bidding against one another, and to
make one common purchase, which they could afterwards
divide among themselves.   The right of *cavel* or of having a
share in these common purchases is more easily traced in
the laws of Scotch than of English towns.   But there is
evidence that a similar right existed at Chesterfield in 1294,
and subsequent cases of town trading, whether they are
survivals or only accidental revivals of a former practice,
throw interesting light upon the conditions which would
render such an institution desirable.   Town purchases of
coal were frequent in Dublin in the seventeenth and eighteenth
centuries.   Many towns made provision for a food supply
by means of granaries in the sixteenth and seventeenth centuries, and the town mills of Edinburgh were an important

part of corporation property until comparatively recent times. But whatever direct pecuniary advantages may have accrued to a townsman from membership of the gild—and the gild did not embrace all inhabitants, while it might include non-residents as members—it certainly conferred a status, which made him a person of credit. There was a substantial body behind him to which appeal could be made in case of default, and the increased security and smoothness of trading transactions would go far to account for the anxiety of many towns to possess their own gild.

Besides these town gilds, we hear in the twelfth century of several gilds in different places, composed of men who followed some particular trade, especially that of weaving. It is not a little remarkable that they should occur in a trade which was not a separate business, but a part of the women's household duties during the Early English period; weaving was, however, already practised with considerable success in Flanders, and many immigrants from that country settled in England within a century of the Conquest. Whatever may have been the origin of these gilds we find that the relations of their members with other townsmen were by no means friendly. It seems more probable that they were separate associations of aliens, authorized and protected by the Crown, than that there was a large class of native English weavers at this time, who found it desirable to develop such institutions on their own account. The story of the weavers' gild in London, of its long independence and eventual submission to the City authorities in 1321, appears to bear out this view of the situation; but it is also noticeable in regard to these early industrial gilds that they occur in trades where authoritative regulation was enforced. Bakers' gilds are as early, though not so widely diffused, as weavers' gilds. The bakers' gild of Coventry has an unbroken existence from

the sixth year of king John. The Assize of Bread and the
Assize of Measures are among the oldest English regulations
for the weight and size of goods : and it may be questioned
whether the origin of these industrial gilds was not due rather
to the need of local administrative powers than to the principle of voluntary association. At any rate, if they were
formed by association, we can see one reason why they
were favoured and fostered by the central authority.

37. Such, on the whole, was the character of the
towns and of their institutions in the time   Affiliation
of Edward I. The more we read of their   and represen-
                                            tation. Na-
intercourse, the more striking is the self-con- tional control
tained character of each borough, and its ex-   of commerce.
clusiveness against *foreigners*. It is, in itself, strange to find
this word used habitually for men who were foreign to the
town, whether they were aliens, or Englishmen from other
places. The legal position of a trader from Norwich at
Stourbridge Fair, near Cambridge, was precisely similar, for
business purposes, to that of a trader from Bruges or Rouen.
A common Merchant Law was recognised in all these places ;
and this, rather than the law of the realm, governed transactions. In each case the *communitas* to which he belonged
was looked upon as responsible for the good faith of a
merchant, whether he hailed from an English or from a
Continental town, so that, at first sight, there would seem
to have been little connexion or common feeling between
English towns as such.

But there were, after all, close ties of connexion between
the various towns. The customs which each maintained
were not an independent creation of its own. Each of the
later boroughs obtained privileges in its charter which were
not enumerated in detail, but which were described as being
precisely similar to those of some other place. In this way we

can *affiliate* the various boroughs to one another, and trace
their institutions back to a common stock.   Thus Derby
derived its custom from Nottingham, Nottingham from
Coventry, Coventry from Lincoln, and Lincoln from London.
In some cases the daughter town might deem it wise to appeal to its mother for advice, as to the interpretation of the
custom.   In some of the Continental cities the filial relation
appears to have involved a direct subordination which was
not in vogue in England.   Still, the filial relationship enables
us to trace out distinct family trees, which lead back to the
several original types of city custom which are found in
London, Bristol, York and Hereford.   The towns on the Welsh
Marches followed the custom of Hereford; those of Ireland
that of Bristol; while the custom of London, as adopted at
Winchester, was more widely diffused.   It was followed, not
only by many towns in the South, but also by Newcastle ; and
from Newcastle it passed to be the common custom of the
boroughs of Scotland.   In their earlier history and before the
Scottish War of Independence, the analogy betwen Scotch
and English boroughs is very close; but, in their later life
and institutions, the Northern towns were greatly influenced
by French and Flemish usages, and followed a line of development different from that of municipalities south of the
Tweed.   By far the largest number of English towns followed
the model of London, which was the source whence a common
body of municipal regulations spread to two-thirds of the
commercial centres of England.   A common custom, which
was so generally enforced by municipal authorities, had an
influence nearly as great as that exercised by Parliamentary
enactments in later reigns.   Indeed it may be said that a
great deal of the early legislation for trade did not take the
form of devising new expedients, but rather of giving wider
scope to regulations already recognised in many localities or

which formed part of the custom of London. The seven
years' apprenticeship enforced in 1563 may be specified as a
case in point.

The affiliation of their customs connected many of the
English towns with one another; but they were also connected by a common interest, since each was a large contri-
butor to the expenses of the realm. Besides the regular
payments which they were bound to make from year to year
to the Exchequer, occasional demands were exacted from
them in special emergencies, e.g. when war broke out. The
most remarkable event of the reign of Edward I was the
formation of a Parliament to which the towns sent representatives, and in which "what concerned all could be
approved by all." The summoning of Parliament gave the
towns an opportunity of making their united voice felt in
regard to the subsidies they could be called upon to pay, as
well as in regard to the rates at which customs should be
charged on exports like wool, or imports like wine. The
organisation of representative government was important
in many respects, and certainly had far-reaching effects
on English trade. By the time of Richard II, the towns
were strong enough to make themselves felt as the principal
factors in controlling the commercial policy of the realm.
In his reign and subsequently, the regulation and direction
of English commerce depended far less on the wisdom shown
by separate municipalities. than on the decisions taken for
the nation, as a whole, oy a national Parliament. From
the fifteenth century onwards, the main responsibility, for
securing the well-being of English industry and for promoting
the development of English commerce, was gradually transferred from municipal authorities to the national Parliament
and to executive institutions, which, whether localised or
not, derived their authority from the central assembly.

But the growth of Parliamentary power at the expense of municipal authority was very gradual. In the fourteenth century, at all events, the sphere of Parliamentary government was still so limited that it did not overshadow local powers; and we find new and active developments of municipal institutions under the Edwards. Some towns continued to flourish in the fifteenth century, but there were many vicissitudes in their story; the Black Death must have been a serious blow to the prosperity of many places. Troubles connected with the Peasant Revolt and the Wars of the Roses must have injured others; and we cannot be surprised to find evidence, in Tudor times, that many of them had fallen into great decay, both materially as regards their streets and houses, and socially as regards their institutions. But when English commercial life was reinvigorated in the time of Elizabeth, we can note more distinctly how much Parliament had advanced in power, and how far town institutions had fallen into the back ground. This general statement of the course of the change becomes clearer when we look at one kind of institution in greater detail.

38. The towns had come into being as centres of commerce; in the fourteenth century we find evidence that they had so far advanced as to be centres of industry, and that a corresponding modification of their institutions was becoming necessary. This may, perhaps, be most justly described as the specialisation of the gild merchant into several new bodies which were known as *craft-gilds*. The distinguishing feature of a craft-gild was not merely that its members all practised one and the same craft, but that they had authority to supervise that craft within some definite area. The privilege was sometimes granted by the king, or by some outside power, as in the case of the Exeter

Craft-gilds —their relation to municipal authority and to Gilds Merchant.

tailors ; but this was not a wise arrangement, as disagreements
and disturbances were apt to arise in a town where any
body of workers, united under royal patronage, were exempted from municipal authority in regard to all questions
connected with the exercise of their calling. By far the
most common type of craft-gild was that which derived its
authority from the mayor, as chief magistrate of the town;
in such cases the rules made by the members could be
constantly overhauled by the mayor in the common interest
of the townsmen. Thus the cordwainers of Exeter had
privileges granted them for one year at a time, and they were
unable to enforce rules which had not been previously submitted to, and approved by, the mayor and aldermen.
In the case of the bricklayers of Hull, we know of some
ordinances which were disallowed by the mayor, and to
which he would not agree. But, subject to this supervision,
the craft-gilds had very extensive powers for the regulation
of their trade. The wardens had the right of search, and
exercised it to see that good materials were used, and that
the processes of manufacture were properly performed.
They also took measures to secure that workmen should be
properly trained by serving a regular apprenticeship, and
they made rules affecting the hours of labour and the
well-being of those who were employed. The purpose of
the institution was to insure, in the interests of the public,
that work should be properly done by qualified men, and
also to secure that such qualified men as did good work
should be adequately remunerated. Throughout the fourteenth and the earlier part of the fifteenth century, the gilds
appear to have fulfilled these duties successfully on the
whole, although it seems probable that a large part of the
urban population were unskilled helpers, deriving but little
benefit from these industrial institutions, which were mainly

concerned with the work of skilled men of different
grades.

The dependence of these craft-gilds upon municipal
authority is clear enough.   It is the distinguishing feature
which separates them alike from the weavers' gilds of the
twelfth century, and from the chartered and patented companies of later times.   But it is far harder to determine
their relation to that primitive municipal institution, the
gild merchant or *hanse*, partly because the traces of this
body in the fourteenth century are very slight and obscure.
According to Dr Gross's investigations, it would seem
that the gilds merchant had almost ceased to take an
active part in the management of business in the fourteenth
century, although they still continued to have a nominal
existence, and were associated with civic pageantry, such as
nas survived in the gatherings of the Preston gild each
twentieth year.   At the very time when we hear most of
the formation and growth of craft-gilds, we almost cease to
find mention of those gilds merchant, which were so prominent in twelfth century charters.   This serves to show that
there was, at least, no violent antagonism between the two
bodies in this country.   Indeed it is far more probable that
the craft-gilds were gradually established, as one or another
craft developed, to carry on one part of that trade regulation
which had previously been exercised more generally by the
gild merchant.   We should thus regard the craft-gilds as
specialised forms of the gild merchant rather than as its
successful rivals.

It certainly appears that the men who enjoyed full
membership of the craft-gilds in the fourteenth century had
a very similar status to that of the members of the gilds
merchant in the thirteenth.   They were craftsmen and dealers.
As craftsmen they would have to buy materials and tools; as

craftsmen they would wish to sell the results of their labour, and therefore, as craftsmen, they had to take part in trading. There is no reason to believe that in twelfth century towns there was any class of store-keepers or merchants who did not practise some kind of manual calling; even the foreign merchant was probably a shipman. The members of gilds merchant in the thirteenth century were, in all probability, craftsmen first and dealers next, as far as the occupation of their time went. The list which Mr Hibbert gives of the Shrewsbury gild merchant seems to show that the members were not mere dealers. When any town increased so far as to have several men of the same calling, who were empowered by the mayor to form a craft-gild of their own, they would have less interest in the general business of the gild merchant. In some such way as this it would seem that most of the members of the gild merchant were formed into craft-gilds, and that these new bodies took over and carried out in detail the sort of regulation, which had been exercised by the same class, but in a more general way, through the gild merchant. The members of the craft-gild had a more effective instrument at their command, but they did not lose the status of members of the gild merchant, though that larger body had lost its importance.

39. The fourteenth century appears to have been the time when these craft-gilds attained their greatest influence and importance. Those in London were especially famous and enrolled various princes as *love-brothers*; but towards the middle of the century we find traces in that city of the formation of new bodies on similar lines, and composed exclusively of men engaged in dealing. They had, of course, skill to judge of the quality of goods, and to blend or sift the commodities sold. But they were store-keepers or ware-

housemen rather than artisans.   The most prominent and
powerful of these companies was that of the Grocers, while
there were others, like the Merchant Taylors, who were
wholesale dealers rather than craftsmen.   Similar trading
companies, in connexion with the cloth trade, were found in
Coventry and other provincial towns in the fifteenth century.
Early in the reign of Richard II an attempt was made to
insist on a specialisation of callings in London, and to
prohibit those who were engaged in industrial crafts and
those who were traders, from interfering in one another's
business.   The formation of these great *Livery Companies*
of traders is of interest in many ways, but chiefly because it
shows the rise of a class of merchant burgesses settled in
the towns.   The trade at fairs was declining, because it was
being transferred from occasional to regular centres of commerce, and was simultaneously passing out of the hands of
alien merchants who frequented fairs, into those of burgesses
with exclusive town rights.

40.   Other aspects of town life were not so satisfactory;

Fifteenth
century diffi-
culties be-
tween gilds,
and with jour-
neymen and
apprentices.
there was some difficulty in defining the range
of the authority exercised by each craft-gild.
The various branches of the leather trade and
the processes which fell within the purview of
the tanners, the cordwainers and the saddlers
were not easily kept distinct; and the confusion gave rise to
much dispute between these bodies.   Similarly, the claim of
the woollen weavers to exercise jurisdiction over linen weavers
was contested in London; and the different trades concerned
in the manufacture of cloth seem sometimes to have formed
separate gilds and sometimes to have been amalgamated into
one, as at Coventry in the fifteenth century.   It is difficult at
this time to see the reason or to understand the bearing of
these changes; but there were other disputes, in connexion

with fifteenth century gilds, which present them in an unfavourable light.   Journeymen, who had finished their
apprenticeship, but who had not set up independent households of their own, appear to have resented their subordinate
position, and in several cases formed combinations among
themselves for a time.   In the light of recent research it
would appear that the journeymen in England, though less
successful than their brethren on the Continent, formed
many gilds of their own.   They certainly had some temporary successes, and the struggle between the journeymen
and weavers at Coventry appears to have resulted in an
arrangement, by which the journeymen's gild was recognised as a permanent but subordinate society, which paid a
contribution to the main organisation.   These journeymen
were of course skilled men, though servants, and it is not
always easy to distinguish their history from that of unskilled
helpers, who were doubtless a larger body in some trades,
but of whose grievances little has been put on record.

  We also hear of difficulties in connexion with the
position of apprentices.   Many obstacles hindered townsmen from procuring boys for service out of rural districts.
The agricultural decay which followed the Black Death
and the progress of sheep-farming caused some anxiety
lest the area of tillage should be so greatly reduced
as to furnish an insufficient food supply.   A statute of
Richard II and, more obviously, one of Henry IV were
intended to prevent the migration of country boys to the
towns, so that an available supply of rural labour might be
maintained.   Nor were these statutes a dead letter.   The
citizens of Oxford distinctly suffered from the restrictions
that were put upon them, and failed to obtain an exemption
from this legislation, such as was granted to London and
Norwich.

      C. & M.   5

But when the masters obtained apprentices they did not always do their duty by them. They did not always teach them properly, and there were some justifiable complaints on the part of apprentices about their *finding*. In Coventry when a master was twice shown to be in fault in this matter, his apprentice was transferred to some other man, and the master was not allowed to supply his place, at any rate not for a time. The apprentice was received into the master's house as a member of the family, and the latter was responsible for his good behaviour. The system thus formed an important element with regard to the police and good order of the town, while it was believed to give opportunities of discipline which were salutary, not only for technical training, but also for the formation of character. In this latter aspect the apprenticeship system is still highly valued by those who support its revival.

41.   It appears that the influence of these associations for the maintenance of order had been considerably weakened before the end of the fifteenth century. At any rate they did not prove effective to control the apprentices under the new temptations to which they were then exposed. An incursion of aliens from Italy, who came to settle in this country, was taking place at this time, though it is difficult to assign any special or definite reason for the occurrence. Of the fact, however, there can be no doubt ; and with it there was a new bitterness against alien workmen, which showed itself partly in municipal regulations and partly in riots fomented by the apprentices. The records of Shrewsbury show that the difficulty was felt far inland, but the most violent outbreak occurred in London in 1517, on what was long remembered as ' Evil May-day.' The City authorities seem to have been quite

Craft-gilds under Henry VII and Henry VIII.—National control of industry.

helpless in the matter, and the populace, incited by a preacher, made an organised attack on the aliens.

There were other sides on which the craft-gilds were failing to discharge their public duties. From the accounts which we have of the formation of the gilds in London, it is quite clear that though the members desired to have exclusive powers, they would not have been entrusted with them, had it not seemed probable that these powers would be used in the public interest, and would help to secure a high character of work, and good quality of wares. Early in the time of Henry VI, however, there were complaints of "the unreasonable ordinances" passed by the Companies. Whether from lack of power or from lack of will the municipal authorities seem to have been unable to control them properly, and in 1504 a statute was passed which did not aim as in 1437 at re-enforcing municipal powers, but rather superseded them and placed the local craft-gilds directly under national supervision. The judges were to decide on the ordinances which might be allowed, and thus a double check was put on the self-interested action of these gilds, where it became injurious to the public. Even these checks seem to have been insufficient, and complaints became more common and more bitter. In York, in 1519, the Mayor resumed the powers of jurisdiction hitherto exercised by the gilds, and reduced them to the position of official informers in his court, while the regulative statutes of Henry VIII show that the grievances, both of apprentices and of journeymen, continued.

To some extent these misdeeds brought their own retribution upon the towns. Journeymen who might not set up independently in the towns where they had served their apprenticeship, were inclined to migrate to other places. This tendency was marked among the clothiers of Worcester, the rope-makers of Bridport, and the coverlet-makers of York. It may, in part, have been due to the burden of taxation and the pressure of the rates in these towns; but as it continued, the difficulty of making these payments was seriously increased, and an attempt was made, in the fiscal interest of the country, to check the migration. The tendency was so strong, however, that the story of urban life in the sixteenth century is rather that of the growth of new industrial centres in suburbs, or on manorial estates, than of any increased prosperity in the towns organised according to the old model. The decay of the older towns reacted unfavourably in turn on their institutions. A statute of Edward VI seems to have limited the powers hitherto enjoyed by the gilds of fixing wages and prices, and the property which they had devoted to religious purposes was confiscated in the same reign: they were not dissolved, but the time had come when they failed to subserve an important economic purpose, and they only survived like the gilds merchant in occasions of hospitality or pageantry. By the reign of Elizabeth, the municipal control of trade and industry had been superseded by institutions which emanated from national authority, even where they chiefly served to protect some locality from the immigration of aliens (§ 64).

CHAPTER V.

THE BEGINNINGS OF NATIONAL ECONOMIC LIFE.

42. IN the preceding pages attention has occasionally been directed to the many signs of a national life among the English; from early times the king was the centre of the nation, around whom they rallied in the defence of the realm.

The personal influence of the Kings. Continental connexions.

In the Norman period the king and his Exchequer are clearly in view. They provided the centre of the whole social system, and the sheriffs, in rendering their annual accounts, formed the connecting link between each separate manor and the authority which ruled over all. The king was also the greatest of all landowners, and all questions of manorial management were of importance to the Crown. He was expected 'to live of his own,' and the royal estates, when well managed, supplied the regular income which was required for administrative purposes in ordinary times. He was also the source of judicial authority, and by the discharge of its fiscal obligations each estate was brought into contact with his officers. Not only was he a typical landlord, but his office was the unifying principle, which combined the separate isolated independent elements into one whole. The personal character of the

king and his personal policy made itself felt in all relations
of life; if the king was too weak to enforce order, the
public suffered from private wars or from the exactions of
petty oppressors; if his policy was unwise, he might burden
the land with excessive, or too frequent, taxation; if his
administration was bad, he might fritter away the royal
resources and leave the Crown impoverished.   The reign of
Henry III is an instance of both these latter forms of mal-
administration, which were alike oppressive and wasteful.

While there was no side of social life and no place in
the realm which was unaffected by the influence of the
Crown, there was one department which was most directly
within the control of the king.   All matters of foreign policy,
whether of peace or of war, were in his hands, and therefore the manner in which communication was conducted
between England and Continental countries was especially
under his control.   Dynastic alliances and foreign ambitions brought England from an early time into contact with
the Continent.   King Offa made our earliest commercial
treaty, when he secured privileges for English pilgrims and
merchants by his treaty with Charles the Great.   At the
beginning of the tenth century the daughter of Alfred
cemented the connexion between England and Flanders
when she granted the manor of Lewisham to the great
Benedictine monastery at Ghent.   The power of Cnut
brought England into closer commercial relationship with
Iceland and Norway, as well as with Denmark.   The
Norman Conquest strengthened the ties with Normandy
and Flanders, and the Angevins established a connexion
with Gascony.   The carefully organised intercourse with
the Low Countries was developed through the influence
of Matilda of Flanders, while the regular import of wine
from the vineyards of Bordeaux seems to have originated in

Plantagenet times. The enterprise of Richard Cœur de Lion and the part which he took in the Crusades first introduced English seamen to the waters of the Mediterranean, and stimulated commerce in the products of the East. John and Henry III are mainly responsible for the firm hold which the Papacy secured in this country and for the heavy taxation which it levied. Thus for good or for evil the royal power was for centuries directly responsible for the economic relations between England and Continental lands.

43. Along with these early trading connexions we find some signs of a definite commercial policy. It was desirable to encourage foreign merchants to import the products and manufactures of other countries, so as to make up for the deficiencies of our native resources ; and

Regulation of foreign commerce and progress of internal development.

the settlement of the men of the Emperor in the Steel-yard in London before the Norman Conquest shows that English kings were glad to give facilities for import trade. Evidence from the same period is forthcoming as to the principle which guided them in regulating the export trade. If the raw products of this realm could be exported at profitable rates, it was desirable to send them abroad. But, from the point of view of the times, there was no object in forcing an export trade unless it was really remunerative ; even before the Conquest limits were fixed and a minimum price was settled, at which goods might be exported ; if they did not fetch this, it seemed wiser to keep them at home. When we remember that the products of England were the necessary materials for food and shelter, and were not of a nature to spoil by keeping, we may be better able to sympathise with the desire to afford Englishmen an opportunity of procuring these things on easy terms, and to insist on making foreigners pay a considerable equivalent for them before they were sent out of the country. The same principle governed much of Edward III's legislation for the wool-trade, and in one form or another affected a good deal of medieval legislation.

So far as internal regulation goes, the direct influence of the Crown was less important economically, but there were various ways in which it initiated change. The influence exercised by foreign artisans on the development of our industries has already been alluded to, but it was with royal approval that they settled here, and under royal protection that they obtained privileges.

Again, each of the several steps of progress taken by the towns received sanction from the Crown; for it was by means of royal charters that they secured the powers of regulating their own internal economy in the twelfth and thirteenth centuries. In some cases, perhaps, enterprising townsmen seized an opportunity afforded by royal necessities, but the foundation of free towns by Edward I seems to have been directly due to royal initiative. The earliest regulations affecting weights and measures or the quality of goods also seem to have emanated from the Crown. Henry I is credited with the introduction of more definite standards, and with the punishment of the officials who brought the royal honour into discredit by diminishing or debasing the coinage. In the time of Henry II we have an Assize of Bread, based on the experience of the royal bakers, and establishing a sliding scale which fixed the proper weight for a farthing loaf according to different prices of corn. As early as the time of Richard I there was an Assize of Measures, which, among other things, settled the length and breadth of the pieces of cloth exposed for sale, and subsequently an *aulnager* was appointed to supervise it. This may not im-probably indicate that there was even then some demand for English cloth abroad, but at any rate it serves to show that in very early times, when industry was least centralised and local groups were most isolated and self-dependent, the central authority was not indifferent to matters connected with foreign commerce or internal production. From the time of Edward I, however, when Parliament took shape, this central influence became much more striking, and it has gradually superseded manorial and municipal powers in the regulation of affairs of every kind.

44. English national life was carefully consolidated in the time of Edward I. His general policy was to abstain from attempts at Continental aggression and to strengthen the realm of England. His successes in Wales and his less successful attempts in Scotland were all parts of the same scheme for making his authority effective over the whole of Great Britain. And as he endeavoured to reduce the whole area to subjection, so he desired to get rid of extraneous and unpliable elements. The constitution of the towns in his day seems to show that most of the foreign settlers were absorbed into the ordinary society of the places where they lived. The Jews, whose religion and habits forced them to maintain an exceptional position, were expelled from the country at a considerable sacrifice to the revenues of the Crown, while Papal authority was repudiated when, as in the case of the alien priories, it interposed to check the royal demands. And while national unity was thus consolidated, national institutions were also improved. The creation of a Parliament, which came to include representation of the boroughs, was less important for what it immediately effected than for the steady development of national self-government which it rendered possible. Some of the contemporary measures, which afforded police

Edward I.
National
unity and
national
institutions.

protection for traders, were not despicable.   The Statute of
Acton Burnel (1283) did not create a new machinery for the
recovery of debts, but it gave a new character and a national
importance to the arrangements which had hitherto existed
locally by the custom of various towns.

Besides creating these representative institutions, Edward I showed that he possessed real administrative genius.
The changes which took place in the constitution of the
towns during his reign gave the municipal authorities a more
complete control over the various discordant elements within
their walls, and diminished the occasions of quarrel with
other authorities.   He also established a new fiscal system ;
he specified the definite ports through which trade should
flow to and from the realm, and he appointed *customers*
whose business it was to collect the duties which traders
had to pay.   During his reign the central authority was
brought to bear, so as to give immensely improved facilities
for internal trade.

45.   When the realm was thus consolidated and when
its national life was regulated internally, it
became more possible to develop a commercial policy, and to make systematic arrangements for foreign trade.   This change becomes
noticeable in the time of Edward III.   He had a vigorous
foreign policy, and apparently indulged in dreams of continental conquest, while there can be little doubt that trading
and commercial considerations helped to determine the
form of his contest with the French king.   England and
Flanders were closely bound together by common industrial
interests, as the former supplied the raw wool which the
Flemings manufactured, dyed, and dressed; and a considerable number of these skilled artisans found it advantageous to emigrate to England in 1331 and 1336.   Had

*Edward III.
Foreign and
commercial
policy.*

the English king been successful in establishing a claim to the
French crown and in obtaining suzerainty over the Flemish
towns, the leading burghers would have warmly welcomed
the political connexion with England. In a somewhat similar fashion the English provinces in the South of France
supplied wine and other products, which England could not
produce satisfactorily from her own soil. Edward's desire
to be acknowledged king of France becomes more intelligible when we see that thus he would have secured a complete and independent sovereignty over this wine-growing
district. It seems to have been his design to bring the
South of France and the manufacturing districts of Flanders
into close connexion with England by common subjection
to the English king; thus he would have laid the foundations of a great commercial empire, each part of which
would have supplemented the requirements of the others.
To establish and maintain free intercommunication between
the different parts of this empire, it was desirable to assert
the king's peace upon the sea, and to diminish the risks
which traders underwent from the attacks of pirates. On
some such grounds Edward III put forward this claim to
the sovereignty of the sea, and gave it expression by the
issue of the noble—a gold coin which was meant to circulate
in Flanders as well as in England.

His conduct confirms the view that some such scheme
floated before the minds of Edward and his advisers; and
the manner in which he asserted his claim to the crown of
France, and then failed to press it when the country lay at
his feet, seems to show that conquest of additional territory
was not, after all, his main object. When the treaty of
Bretigni was signed in 1360, circumstances had so far changed
that he did not stand out for the scheme described above,
in its entirety. He appears to have been satisfied to pur-

chase immunity from Scotch attacks by sacrificing his
pretensions in Flanders; but his schemes appear to have
been statesmanlike, and so much progress was made in his
reign as almost to justify the appellation which he afterwards received of 'Father of English Commerce.'

46. In so far as this view of Edward III's foreign
policy is correct, it serves to explain the line
which he pursued in dealing with aliens in
England. Alien merchants had always been
welcomed in this country, so long as they furnished the
realm with useful products from abroad, and while they
confined themselves to wholesale trading and did not compete with Englishmen in retail and internal trade. Under
Edward III, who desired to encourage frequent intercommunication with Flanders and Gascony, the privileges of
aliens were interpreted in the largest sense, so that the
whole of the shipping trade of the country fell into their
hands, while they also intruded in much of the internal
business. The invitation and encouragement extended to
weavers from abroad, and also to men who practised other
callings, may all be regarded as part of the same policy.
It seems, however, to have awakened among Englishmen a
decided jealousy of aliens. This took effect in the following
reign, when the reaction against the policy of Edward III
made itself felt in many ways, and obtained the support
of Parliament and the assent of the Crown.

There was one direction, however, in which the influence
of Edward III and the legislation of his reign was much
more permanent. He revived and reorganised more completely the institution of staple towns to which all English
products should be consigned, and in which the English merchants of the staple should do their business with continental
traders. Such staple towns had been a common system of

mercantile policy from the earliest times. Carthage was a staple town for the products of the Western Mediterranean and of a great portion of Africa: the trading cities of Italy, Greece, and the Ægean were forced by Carthaginian fleets to frequent this staple, and prevented from dealing directly with Spain or with the other lands which lay within the sphere of their influence. In a somewhat similar fashion Bergen was a Norwegian staple, whither the products of the Northern Seas were brought, and where other European merchants were forced to buy them, if they wished to enter on this line of trade at all. The concentration of trade at a single point was certainly convenient for the collection of revenue, and the customs derived from the staple commodities were, throughout the fifteenth century, a very important item of the royal revenue. But the organisation of staple towns would scarcely have been so general and so long continued if it had not been advantageous from the merchant's point of view as well as in a fiscal aspect. When the streams of commerce were feeble and intermittent there was a real advantage in concentrating them in one channel. Buyers and sellers were each more sure of a good market, while they could hope to sell and to purchase goods on satisfactory terms. It was possible too to provide rights and privileges which rendered the merchant's goods and warehouse secure from arbitrary exactions, and which gave him the means of recovering his debts by simple legal processes. Though they finally adopted it, there is reason to believe that Edward III's advisers were not clear as to the advisability of the institution in the earlier period of the reign. Even after the staple was reorganised in 1353, there was still some doubt as to whether it was wiser to fix on an English or on a Continental town as the depot for English goods. Eventually the problem

was solved by assigning the position to Calais, an English
town across the Channel; and the merchants of the staple
formed the first of the great Companies of English merchants
who had special privileges assigned them for carrying on one
branch of foreign trade.   They dealt in the four staple commodities, wool, wool-fells, hides, and lead—all, as may be
observed, raw products—and they shipped them to be disposed of at the staple town of Calais.   Their work continued
to be of real importance, although it diminished somewhat
as the English advanced in the knowledge of industrial arts,
and ceased to export raw products so largely, because they
worked up these materials within the realm.   The loss of
the town of Calais put an end to their active trade there,
although the merchants continued to have a certain status.
The Company, though shorn of its former glory, is not even
yet extinct.

47.   With the reign of Richard II the national economic life of England seems to enter on a new
phase.   Various causes were at work which
were tending to transfer the business of the
country from the aliens who carried on the trade at fairs,
and to place it in the hands of English merchants who
conducted their business at their houses in the towns.
A class of wealthy native merchants was coming into notice,
and they were powerful enough to make their influence felt
in the proceedings of Parliament.

New devel-
opments under
Richard II.

Attention has been called in a previous paragraph (p. 69)
to the personal influence exercised by the king, but the end
of the fourteenth century was the time when an effective
public opinion began to influence economic legislation.
This may be noticed in the Good Parliament of 1376, but it
seems to have exerted itself more successfully in the reign of
Richard II.   As time went on there came to be occasions

of grave difference between the economic policy which com-
mended itself to the public opinion of the country and that
which was pursued by the king and his advisers. But in the
fifteenth century Parliament and the Crown appear on the
whole to have co-operated together; though the personal
character of the king was no longer of such exclusive importance. There are some signs of a real public opinion from the
time of Richard II onwards—not necessarily the opinion of
a large public, but one that embodied the common opinion
of local aristocracies of wealthy burgesses.

By the time of Richard II, too, the process of superseding
local by national administration, which has been described
above (p. 59), had gone a considerable way. It was much
more possible to enforce similar trade regulations in all
parts of the country, and even to carry out a similar trade
policy, than it would have been in the days of Richard
Cœur de Lion.

48. But most important of all, we see that the policy
which was pursued by Edward III was defi- Plenty and
nitely discarded by his grandson; and we Power.
find indications of another course, which, when finally
adopted and regularly pursued, was known as the Mercantile
System. There is, however, no evidence that it was
consciously thought out and deliberately followed before
the time of the Tudors.

Probably different parts of the system were introduced
under immediate pressure, and because they favoured the
aspirations of English merchants. Even when thus fitfully
adopted, the new policy amounted to a deliberate rejection
of the methods approved by Edward III. In later times,
when it was completely systematised, as for example under
the Tudors, it is seen to be a commercial policy which
aimed not merely at securing plenty of foreign products,

but also tended to increase the power of the realm. This, as Bacon saw, was the crucial difference; Edward III, by favouring the easy access of alien merchants, pursued a policy of *plenty*, since they brought large quantities of foreign goods in their ships; he imperfectly anticipated the free trade policy of England at the present time, which aims at securing plenty of foreign food and foreign materials for English consumers Those on the other hand who advocated the mercantile policy, aimed at promoting the political *power* of the realm, and were ready to subordinate the convenience of producers and to sacrifice the comforts and tastes of consumers to this great national object

This was the one great aim which more or less consciously dominated our economic policy for centuries; when we bear it steadily in mind, much of the fidgety and petty legislation of the seventeenth and eighteenth centuries becomes intelligible, even if we still regard it as unwise. The Mercantile System, as completely thought out, rested on the principle, not of fostering industry and commerce for their own sakes, but of trying to guide them into such directions that they should subserve the political power of the realm. Similar schemes were in vogue in different countries, in Spain, France, Holland, and elsewhere, but the special form which economic policy took in our case was due to the special conditions of our national life. An island realm can only be strong either for defence or offence when it is a naval power; and hence, the development of our shipping and the encouragement of our commerce gradually came to be the most prominent features in the economic policy of the realm.

There are three elements in political strength which may be considered in turn. First, sufficient food must be procurable to provide for the maintenance and rearing of a

well-nourished population from which soldiers and sailors
may be drawn: secondly, a sufficient supply of money or
treasure must be available in the royal coffers to meet any
emergency, and this in a realm that has no mines can
only be amassed by the careful regulation of industry and
trade ; last and not least in the case of England, it has
been necessary to develop shipping with its subsidiary employments. Great pains have been taken at different times
to strengthen the country on all these sides. It is not
possible to separate them altogether from one another, for
each factor in our industrial life has had a double bearing,
and success in one direction has often reacted favourably
on another. Thus (i) the obtaining of an adequate food
supply, (ii) the progress of industry, and (iii) the development of commerce were partly pursued as independent
objects, but there was also (iv) an underlying policy, which
insisted on treating them with conscious reference to the
offensive and defensive strength of the realm. Keeping
these main points in view it may be convenient to deal
with them in turn, and to indicate the various ways in
which the strong hand of the central authority has exercised
its influence on each.

CHAPTER VI.

THE VARIOUS SIDES OF NATIONAL ECONOMIC LIFE

I. The Food Supply.

49. THERE were special circumstances in the time of Richard II and in subsequent reigns which gave rise to anxiety with regard to our food supply. The disorganization of rural society and the increase of sheep-farming, which ensued on the Black Death, seemed to threaten wide-spread disaster. If the land were allowed to go out of cultivation, it would be impossible to procure sufficient corn for the subsistence of the people; and hence we have a succession of legislative measures which were definitely intended to promote tillage.

The migration of the rural population.

Among the earlier regulations of this sort were restrictive laws, which were devised to prevent the migration of the rural population to the towns. This may have been, to some extent, a military precaution, as it was generally believed that an outdoor country life was favourable to the development of a population, which should be physically capable of rendering effective service in time of war; while the depopulation of the coasts was also a military danger, since the sheep and their shepherds could offer no effective resistance to the landing of a hostile force. But the main object of the measures, which restrained the country people from migrating to the towns, was that of maintaining sufficient rural labour to carry on cultivation. Although, in some cases, those who were ready to work were evicted to make room for sheep, yet in the fourteenth century it was a matter of more common complaint that labourers could hardly be obtained in agricultural districts. There is much said in the present day about the flocking of the rural population to the towns, but it is not a new phenomenon; for active efforts were made to check it nearly five centuries ago. In the time of Richard II legislation only affected adult labourers, but under Henry IV and Henry VI stringent measures were passed to prevent the children of rural labourers from becoming apprentices. Efforts were made to keep the rising generation on the soil; that these measures were not inoperative is shown by the complaints of the men of Oxford as to the decay of their trades, and by their fruitless efforts to obtain exemption. In the great Statute of Artificers (1563), this principle was incorporated. Special facilities were given for training boys to those employments which were subsidiary to agriculture, if not to agriculture itself. And the distinction was so far maintained and acted upon that this point was noted as an important factor in the decay of the domestic system, and the growth of factories as late as 1804[1].

50. Another method of favouring tillage and preventing the development of sheep-farming is found in the statutes restricting the number of sheep which any one man might possess. Two

Restrictions on sheep-farming.

[1] Mr Cookson of Leeds argued before a Committee of the House of Commons that it was desirable to modify the Act of 1563, so as to favour apprenticeship to the clothing trades in rural districts.

thousand was regarded as an outside limit in the time of
Henry VIII, and Edward VI expressed himself personally
in favour of such a course.   But it is difficult to see how a
statute of this kind could be enforced, since evasion was
not difficult.   Another series of measures with a similar
object was also enacted.   These rendered land-owners responsible for re-erecting any houses of husbandry that had
fallen into decay within a given period.   The most celebrated
of these measures followed on the official enquiry of 1517,
which disclosed a considerable amount of depopulation during
the previous twenty-eight years.   Similar measures were passed
under Elizabeth when the price of wool was, on the whole,
very high.   In 1592 it had dropped, and with the lowered
price of wool Francis Bacon thought that the motive to de-
populate no longer came into play.   In the five following
years, with a higher price there was some recrudescence
of the tendency, but it appears to have so far ceased
to operate in the early part of the reign of James I that
such restrictive measures were no longer necessary.

51.   Other schemes for the encouragement of tillage
were also organised and maintained: the fa-
vourite expedient in the Elizabethan time
aimed at securing that the farmer should have
a remunerative price for his corn.   The traditional method
of securing cheap food had been embodied in Solon's legislation and prohibited export; but in a country where there
was any choice about the kind of cultivation or the extent
of cultivation, such restrictions were apt to defeat themselves.
A wiser course, suggested as early as the time of Richard II,
was that of giving greater liberty for export, especially when
corn was unusually cheap.   In this way the farmer could count
on getting a remunerative price even in very plentiful years.
This line of policy was embodied in the celebrated Corn

(marginal note:) Maintenance of the high price of corn.

Bounty Act of William III (1689), which appears to have accomplished its object with wonderful success. Probably corn was not as cheap as it would otherwise have been, especially in plentiful years. But the price was kept exceedingly steady at a moderate level, which yet afforded an ample profit to the agriculturist. Under these circumstances he was encouraged to farm on a larger scale and by improved methods; so much land was thus brought into cultivation, that even in unfavourable seasons there was a sufficient supply of native grown corn and the price rose but little.

52. Well adapted to its ends though this policy appears to have been, it could not be indefinitely pursued. It was only practicable when a large area of land was available for cultivation at a moderate expense. When population increased, and with it the demand for additional food, this could not be remuneratively procured from England alone. Till 1773 England was able to supply her own wants entirely, and generally to send some surplus corn to Sweden and other countries. But from 1773 to 1793 there was a period when the demand and the supply were almost equally balanced; when there was very little export of corn, and when importation was often necessary (§ 118). From 1793 onwards the change was complete, and England became permanently and regularly dependent on foreign countries for a supply of food. The problem of national subsistence thus assumed a new form, and the Corn Laws, which had been devised for entirely different circumstances, ceased to serve their purpose.

Changed conditions of corn-growing.

53. In the last decade of the eighteenth century the difficulty of procuring sufficient food for the population of England made itself felt in the severest fashion. There were

several successive seasons of exceedingly bad harvests; and

Scarcity and
the allowance
system. during the time of war, it was almost impossible to procure from foreign countries the supply of corn which the nation now required, even in fairly good years. The distress of the labouring poor was terrible, and all sorts of expedients were devised to meet it. Some benefit may have accrued from the efforts which were made by the wealthy to restrict the consumption of corn in their households; thus the inhabitants of Kensington on one occasion decided to abjure pastry. But, after all, such devices, though testifying to a wide-spread sympathy for the poor, would add comparatively little to the stock of corn available for their support. There was a general demand, which found favour in many quarters, for the regulation of wages by a sliding scale, so that the working man might have more power of purchasing food; but this scheme, though plausible, was felt to be impracticable as a measure of relief. It would only increase the effectual demand for corn, even at a high price, and thus tend to drive the price higher and higher with each new advance of wages. The method eventually adopted was fraught with disastrous consequences in pauperizing the rural population. This was the system introduced by the Berkshire Justices in 1795 of giving allowances (under Gilbert's Act of 1782) to supplement the meagre earnings of the labourer. It seemed to be the common sense way of meeting the difficulty, in the most direct manner, with the least dislocation of ordinary trade. It was evidently intended as a temporary expedient, and had it been merely temporary it might have served its purpose in the least costly fashion. But the continuance of war, together with the decay of by-employments in rural districts which followed on the introduction of machine spinning, rendered it impossible to revert to the

old order; and allowances, with all their demoralizing and
pauperizing effects, came to be an integral part of our industrial system. They served, indeed, to tide over the worst
period of distress, but at the cost of a serious deterioration
in the character of the rural labourers.

54. Much controversy ensued and many interests
were sacrificed before the English Parliament
determined to accept a position of per-   Excuses for
manent dependence for a substantial portion and effects of
of our national food supply on foreign corn, the Corn Law
                                             of 1815.
purchased with the results of national industry and with
national mineral wealth. While foreign corn was practically
excluded by the war, the rural classes, landlords, farmers,
and yeomanry had been very prosperous; and owing to the
high price of corn they had not seriously felt the great increase of the rates. To them the admission of foreign corn
and a sudden fall of price would have meant ruin (§ 120);
and the ruin of the agricultural interest would, it was said,
be followed by the still deeper misery of the agricultural
labourers. The analogy of the earlier part of the eighteenth
century seemed to show that an artificial method of rendering agriculture remunerative was quite compatible with
the prosperity of all rural classes, and with the comfort of
the artisans, if only they were sufficiently paid. The analogy
was false, for circumstances had greatly changed, and
our soil no longer afforded an ample home supply of food
with a margin for export. Still, the project was so far
plausible that Parliament passed the Corn Law of 1815,
which prohibited importation till corn should reach the price
of 80s. per quarter. The landed interest had their way, and
they were inclined to urge that the distress in the manufacturing towns should be met by a rise of wages.

But this expedient was impracticable. The close of the

war did not open up any new markets for English goods.
They had previously been smuggled into the countries from
which they were officially excluded, and the poverty, which
followed in the wake of the Napoleonic wars, prevented any
active demand from the Continent. Besides this, some of these
countries had little but corn with which to pay for English
goods, and the Corn Law prevented them from purchasing
with the only commodity that was available to them.   With
such reduced demands from abroad, English manufacturers
could not give much employment, far less could they raise
the rate of pay.   Even as regards the home market, the
poverty of the working classes and the dearness of food
rendered it impossible for them to spend as much as they
had previously done on manufactured goods. The Corn Laws
interfered with the foreign demand for our commodities, and
by causing a high price diminished the home demand. Hence
it was that the manufacturers, headed by Cobden and Bright,
demanded the repeal of the Corn Laws   They urged that
apart from their injurious effects, they were unnecessary, since
the prosperity of our manufactures would enable us to purchase a sufficient quantity of food.   Thirty-one years after the
landed interest had been buttressed by the Corn Law of 1815,
the manufacturing interest procured its repeal (1846).   According to the new policy then entered upon, our national food
supply is not mainly produced at home, but is chiefly purchased
from abroad, and the maintenance of our commercial supremacy, and the success of our manufacturing industry, have
come to be essential for procuring national subsistence.

55.   When this change was brought about there were
those who argued that such dependence on
food supplies from abroad would be a grave
political danger, and that in time of war our
enemies might cut off our supplies and starve

Political and economic results of its repeal.

us into complete submission. So far this fear has not been realized; the warning failed to attract much attention, because it was clear, from the experience of the twenty years after Waterloo (1815), that the Corn Law with all its disadvantages did not render us really self-sufficing, or give us complete immunity from this danger. But apart altogether from the political question, it may be said that our economic prosperity, if far greater, rests on a less stable basis than it did in earlier days. A country, which has its own resources of food and the materials for its own manufactures within itself, is liable to fewer risks and dangers than one which is dependent on outside supplies for the very necessaries of existence. The sudden collapse of the industrial and commercial greatness of Athens is, at least, a warning of the inherent weakness of any society which can only procure its food and its materials through the efficiency of its marine.

II. Industrial Life.

56. WHEN we trace the history of the seventeenth and eighteenth centuries, it is easy to see that in the regulation of industry, as on all other sides   Labourers' wages. of economic life, the promotion of national power was a paramount consideration. Every effort was made to provide employment for the people, so that an effective population might be maintained ; and a distinct preference was shown for those kinds of industry which favoured the influx of the precious metals, and thus gave the means of accumulating treasure in the royal coffers.   These points may be brought out below; in the meantime it is more important to notice how the national machinery for regulation was slowly formed, and to show what a firm grip it had on every side of industrial life. National administrators began to do more effec-

tively what manorial and civic authorities had hitherto attempted, and to make wise regulations for the quality of goods and the conditions and terms of employment.

The Black Death marks the time when these matters were first taken cognisance of by Parliament. So far as questions of the times of work or the reward of agriculturists arose before that epoch, they were apparently decided in each particular manor in accordance with its custom. The Statutes of Labourers, passed by Edward III, confirmed customary wages in some callings, and entrusted the enforcement of the law to the Justices of the Peace. These officials also possessed discretionary powers to fix wages in a few occupations, but in the reign of Richard II (1389) they were empowered to assess wages more generally, and according to the plenty or scarcity of the time. In subsequent reigns their duties were more commonly limited to the proclamation and enforcement of statutory rates, fixed either absolutely or within certain limits by Parliament. Occasionally they were authorised to assess as well as to proclaim a scale of wages: this latter plan was definitely adopted by Elizabeth in the Statute of Artificers (1563), and very severe penalties were threatened against those justices who neglected their duty. There seem to have been serious efforts to carry the law into effect in various parts of the country up to the time of the Civil War, and the Council occasionally brought pressure on the local authorities to perform this duty. In the latter part of the seventeenth century the practice probably fell into desuetude, though it seems to have been maintained in Yorkshire and possibly elsewhere. Apparently in the earlier part of the eighteenth century it was not in general use, although it was occasionally acted on in Shropshire. On the other hand, the attempts, which were made in 1728 and 1756 to enforce a similar line of policy in the interests of the clothing trade in Gloucestershire, show that this measure was quite neglected and practically unknown in that county.

During the period of great distress at the end of the eighteenth century, when food was so dear and remuneration was so inadequate, it was proposed in Parliament to amend the old law and to impose on the justices the duty of fixing a minimum wage. Some of the reasons against this attempt have been indicated in a preceding section (p. 86), but it was also obvious that an attempt to raise wages suddenly might lead to the dismissal of all the aged or inefficient, whose work was not worth a high rate of pay. This seems to have been the last attempt to revive this policy for rural districts ; but at a time of terrible distress, the cotton operatives in Lancashire fell back on the provisions of this Act as a means of securing the object they had in view—the legal determination of 'a living wage,' which should be regarded as a minimum. The employers and the magistrates appear to have been favourable to the plan, but Parliament pronounced against it, and repealed the clauses by which the justices had been required to regulate wages (1813). This great department of national well-being, which had been regulated in early times by the several customs of distinct manors, was treated as a proper subject for supervision by royally commissioned officials from the time of Edward III till 1813, when the policy of *laissez faire* triumphed, and this with so much else was left to be adjusted by private bargaining and free competition.

57. The methods for relief of the poor adopted in London and other towns gave suggestions for Tudor legislation, but little help could be derived from ordinary medieval practice. The charity of which we hear most was that distributed by the

Poor Relief under Elizabeth.

monasteries in doles; while a large portion of the rural
population were restricted to, and had rights on, the land.
The problems of rural pauperism must have been very different from those which we have to face at the present day.
In Tudor times, however, the increase of sheep-farming
and the diminution of agricultural employment combined
with other causes to bring out the necessity for organising a
regular system of poor relief.   And Parliament encouraged
the ecclesiastical authorities to deal with the matter.   The
parish, an ecclesiastical division, was taken as the area to
be dealt with, and ecclesiastical officers, the churchwardens,
were originally authorised to exercise compulsory powers in
gathering money to be used as poor relief, though additional
overseers were subsequently appointed.   A new national
system was completed in 1601 to meet this need   Until the
time of the Civil War the Council and the justices appear to
have exercised very effective control over the parochial authorities in the execution of their duties.   In the eighteenth
century each parish became practically independent in the
matter till central control was re-introduced by the reform
of 1834.

58.   The available resources, in different parishes, dif-
Parochial   fered greatly, and in the seventeenth century
settlements.   vagrants were inclined to fasten themselves on
some parish, where the common waste was good, and the
parish stock was large.   With a view to guarding against this
unfairness, a Law of parochial *settlements* was passed under
Charles II (1662), which carefully defined for what poor
each parish should be responsible.   This measure had many
unexpected and disastrous effects.   Each parish was able
to prevent the ingress of outsiders to reside within its
bounds, if there seemed any danger of their becoming
chargeable on the rates.   And by this means a new obstacle

was created, which acted almost as serfdom had done, in tying the labourer to his native place and preventing him from seeking better employment elsewhere.

The mutual jealousy of parishes and a desire to reduce the pressure of their rates led at times to great harshness in the treatment of the poor, and to a war on cottages on the part of some landlords. In some *open* parishes, where there were many small proprietors and no common policy among them, many houses were run up, and the cottagers who were expelled from neighbouring parishes resorted thither. Castle Acre in Norfolk was particularly notorious in this respect; there a demoralizing practice arose in the present century of forming gangs of mere children, who were little better than the slaves of a master, and who were hired in masses to do field labour in thinly populated parishes. This was a serious if exceptional evil to which attention was directed in 1843.

59. There were other evils connected with the administration of poor relief; assistance was given as outdoor relief, and there was a curious alternation between heartless stringency and undue laxity in the method of administration. During the seventeenth and eighteenth centuries there was a continual struggle to find some system by which work might be provided, so that the idle might be discriminated from the unfortunate. In the seventeenth century the chief expedient was to teach spinning, and the wide diffusion of this art in the eighteenth century was not improbably due to the efforts of local authorities to popularise it. At the close of the seventeenth century pauperism increased by leaps and bounds; this gave rise to wide-spread alarm, and resulted in attempts to institute workhouses, where the adult poor might find employment. There were, however, grave diffi

culties in making them remunerative, and the check which pauperism received during the earlier part of the eighteenth century can hardly be ascribed to their influence. It was more probably due to the improved agricultural conditions of that time, which removed some of the causes of poverty, and to the demand which arose for able-bodied labour in the American colonies. These circumstances, together with the general severity of administration which came into fashion, kept down the evil in a somewhat ruthless way, but towards the end of the century, there was a reaction in favour of a more generous treatment of the poor. Two enabling measures, in 1782 and 1795, then permitted the formation of Gilbert 'incorporations' in which the funds were better administered, and sanctioned the action of the justices in granting allowances from the rates to supplement the income of labouring families.

60. The circumstances which called forth this disastrous measure have been described above (p. 86), but a wool famine which occurred about the same time threw many spinners out of employment, or forced them to work at unremunerative rates. The allowances seem to have been an expedient for giving a temporary substitute in lieu of the earnings of women and children. But as domestic spinning never revived, this temporary measure came to be a permanent institution, and during the first thirty years of the present century outdoor relief was largely given in forms which tended to foster a pauper class.

Allowances and the new Poor Law.

These various evils were so crying that a drastic measure of reform was rendered necessary in 1834. A central board was created, which exercised wide control and gave a more uniform character to the administration of poor relief in different districts. It was a time of great national distress, both rural and urban, and the new authority carried out its first reforms under adverse circumstances. But it has suc-

ceeded in abolishing the worst abuses of the old days.
If national poor relief is unsympathetically given and
unthankfully received, it is at least less harsh and less
pauperising than it was at various times in the eighteenth
century.

61. National organisation has come into vogue in
another direction to provide facilities for   Internal
internal communication. This was recog-   communica-
nised as a national duty from the earliest times   tion.
as part of the *trinoda necessitas*; but it had, in all probability,
more reference in those days to military than to commercial
convenience. Throughout the Middle Ages and indeed
until the reign of Queen Mary the repair of the roads
appears to have been left to private munificence. It was
an object to which the charitable devoted money in their wills,
and to which the monasteries in their more prosperous days
gave considerable attention. When Parliament took the
matter up, it supplemented rather than superseded the
action of local authorities. As in the case of poor
relief, the ecclesiastical organisation was used as the agent
for effecting this important piece of civil work. Each parish
was rendered responsible for the care of its roads, while the
justices were called upon to exercise a general supervision
and to see that the parochial authorities did their duty.
Increased prosperity in the eighteenth century rendered
improved roads a commercial necessity. A General Highway Act was passed (1741), and the principle was adopted
of collecting tolls, so that those who used the roads might
contribute to their repair. The immediate effect of this
measure was surprising; in the early part of the eighteenth
century English roads had been disgracefully bad, but before its close they had attained to a very high standard of
excellence.

62. From a very early time the central government
Quality and price of bread and cloth. devoted some attention to the quality of goods and to the regulation of fair prices.
The necessaries of life first received consideration. According to the Assize of Bread already referred to (p. 72), efforts were made to devise a self-acting system, which should prove fair both to producers and to consumers by providing sufficient remuneration for the baker and his men, while it secured that the public should obtain loaves of the right size and weight for their money ; the loaf was to be larger or smaller according as corn was cheap or dear. The due execution of this Assize and the effective punishment of those who infringed it was part of the ordinary duties of manorial and other local courts. As it was one of the earliest, so also was it a long-continued piece of national regulation. Early in the eighteenth century (1709) it was re-issued in more modern phraseology, and in 1757, when the harvest had failed, the London magistrates tried to carry out this policy stringently. The results were, however, sufficiently disastrous to prove conclusively that the time had gone by when such measures could be advantageously enforced.

The next great department in which we hear of national regulation was in regard to clothing. A royal official, the *aulnager*, was appointed, whose business it was to see that the cloth exposed for sale was of the proper length and breadth. At first his attention was partly given to imported cloth, but there are indications that he was also called upon to supervise the product of English looms. There were various towns which got into trouble for stretching their cloth unduly, and the aulnager's seal was intended to be a guarantee that the cloth was of sufficient size and weight, and to render it acceptable to consumers either at home or abroad. The traditional character and objects of

the institution are perhaps most easily seen in the time
of Charles II, when attempts were made to foster a clothing
trade in Ireland.   The appointment of an aulnager in that
country in 1665 appears to have been regarded as a step of
first importance, if there was to be successful competition
with the established industries of other lands.   And though
English economists and politicians took measures to repress
this growing industry, the aulnager and his salary survived.

    With the steady growth of the English cloth manufacture
the duties of the aulnager must have become more and more
complicated.   There are complaints from Norfolk of the
exactions of this officer in 1328, and there were special
difficulties when Flemish weavers, accustomed to different
measurements, settled in this country in the time of Edward
III.   The variety which had been introduced into the trade is
most clearly reflected in the legislation of Edward IV, which
enumerates a large number of cloths of different sizes and
qualities, made in various parts of the country.   From this
time, legislation affecting the quality and weight of cloth
was very frequent; the various measures are enumerated in
the statute of 1809 which repealed them all.   At this
date all such attempts at regulation were discredited;
Englishmen were pushing their trade in all parts of the
world, and it was not desirable to define too rigidly the
character of the goods made for so many markets.   To
have maintained the old rules would have hampered
manufacturers in catering for public taste.   There was
no longer the same necessity to preserve these rules as a
security for quality, since a new guarantee was afforded by
manufacturers' trade-marks.   While cloth was made on the
domestic system, such marks could not become a well-known
guarantee, but under the system of factory-production, the
trade-marks of the large houses came to be widely known,

and their reputation served, to some extent, to warrant the character of the goods that they supplied.

63. There were, especially during the Stuart period,
Patents and monopolies. various other instances in which the supervision of a certain department was entrusted to particular officials; this was attempted in the case of alehouses, gold lace and gunpowder. A more common expedient was that of granting special privileges for this purpose to a body of persons thoroughly acquainted with, and actually engaged in, some trade, who could effectively bring home responsibility for defects to particular persons. Some of the London companies, like the Tanners, acquired an extensive right of search of this kind, while others had reserved to them exclusive rights of production. This method of granting exclusive privileges by patent had been relied on by Burleigh, but gave rise to dissatisfaction even in the time of Elizabeth and under James I. Even though plausible reasons were alleged, and the intentions of the Crown were disinterested, the public was badly served by the patentees or their agents. Under Charles I the system received farther development, when he granted exclusive patents for the production of some articles of common consumption. Thus he hoped to secure a revenue, similar to an excise, by granting a patent for soap. It was carefully devised so as to evade the terms of the statute of 1624, but the indignation, which it aroused, rendered it impossible for Charles to proceed, while it brought the whole of this system of national regulation into discredit.

64. National regulation had, however, served a useful
Alien workmen. Incorporated Companies. purpose in various ways. English kings were, from a very early time, alive to the importance of trying to plant new industries within the realm. It was under the shelter of royal

protection that the Dutch Bay makers established their industry at Colchester, and that the Walloons carried out their careful system of trade regulation at Norwich. The benefit, which accrued to the nation from these new trades, was undoubted ; but it was not readily recognised in the localities affected, and Crown patents and protection were necessary to give a proper footing to the new-comers. In subsequent times exclusive privileges in a calling were occasionally conferred on individuals by Act of Parliament, as in the case of the Kidderminster Carpet weavers and the Sheffield Cutlers. It is noticeable that the companies, specified by Adam Smith as chiefly to be deprecated, were bodies of this type. Though thus used to plant new industries, it appears that the same system of trade regulation by charter from the Crown was occasionally used to shelter the inhabitants of certain towns from the incursion and competition of aliens. Exclusive privileges for the carrying on of some industry were granted by charter to local com-panies, who could then exclude the alien workmen of that craft. In some cases the number of separate callings united in one exclusive company is so large that it is impossible to believe that there could have been good common super-vision over such a varied assortment of wares. In the formation of these exclusive companies in Newcastle, Carlisle, and London, and in their attempted formation at Hull, we may perhaps feel that the regulation of industry was a mere excuse. The maintenance of exclusive rights was, very probably, the real object, which townsmen had in view in procuring the expensive privilege of a royal charter. But whatever their precise object may have been, the accounts of the rapid formation of these industrial companies in the sixteenth and seventeenth centuries prove that national authority not only took the place of the towns

in commercial regulation, but that it also completely superseded merely municipal organisations for the regulation of
industry.

65. These various measures may be regarded as
methods for regulating craftsmen, but they
were all intended to be expedients for
fostering native industry. The policy of protection in
some form or other was very old; there are signs of
it in the cloth trade in the thirteenth and fourteenth
centuries, and it developed very rapidly in many employments under the Yorkists and the Tudors. In some
of its phases it is hardly to be distinguished from
the jealousy of alien workmen, to which allusion has
been already made; but in the seventeenth century it was
deliberately pursued on carefully reasoned, if mistaken
grounds. Every effort was made to plant new industries,
so as to render England, as far as possible, independent of
foreign nations for her supplies. As this matter is dealt with
more fully below (§ 87) it may suffice to indicate here that if
we bought few manufactured goods from foreigners, and had
much to sell them, they would be forced to pay us in bullion
and thus to augment our treasure. Such was the argument,
and even when its unsoundness was becoming apparent to
far-seeing men, it yet served to make men eager to plant new
industries, to import materials cheap, to open up markets
for our surplus wares, and in every way to encourage native
industry. The doctrine that labour is the source of all wealth
gave additional force to the desire to provide employment
for hands at home, and to incur no unnecessary expense
in purchasing the results of foreign labour. It was only
after the time of Adam Smith, when international economic
jealousy had become less keen, that it was possible for
the ordinary politician to regard different nations as co-

operating for the common advantage, rather than as un-
scrupulous traders who were always striving to gain at each
other's expense.

66.   The general result of the tendencies described in
the foregoing paragraphs may, perhaps, be   Economic
most clearly indicated by noting how great   freedom.
a change was gradually brought about in the   Migration.
condition of the individual.   He gained freedom in many
ways—freedom of movement, freedom of employment and
freedom to associate.   In the earlier Middle Ages, when
local authority was a leading influence in economic affairs,
freedom of movement was impossible for the industrial
classes.   In the rural districts the peasant was *astricted* to
the manorial estate (p. 34), and could not attempt to better
his condition by seeking for work elsewhere.   So too in the
towns.   The craftsman had his privileged position in the
particular community of which he was free, and would not,
generally speaking, desire to effect any change.   In some
ways Parliamentary authority was used to bolster up these
restrictions when they were beginning to break down.   Under
the Lancastrians, attempts were made to prevent the rural
population from migrating to the towns, while the Tudors
aimed at hindering artisans from forsaking the impoverished places in which they dwelt.   But, on the whole,
national regulation of the labourer's position by successive
Statutes of Labourers, and the more general administration
of the law by Justices of the Peace tended to bring about
the recognition of a class of free agricultural labourers who
worked for wages, and who were not hindered from moving
about in search of employment.   In the time of Charles II
a system of astriction was re-introduced in connexion with
the parochial administration of poor relief; the manner in
which this law of settlements (1662) interfered with the

fluidity of labour has been remarked upon above (p. 92). Here it may suffice to say that the evil was soon recognised, and that attempts were made to rectify it. Considerable improvements were introduced in 1795, and the conditions were still further modified when the whole poor-law system was re-cast in 1834.

67. Freedom of movement within the realm was not easily secured; freedom to leave the realm was a boon which was still longer delayed. It was not to the interest of the country that Englishmen should go abroad, since the Crown would, in that case, be unable to rely upon their services for the defence of the realm. When England had attained an industrial reputation it was considered even less desirable than heretofore that Englishmen should emigrate and plant our industries in foreign countries or even in our own colonies. Only under exceptional circumstances did bands of colonists obtain Royal or Parliamentary leave to emigrate to Ireland or to America for the purpose of settling a plantation or of founding a colony. There was, however, no scruple in getting rid of unruly elements. The man who was guilty of homicide could escape the punishment of his crime by abjuring the realm. Disbanded soldiers and other vagrants appear to have been shipped to the New World in considerable numbers. Still it was not until 1824 that restrictions on emigration were abolished; before that date permission to emigrate had only been accorded as a special favour, except in cases where it was enforced as the penalty of misconduct. In the early part of the present century public opinion underwent a great change through the influence of Mr E. G. Wakefield, who had studied the subject of colonial development with much care, and who carried on an agitation in favour of granting this liberty to all subjects.

[Marginal note: Freedom to emigrate.]

68. Along with increased freedom of movement we
may also notice increased freedom in the   Freedom
choice of employment.   Under the manorial   to change
                                             employment.
system this was not possible for the great
mass of the people, and, as we have seen, the legislature
intervened to prevent the rural population from taking up
employments other than agriculture.   Elizabeth's Statute of
Artificers did something to perpetuate this restriction.   But
it also imposed a new difficulty, throughout the country
generally, in preventing a change of trade by artisans.   No one
was allowed to work at a craft to which he had not served a
seven years' apprenticeship, and this rendered it practically
impossible for any one to change his occupation.   In the
eighteenth century, when England was supplying foreign
markets with goods, and the prosperity of different trades
depended on variations in foreign demand, it was difficult
to make the readjustment necessary to suit new conditions ;
for this restriction on change of trade combined with the law
of settlements to prevent workmen from leaving a district
where industry was declining.   According to Defoe the cloth
trade in Essex had diminished, and some villages, such as
Bocking and Braintree, afforded instances of an evil which
became more marked as the eighteenth century advanced.
On the other hand, it may be said that, apart from the
incidental effect of the Poor Law, the Act of Elizabeth
gave increased freedom to the skilled artisan by fixing one
standard of training and skill for the whole realm.   It
gave each skilled craftsman a better opportunity of pursuing his calling in any place which he preferred, instead of
restricting him to work in that town of which he had, by
serving his apprenticeship, become free.

The case of London presents many points of special
interest.   It was exempted from the operation of the Eliza-

bethan Act, and continued its own system of apprenticeship. The custom of the City appears to have permitted a remarkable liberty in the change of occupation. Those who had served a seven years' apprenticeship claimed the liberty to practise a trade other than that to which they had been apprenticed. This liberal custom held its own, but not without a struggle. In the time of Richard II an effort was made to insist that every citizen should choose one calling by which he would abide, and that he should not endeavour to practise more than one, even if he was free of more than one company. In the time of Elizabeth a serious contest arose. There was one party which desired to impose a restriction similar to that in the Elizabethan Act, and another which desired to obtain Parliamentary confirmation for liberty of change. Neither could have their way, but in the long run the old custom of freedom of change was able to assert itself. It appears to have been one of the elements which gradually brought about a severance between the various companies and the actual crafts with which they were nominally connected. The liberty, thus reasserted in London, was only secured in the country at large by the repeal of the apprenticeship clauses of the Elizabethan Act in 1814.

69.   Unauthorised trade associations have been viewed

Freedom to associate.   with much suspicion from early times, and it is only recently that freedom to combine for trade purposes has been accorded. That there were many advantages in combination was recognised from early times, and authorised associations were formed both by the Crown, by municipal authorities, by manorial lords, and by Parliament. But the unauthorised association of irresponsible persons was viewed very differently. They were at least under the suspicion of being a *ring*, formed to engross and enhance the price of some commodity, in a way which was

detrimental to the consumer. Every attempt on the part of
a section of the community to get gain at the public expense
was strongly condemned. Even authorised associations, such
as the craft-gilds under Henry VI or the patentees under
James I, might be guilty of misusing their powers. But
unauthorised association laid the members open at least to
the suspicion of criminal intent, and Henry II imposed
heavy fines on the adulterine gilds of his time. The possibility of unfair combinations among dealers was kept in
view all through the Middle Ages, and there was a cog-
nate feeling about combinations of labourers, since wages
were the chief element in price; the demand for higher
wages seemed but little removed from a conspiracy to raise
prices for the benefit of individuals, but at the public
expense. This feeling gave rise to the Statute of Labourers
(1351) under Edward III and to various subsequent measures, which limited the rates of wages. In the time of
Edward VI a combination law was passed (1548), which
seems to condemn much that had been commonly done by
the old gilds. But it was not until the eighteenth century
that the matter assumed much importance. Early in that
century the masters in certain trades were suffered to combine for certain specific objects, such as that of prosecuting
fraudulent workmen. Combinations among workmen were
not unknown. They are mentioned by Adam Smith. But
their history and objects remain obscure until 1799, when a
measure was passed which gave the whole question a new
prominence. The government of the country was suffering from a panic about seditious associations. Debating
societies and freemasons' lodges were looked upon with
grave suspicion, as possible cloaks for treasonable assemblies,
and a Government measure was hurried through the Commons, which treated all associations of workmen as criminal

bodies.   The economic conditions of the times rendered it specially hard that workmen should not be in a position to combine to drive a bargain with their employers.   The Act of 1799, amended in 1800, compelled them to keep such combinations secret, and gave them the character of the devices of desperate men.   Occasional prosecution for belonging to such associations gave rise to immense bitterness, and the injustice was so patent that in 1825 the obnoxious measure was repealed.   It had, however, wrought infinite mischief while it lasted, and its repeal was undertaken with some hesitation.   The economists of the day had a decided opinion that unions were powerless to effect any real improvement in the position of the worker, and while they were in favour of removing the criminal character of such associations, they were wholly averse to encouraging the principle of combination.   Events have since seemed to falsify the calculations of the time.   With the power of combination workmen have succeeded in securing improved conditions, and the existence of unions is now recognised in many trades as a convenient means for making arrangements between employers and employed.   The precise objects for which combination is allowable, as well as the possible means of enforcing the policy of a combination, have given rise to much discussion and to occasional legislation.   But since 1825 the existence of unions among labourers has been permitted to an extent which was never possible in earlier times.

70.   The preceding sections have brought out a definite line of progress in favour of economic freedom

Laissez faire and philanthropic legislation.

on the part of the individual.   This movement attained its greatest development during the first half of the present century, when the principles of *laissez faire* were deliberately applied to all the institutions of the country. Since the middle of the century, however, there have been signs of a reaction against this attitude of opposing regulation of every kind, and public opinion has come more and more to favour the interference of the State in matters which were at one time left entirely to individuals.

The first signs of this new era of regulation were in connexion with children's labour. It was said that they were too young to fight their own battles and that, as a matter of fact, they did not drive their own bargains. On this account men like Sir Robert Peel, who were uncompromising advocates of *laissez faire* with respect to adults, were eagerly engaged in promoting measures for the protection of children. The whole of the Factory legislation of 1802 and 1833 rested on the supposition that children were not free agents, and that it was a matter of public interest to secure that they should not be overworked, so that the rising generation should be able-bodied and effective citizens. There was a direct object of national importance in view, and the earlier measures, at all events, were merely concerned with the labour of children. Within these limits State interference is readily accepted as advisable by most persons in the present day. Whether it is expedient to do more than this may perhaps be doubtful, but the general tone of feeling has hitherto been that of leaving it to adults, so far as may be, to drive their own bargains and to secure satisfactory conditions for themselves.

The first and most definite departure from this principle of freedom for adults has been in the case of mines, where the Government has, by regulation and inspection, insisted upon the use of precautions which would not have been so readily introduced, had it not been for outside pressure. The very risks of the miner's life may sometimes render him reckless and inclined to disparage the safeguards which are recommended on scientific grounds. In cases of this sort a public authority may be more far-seeing and careful than any of those whose interests are directly concerned, and it may be possible to give greater security for life and limb by Act of Parliament. A very great deal of the regulation incorporated in more recent Factory and Workshop Acts is of the same character, while the general approval with which they meet, and the frequent demand that they should be further extended, mark how far public opinion has veered from the *laissez faire* principles.

71. Despite this mass of legislation, however, there is still a tendency in some quarters to speak of it as exceptional, to assert the old *laissez faire* principles, and to argue that it is best to leave adults to fight their own battles and secure advantages for themselves. But here the difficulty arises that, isolated and alone, the individual artisan has but little real economic freedom. His comparative poverty may render it impossible for him to stand out for a bargain, and the difficulty of moving his home limits the field within which he can seek work. The fluidity of labour is much less than economists sometimes seem to assume; and on this ground the labourer may fairly contend that effective economic freedom can only be assured to his class by securing him an effective right to combine.

This was strenuously denied by the *laissez faire* economists at the beginning of the century. During the period before 1825, when the unions were treated as criminal bodies, they were forced to maintain their position by secret and sometimes by violent methods, and the legislature has always been inclined to protect the individual who is satisfied with his independent position from those who wish to induce or to force him to throw in his lot with a trade combination. The State, in admitting liberty to combine, has been anxious to maintain, on behalf of other workmen, the liberty not to combine. It has been a difficult problem to hold the balance evenly between the two. Wherever the unions have attained such a position as to be really effective economic forces, they have been able to exercise a dominating influence on the conditions of the trade ; and the story of their early struggles and of the gradual growth of their organisation is one of supreme interest. But it is not clear that their policy has been wiser, or that it has been enforced with less friction and suffering than would have been the case, if serious efforts had been made by public authority to continue to regulate the conditions of labour and terms of employment in a fashion similar to that attempted in the Elizabethan labour code.

III. Commercial Development.

72. IT has been pointed out above that national regulation of industrial life gradually superseded that which had been undertaken in early times by local authorities. But this is much less true *Municipal and national regulation.* of commercial affairs. Our shipping and commerce were so little developed in the thirteenth and fourteenth centuries that the institutions for fostering and developing them had to be almost entirely created by the Crown or by Parliament. To some extent, indeed, the new system was grafted on to the practice and custom which had prevailed in municipal commerce, and in the thirteenth and fourteenth centuries we see the points of transition most clearly.

Thus in dealing with internal commerce and the alien merchants who visited English marts, the State was at first content to enforce, with additional authority, the old municipal arrangements. The Statute of Acton Burnell (1283) at most extended to new centres a system of trading security for the recovery of debts which was already familiar in other localities. But in later commercial legislation there are fewer local limitations, and the facilities for trade, which were organised in the fourteenth century, seem to have been devised with reference to all portions of the realm. The organisation of a great national institution like the merchants of the Staple must have told against the status and importance of local mercantile communities.

The nation could also do much for the protection of the person and property of the merchant, which lay beyond the cognisance of any single city. The towns had attended to matters of local police, but the security of travellers on the roads could only be undertaken by the king or by Parliament. In the time of Edward I we see that the importance of affording to merchants immunity from attack on the king's highway was clearly recognised, and serious efforts were made to ensure it in the Statute of Winchester (1285).

73. During the fourteenth century Englishmen were beginning to take some part in foreign trade, and this new departure brought to light a new series of responsibilities, which the king and Parliament were forced to undertake. The effort to put down piracy was partly intended to preserve the coasts from attack, but it also served to give protection to merchant vessels on the seas. When Edward III claimed the sovereignty of the sea, he became bound in honour to maintain the king's peace on the sea as well as on the shore. The duty was, indeed, inefficiently done; merchant vessels which paid for a convoy did not always secure an effective escort. When the armaments of Edward III and

The perils of the sea.

Henry V were scouring the Channel merchant shipping
may have been fairly well protected; but in the time of
Henry VI national energies were severely strained, and no
sufficient pains were taken to render the seas safe for
traders. Piracy assumed frightful proportions; organised
fleets like those of the Victual Brothers and the Rovers
of the Sea destroyed our shipping and attacked our coasts.
Privateering was not discouraged, and the commercial
jealousies of Englishmen and Hansards gave rise to occasional quarrels and to bitter reprisals. Towards the close
of the fifteenth century a series of treaties rendered trade
more secure, and the efforts of different commercial communities put down the Northern piracy, from which all
suffered in turn.

74. As English trade expanded more widely, it became
necessary to deal with the old difficulties on
a larger scale. Trade in the Mediterranean   Commercial treaties.
was seriously interfered with by the pirates of   Trading Companies.
Algiers and Morocco. These petty states be-
came the resort of desperate characters of all nationalities,
and the attempts of James I to obtain Spanish co-operation
for the extermination of the evil proved a failure. They did
not confine their depredations to merchant shipping. In
1631 the town of Baltimore in the South of Ireland was
utterly destroyed, and the surviving inhabitants carried into
slavery. When such depredations could be successfully
carried out, there was at least some excuse for Charles I's
demand for a payment of ship-money to defend the realm.
The sailors of the Commonwealth had some temporary
success, and the negociations of Charles II were not without effect, but it was not until English power was completely
established in the Mediterranean that this mischief was
really brought to an end and that piracy ceased to be a

serious danger for merchants to face in European waters (1818).

There were several important commercial treaties in the time of Edward IV and Henry VII which not only served to diminish hostilities on the high seas, but also gave a footing to English merchants in foreign countries. In some cases a factory was secured to them, where merchants could live on moderate terms, and warehouse their goods. Sometimes a consul or representative was appointed, who was able to look after the interests of any merchant who visited the port. Successive appointments of this kind serve as landmarks to show the gradual expansion of English trade, not only in the Low Countries where the Merchant Adventurers had their factories, but in Pisa, Crete, and Smyrna where consuls were established in the time of Edward IV and Henry VII. Arrangements of this kind, though of the first importance for commerce, were really political in character. The English cities never aspired to be independent states, and attained neither the wealth nor the position which would have enabled them to procure privileges and to push English trade in these new and distant ports.

From this point of view it is clear that many of the mercantile organisations, which seem at first sight to be merely municipal, were really national in character, and could only have been authorised by national authority. So long as the Mercers confined their attention to wholesale trade in cloth within the realm, they might be satisfied with the sanction they received from the Mayor and Aldermen, though they preferred the additional status conferred by a royal charter. But when some of the brethren devoted themselves to shipping goods abroad, and it was desirable that the trade should be organised and put on a sound footing, the Company of Merchant Adventurers obtained powers of self-government at a foreign mart and of exclusive trading as against other Englishmen. This could only be granted by national authority. Similarly when the Grocers concerned themselves not only with *garbling*—or sifting spices and dealing in imported goods, but took to shipping them from the Levant, they were organised by royal authority as the Turkey Company. These London Adventurers affiliated similar organisations which were formed by royal authority in the out-ports for various branches of foreign trade. It is only necessary to specify the Merchant Adventurers of Exeter, founded by Queen Elizabeth, and the Merchant Adventurers of Newcastle. To regulate trade within a city was comparatively easy, but to shield and to organise Englishmen in their trading with foreign lands was a political duty which could only be undertaken by the highest authority in the realm.

75. The Tudor kings were all interested in maritime affairs, and from their time onwards we find more systematic efforts to diminish the physical risks which seamen had to run on our coasts. There were constant efforts to improve the harbours; while the Brethren of Trinity House at Deptford were especially encouraged to erect sea marks and lighthouses and to concern themselves with the training of pilots. A similar institution with more restricted powers was formed at Hull, and their united efforts resulted in greatly increased safety for our shipping by improving the access to harbours, by rendering harbours more secure, and by marking out the course which it was wise to pursue, or the points it was necessary to avoid. Such work was, in itself, of the highest importance; and it also serves as an interesting illustration of the nationalisation of local institutions, when

The protection of the coasts.

we see how an association of Thames pilots was taken up and employed by royal authority to exercise a guardianship over the whole of our coasts.

76. The re-discovery of America (p. 11) and the discovery of fresh routes to the East gave a fresh stimulus to the ambition of Englishmen. When they seriously endeavoured to enter into competition with foreign nations in these new directions, they went out under royal patronage and with royal approval. There was, of course, much individual enterprise, as was shown, for example, in the expedition fitted out by a Bristol merchant in 1480 to seek for the island of Brazil. But a regular trading expedition, which required a valuable cargo, could only be undertaken by the co-operation of several merchants; and they naturally desired to obtain the prestige of a royal introduction in the distant countries which they visited. A Russia Company was organised under Edward VI, which, though it consisted of London merchants, was really a national undertaking. These merchants opened a trade with Archangel, and before long they pushed their way by the Russian rivers and the old caravan routes to Persia. This was the first attempt made by Englishmen to open up communications with the East, and to obtain a share in the profitable trade from which the Portuguese derived so much wealth. The Company's agents were provided with royal letters, written in Hebrew and Greek, which it was thought might prove intelligible to Oriental princes and recommend the subjects of the king of England to favourable consideration.

The New World and new routes to the East.

77. Another such company endeavoured to win for Englishmen a share in the direct trade with India by the Cape of Good Hope. The East India Company was organised by London

Joint-stock and regulated Companies.

merchants, but was under Court patronage; and at one
time the shrewd City men who started it feared lest the
influence of the Court should introduce into their ships
some gentlemen adventurers, who would be more likely to
direct their attention to fighting than to trade. Those who
entered the Company did not trade as individuals, but combined to take shares in fitting and loading several ships one
year, and then formed a new subscription for each subsequent voyage. The private trading of individual merchants
or of the Company's servants was sedulously put down, and
each voyage was made upon a joint-stock. There was,
however, an unnecessary complication in such a system,
especially when the charges of the establishments at home
and abroad were considered. In 1612, the charter of the
Company was renewed in a different form, and it became a
joint-stock company, in which all the partners had larger or
smaller shares. Such a joint-stock company, which traded
as a single corporation, was in a strict sense a monopoly,
since it had the exclusive right of trading. Other companies,
such as the Russia and Turkey Companies, were composed
of men each of whom traded on his own account and competed with others, while he recognised some general regulations, which were thought to be beneficial to all: such
traders also had the advantage of special privileges and
conveniences in the towns where they carried on business.
Any English subject could belong to these regulated companies upon payment of a comparatively small fee for
admission, and part of their trade regulation was intended
to prevent the richer merchants from concentrating business
in their own hands, and to allow younger men to have
their chance. Both regulated and joint-stock companies
were national institutions for the development and control of
foreign commerce. Both obtained their powers by charter

from the Crown, but whereas the joint-stock companies were really monopolies, the regulated companies do not deserve that name.

This system of company-trading was, to a large extent, an English institution, and did not develop so fast, or on quite the same lines, either in Holland or in France. There was much doubt in England during the seventeenth century as to whether the system was wise or not. The East India Company was the one most frequently attacked, but even the regulated companies were severely criticised as being injurious to trade. In 1608 the privileges of the Merchant Adventurers were suspended, and at a later date the Russia and the Turkey Company aroused considerable hostility on the part of the *interlopers*, as those English merchants were called who defied the exclusive claims, and competed in the trade of the Companies. Under James I a special commission on trade was appointed, and it was one of their chief duties to consider the policy of allowing companies in trade. The Commissioners did not pronounce against it, and further attacks, made in the time of Cromwell, were successfully resisted. Before the period of the Revolution, however, the constitutional rights of interlopers to trade were upheld, as against the joint-stock companies, in a case which was brought by Sandys against the East India Company (1684). With the Revolution and the Bill of Rights, the position of these bodies, which depended on charters granted by the Stuarts, was weakened, and the rivals of the East India Company seemed likely to get their way. The interloping merchants were empowered to form a new general or regulated East India Company, which seemed likely to supersede the old London or joint-stock company. The two entered on an unseemly and disastrous competition, but eventually their competing interests were reconciled,

and the two bodies were amalgamated. At this juncture
the principles for which the joint-stock company had con-
tended may be said to have triumphed, and Parliament
appeared to acknowledge that in distant trade with peoples
with whom we had no regular diplomatic relations, it was
expedient for Englishmen to present a united front.

78. The later history of this great Company, and the
steps by which it was transformed from a   The East
trading body to a political power need not be   India Com-
detailed here. It continued to pursue the   pany.
policy of corporate trading, with which it had started,
but it did not prevent its servants from engaging in
private trade on their own account within India itself.
The relations of the Company with its servants and of
the Home Board with its officials abroad were complicated and often unsatisfactory. Commercial and political
interests conflicted, and the common trade of the Company
was sometimes said to be sacrificed to the private trade of
the servants. The wealth of these servants, when they
returned, and the high profits of the Dutch Company, which
was managed on different principles, made the shareholders
suspicious, and tempted the directors to gratify them by
paying extravagant dividends. The Company was brought
to the verge of bankruptcy by the middle of the eighteenth
century, and when reconstituted it came to be more and
more political in character. At the time when the trade to
India was formally thrown open (1813), the shipments of
the Company had come to be very trivial, but it retained
its exclusive trade with China for a longer period (1833).
Tea was an article of common consumption of which the
Company had the monopoly and could regulate the supply.
It is in connexion with this article that we see the last
remains of the controversy on the advantages and disadvan-

tages of corporate trading. That there were some advantages
may be gathered from the strained relations with China,
which immediately followed the abrogation of the trading
monopoly and the independent efforts of competing tradesmen to push the sale of their wares.

79. In the present day when the British mercantile
marine is so very large, it is strange to recall
the fact that through a long period of our
history we had very little shipping at all, and
that our commercial supremacy is of quite

*The Navy
and joint-
stock Com-
panies.*

recent growth. But it is perhaps more important to
remember that our naval power has grown along with
our commerce, and that owing to that naval power our
commerce is far less fettered than was formerly necessary.
In former days the Government was unable to protect the
mercantile marine effectively from the attacks of pirates,
or to secure our merchants due respect in distant lands.
But now-a-days our naval power serves to protect our commerce everywhere, and to give our merchants a firm footing
in the most distant parts of the globe. We are dependent
on our navy for the regularity of our food supply. We are
dependent on it too for the protection of our commerce,
and for all the industrial success which is bound up with
our commerce.

In old days, when *adventurers* could look for little
effective support from the home Government, and were
forced to provide for their own defence themselves, there
was much excuse for conferring a trading monopoly on
those who undertook this difficult position. The practice
of chartering monopolist companies for distant trades with
half-civilised peoples did on the whole justify itself. But
now that English political power is more widely and more
effectively felt, there is no longer the same excuse for con-

ferring a monopoly on trading companies that undertake
political risks. But even though English subjects all over
the globe can look to the Government for protection, the
recent formation of the Chartered African and Borneo
Companies shows that the old expedient is still resorted to
for pioneer work.

But though these companies have not their old political
character, the commercial principle on which they were formed
still holds good, and has been applied in every sort of way.
From very early times, several owners might combine to fit
out a ship and buy a cargo, when none of them was able,
separately, to risk a very large sum in ventures by sea ; and
this practice received a new application when a permanent
joint-stock company, like the East India Company, was
formed to undertake the difficult task of opening and
maintaining friendly relations with distant peoples, whose
civilisation was very different from our own. Such trading
connexions could not be permanently maintained by individuals singly, and the risks of trading were minimised
for each, when the shareholders acted together as one
body. By this means the owner of a comparatively small
sum of money can club with others, so as to share great
risks, and, if he is successful, earn large profits. At all
events this method of associating for business purposes has
been more and more adopted. Adam Smith attempted to discriminate between certain kinds of business which could not
be satisfactorily undertaken in this fashion, but since his day
enterprises of every possible sort have been carried out on a
joint stock. It seems, indeed, that unless this form of conducting business had been generally understood, the gigantic
undertakings of the present day—such as the construction
of railways—could hardly have been accomplished ; there
would have been no capital available. But every kind

of undertaking—financial, commercial, agricultural, shipping, mining, manufacturing—is now successfully conducted on this basis. Though there are obvious disadvantages in the system—since the management may be lacking in keen personal interest, and the owners of the property deficient in a sense of personal responsibility for the conduct of affairs— it is steadily gaining upon private enterprise. Year after year we see private firms reconstituted as joint-stock companies, and there are some lines of business, such as banking, from which the private firms have been almost wholly ousted.

IV.   *Economic Policy.*

80.   In the preceding paragraphs an attempt has been made to trace out the different sides from which the State interfered with and controlled the development of our industry and commerce.   But it is also worth while to gather these various threads into one, and to show that a common purpose underlay all the efforts at regulation and control. This has been already indicated in connexion with the reign of Richard II, which proved such an important turning-point (§§ 47, 48); but the whole becomes clearer when it is looked at retrospectively as well as prospectively. The central authority kept a firm hand on all sides of economic life, and it employed them all so as to promote national power, and to render England stronger relatively to other nations.   Though there were strokes of good fortune, on which the mercantilists could not have counted, and which aided their efforts, we need not deny them the credit of success in attaining the object they had at heart.   In the time of Richard II, England was a small power in Europe, with no marine to speak of.   At the beginning of the nineteenth

(marginal note:) Elements of power. Shipping and treasure.

century, England was strong enough to hold her own against
the world, and her fleets guarded a world-wide commerce.
While the Mercantile System was in vogue, the highest
ambition of those who designed it was accomplished, and
England attained to a position of immense power and
prestige among the nations.

As already stated, there are some objects which may be
regarded as common to all countries that seek to increase in
strength. A sufficient food supply is one of them ; the
means taken by England to attain this end were by no
means common and have been sufficiently described above.
But two other objects were kept in the forefront by the
Mercantilists ; one of these was specially thought of by
Englishmen—the increase of our shipping and the strength-
ening of our wooden walls. It was of obvious importance
in the case of an island realm, and the efforts to encourage
our shipping and seamanship ramified out into all sorts of
subsidiary regulations. Further, the providing of a large
treasure of the precious metals to meet political emergencies
presented a difficult problem in the case of a country which
had no mines ; in attempting to solve it the Government
devised expedients which affected many branches of enterprise and employment.

81. Deliberate attempts to encourage English shipping
are found as early as the time of Richard II.
The policy of Edward III had practically
discouraged Englishmen from engaging in
trade, and their ships had suffered so much
from the requirements of the king's military expeditions
that the English mercantile marine was almost destroyed.
To remedy this evil, an Act was passed in 1381 which
insisted on the employment of English ships, although in the
following year this was modified into giving a preference to

The objects
and effects of
the early Na-
vigation Acts.

English ships.   This policy, though politically advantageous, entailed numerous commercial disadvantages ; even after the first few years of trial it appeared that shipowners were charging exorbitant rates, so that fewer goods were imported, and, consequently, the prices for imported commodities ranged higher than would otherwise have been the case.   The grievance was so great that the navigation Acts were not steadily enforced during the fifteenth century; and in the sixteenth, Wolsey was definitely opposed to a restriction, which, though it might eventually increase shipping and power, in the meantime diminished plenty.   He saw that a navigation Act would be likely to involve a reduction in the quantity of wine imported: and a double mischief would ensue—to the king from the reduction of the customs on wine, and to the consumer from a diminished supply and a consequent increase of the price.   Thomas Cromwell was in favour of a strict navigation policy, but the old difficulties recurred under Edward VI; and the measure which was passed under Burleigh's administration was discriminating in character and aimed at the encouragement of English shipping, while it minimised the evils of restriction.

82.   The next legislative change was in the time of the

Effects on Holland, Scotland, Ireland, and the Colonies.

Commonwealth, when the commerce of Eng land had considerably increased, and when a stringent policy was re-enforced, not only for the sake of fostering English shipping, but also in the hope of striking a blow at the carrying trade of the Dutch, and bringing the American and West Indian colonies into closer commercial relations with the mother country.   Whether, as is commonly supposed, the Navigation Acts (1651, 1660) inflicted serious injury on the Dutch or not, they certainly entailed inconvenience not only on English consumers but also on English colonists.   These were restricted in their trade with one another and with European countries, and if the connexion with the mother country became firmer, it also became more galling.

The navigation laws were merely intended to encourage the trade of England, but they told against the progress both of Scotland and of Ireland. The Scotch, in the earlier part of the seventeenth century, had supplied the colonial markets with a good deal of coarse cloth which had been exported in Dutch ships. With the passing of the Navigation Act (1651) this channel of trade was closed, and after the Restoration they were also prevented from using English ships. The restriction was thus a serious blow to the struggling industry of Scotland, and the great popularity of the Darien scheme was undoubtedly due to a general belief that it would serve to give Scotch merchants and Scotch manufacturers a footing in the distant markets, which had recently been closed to them. The Act of Union (1707), by uniting the two nations into one kingdom for commercial purposes, served to include Scotland in the benefits of the Navigation Act. Ireland, which had not been excluded by the Act of 1651, came under restrictions in 1663, and continued to be at a disadvantage through the greater part of the eighteenth century. She was treated as a dependency, and was excluded from direct trade with the colonies; Galway in particular suffered seriously from this restriction. The victualling of ships was a business for which Ireland was specially well adapted, and in more than one way her native interests were sacrificed to those of more distant colonies, as in the matter of Virginian tobacco (§ 90) and West Indian rum. Commercial disabilities undoubtedly retarded the development of Ireland, and served to open to the manufacturers of linen in Scotland advantageous markets which were closed to Irish linen (p. 137).

It may thus be said that the interests of consumers in England and of producers in Scotland, Ireland, and the colonies were to some extent sacrificed by the Navigation Acts. That they had this effect was manifest, the only defence, and it seemed to those who maintained them a sufficient defence, lay in the fact that they attained their object. Under their influence, and apparently in consequence of them, the mercantile marine of England developed from being merely insignificant till it attained the supremacy of the world. The acquisition and maintenance of power was the end at which the framers of the Navigation Acts aimed, and power they succeeded in securing. The marine of England decided the issue of the struggle between France and England in India and America. The mercantile marine of England rendered her superior to all the military strength of Napoleon; she found the sinews of war in a world-wide commerce, which extended over seas where none but the English flag was ever seen. It is easy to show that the system was costly: it is not so easy to be sure that the cost was excessive, considering how completely successful the policy eventually proved.

83. Closely connected with this scheme for the encouragement of shipping were other measures affecting (α) the training of seamen, (β) the development of ship-building, and (γ) the providing of materials and naval stores.

Subsidiary callings. Fisheries, ship-building and naval stores.

α. The trade which did most to foster a class accustomed to a seafaring life was that of fishing; and many curious enactments were passed under the Tudors and in subsequent times for promoting this kind of enterprise. The simplest means was to bring about an increased demand for fish, and with this object a sumptuary measure was passed insisting that a fish diet should be used on two

days a week throughout the year as well as during Lent.
Serious attempts appear to have been made to enforce this
measure for nearly a hundred years. After it fell into disuse, a new expedient was tried by the granting of bounties
in connexion with the herring trade. These gave rise to an
immense amount of fraud, and it may be doubted whether
there was any equivalent advantage; at the same time it is
noticeable that, whether through this help or apart from it,
English fishing developed more and more. At the beginning
of the seventeenth century the Dutch fished largely in the
immediate neighbourhood of Yarmouth, and with vessels of
a build superior to anything that Englishmen possessed.
By the close of that century, the latter had been so far successful in outrivalling the Dutch on their own methods as to
get the local herring trade entirely into their hands. During
the eighteenth century Englishmen also made considerable progress in " the pleasant sport of catching the whale ";
while all through the long period from the discovery of
Newfoundland to the present day, they have at least held
their own in the recurring contest with Frenchmen in the
cod fishery.

β. Englishmen have so long excelled in the art of
ship-building that it is interesting to note how much pains
had at one time to be spent in fostering this form of skill.
Henry V built several large ships of war in imitation of the
Genoese vessels, and in the succeeding reign John Taverner
of Hull and William Canynges of Bristol showed special
enterprise in similar undertakings. Henry VIII and his
successors shared this enthusiasm, although they were badly
provided with dockyards and arsenals; but some pains
were taken to remedy this fault by creating an establishment
at Deptford in 1513. The direct encouragement which was
given to English shipping under Elizabeth and in subsequent

reigns, was a means of encouraging ship-building, not only in England but in the American colonies.

γ. The policy is still further illustrated by various efforts which were made to ensure that the realm should be amply provided with naval stores. Special pains were taken to insist on the growth of flax and hemp. So far as maintaining a sufficient home supply of wood for ship-building was concerned, the interests of the navy were more or less sacrificed, as regards both England and Ireland, to the exigencies of the iron trade and the demand for fuel. But this seemed of less importance, as there was an abundant supply in the American colonies. To some writers it appeared as if the chief advantage derived by England from these dependencies was due to the ample supply of wood and tar which came from them, since this country had hitherto been dependent on Norway and Sweden for such stores. This was, indeed, a dominant element in the scheme of policy pursued towards the colonies. They were restricted in various ways, but they received every encouragement to open up their resources so as to supply those products in which England was deficient. So long as they expended their energies in this direction they would strengthen the mother country, and would certainly not injure her by successful competition.

84. To secure a supply of treasure was another great point of economic policy. Without wealth in the form of bullion it was not easy to meet any sudden emergency, or to raise and equip an army or a fleet. Treasure was, therefore, an important element for supplying the sinews of war and for increasing the power of the realm by providing the means of meeting any emergency. Hence we find various measures which were intended to bring a supply of bullion from abroad to this country.

The bullion-ist policy for treasure.

Such legislative effort can be traced back to the time of
Richard II, but no earlier.   There had been a good deal of
legislation under the Edwards concerning the importation
of coin, but these were really mint regulations intended to
provide a sufficient currency for the realm and to keep
the debased coins of other countries out of circulation in
England.   From the time of Richard II, however, we find
that there was a systematic endeavour to accumulate bullion
which might be hoarded as treasure, and thus maintain the
power of the realm.   As England was a country in which there
were no mines, the precious metals could obviously only
be procured from abroad, and they were brought in as the
result of trade.   To this end *statutes of employment* were
passed, which required that those who came to buy English
commodities should pay for them, or for a portion of them,
in bullion.   At the same time the export of bullion from
the realm was prohibited, so that while this bullionist policy
aimed at forcing merchants to bring gold and silver to this
country, it also prevented them from taking it out.   This
system was followed in many lands, and was specially
favoured in Spain by Charles V and his successors.   It was
not, however, very easy to enforce, as the precious metals,
having great value in small bulk, are easily smuggled; and
early in the seventeenth century, it gave place to what is
more properly spoken of as a mercantile theory.   Indications
of this are found as early as the time of Richard II, and it
was well understood in the days of Edward VI.   But it did
not come to the front until the time of James I, when it was
put forward by the members of the East India Company as
a justification of commercial transactions which the bullionists condemned.

85.   The mercantilists, like the bullionists, aimed at
increasing the treasure in the country, but they adopted

entirely different measures to this end. Instead of trying
to legislate directly for the precious metals,
they held that, by legislating for the trade in
commodities, they could induce conditions in
which the precious metals would naturally
flow to this country. If we sold a large quantity of goods
to other lands and bought very few of their products, they
would be bound to pay us a balance in bullion. Hence it
appeared that by using expedients to limit the quantity and
value of our imports, and to increase the quantity and value
of our exports, there would be a balance of trade which
could only be defrayed by payments in bullion from abroad.
As thus recast, the effort to procure treasure ramified out in
many directions, but it should not be forgotten that the
fundamental reason for desiring bullion was the political
one of acquiring treasure. Those who were most decided
about the advantage of procuring treasure, were equally
clear that gold and silver were only valuable by convention
and not in their own nature ; and in so far as mere economics were concerned, there was no tendency to regard
bullion as a specially important form of riches or wealth.

The Mercan-
tilists and the
East India
Company.

The practical question over which these two schools of
economists, the bullionists and mercantilists, came into
collision was of vital importance to the East India Company.
The direct trade with India could not be carried on without
the export of bullion. There was no market in India for
the cloth or other bulky products of this country, and silver
had to be exported in order to procure the silks and spices
of the East ; the bullionists protested against permitting
any export of bullion at all. But the champions of the East
India Company alleged that, by sending some silver abroad,
they were able to drive a trade which enabled them eventually to procure much more silver on the whole. They

argued that the silver sent to India was like the seed which
seemed to be wasted, but which yielded a plentiful harvest.
They held that if London were a depôt for East India
goods, we could procure silver by selling them to other
European countries.   Hence they argued that it was unnecessary to impose restrictions on the export of bullion, so
long as an effort was made to ensure that the commodities
exported by the country as a whole should exceed the value
of the commodities imported.   Gold and silver they argued
must come in somehow, if the trade in merchandise were
carried on in this fashion.

86.   The triumph of this mercantile policy gave a new
importance to the efforts which had been
made, from time to time, to plant new indus-   The general
tries in this country.   In so far as we could   and particular
manufacture at home any goods which had   balance of
                                            trade.
hitherto been procured from abroad, the amount and value
of our imports would be diminished with a corresponding
improvement in the balance of trade.   It was on this
account that attempts were made to foster the silk trade
and to discourage the consumption of any foreign commodities for which bullion was habitually paid.   Authorities
began to discriminate between the relative advantages of
trade with different nations, and to note the particular
balance with each country, as well as to sum up the
general balance with the world as a whole.   The inter-
ramifications of trade are so many that this attempted dis-
crimination between particular trades was probably quite illu-
sory, as was seen by Dr Barbon in the time of William III.
But it took a firm hold on the public mind and gave rise to
an immense amount of argument and to some legislation.
There was a strong desire to cut down intercourse with
France to a minimum, as the particular balance seemed to

be against England in that trade. On the other hand it seemed desirable to encourage intercourse with Portugal, as the particular balance with that country was in our favour. In this fashion it came to be considered patriotic to drink port rather than burgundy or claret. And the tastes of consumers were treated with scant respect in consideration of the political advantages of fostering such a trade as tended not to diminish, but to increase, our treasure.

87. Besides the legislation which aimed at attaining one or other of these various elements of power, many measures were passed with a view to foster the general prosperity of the country, and thus to give a "fund" from which revenue might be drawn for the defence of the realm. It was from this cause that the regulations of the mercantile system had so much vitality; but for this clear recognition of industry as a source of national wealth the mercantile restrictions might have died out at the end of the seventeenth century. From the time of the foundation of the Bank of England, when public borrowing came to be habitually used for meeting emergencies, the political importance of treasure declined, and thus the whole of the economic system which rested upon it might have been expected to collapse. But it was too firmly founded to be easily broken up. The balance of trade was coming to be regarded in a new aspect, as a criterion of the industrial prosperity of the country and of its growing ability to bear the burden of taxation. If the balance of trade with Portugal was in our favour, it was thought that by our intercourse with that country our native industry received a stimulus. If, on the other hand, we had constantly to pay a debt to France, it appeared as if this intercourse fostered their industry more than it did ours. If the general balance of trade were in

our favour the whole business of the country was apparently
being done at a profit.   But if the particular balance with
any nation were against us, it seemed to show that they were
gaining at our expense, that we offered a better market to
them than they offered to us, and it was feared lest in
this way they would gradually outstrip us in industrial prosperity and consequent wealth.   It is here that the close connexion between the doctrine of the balance of trade and the
pursuit of political power makes itself felt.   The power
of one nation is relative to the power of other nations.
If a country increases its armaments, but does not increase
them so fast as a rival does, it is really becoming less
powerful relatively to its possible enemy.   And hence, according to the ideas of the time, political jealousy gave rise
directly and immediately to commercial hostility.   It was
not until the time of Adam Smith that this narrow view of
trade was set aside.   He regarded wealth as the main object
to be pursued ; he held that if the wealth of the subjects
increased, the sinews of power would somehow be available,
and hence he argued that any intercourse between trading
nations, since it benefited both in some degree, might be wisely
continued.   Each was really aiding the prosperity of the other,
and since he regarded it as impossible to discriminate which
gained most, he was prepared to hold that free intercourse
between nations would be for the mutual advantage of all.

88.   Since the desire to promote power lay at the root of
the whole system, there was no scruple about
sacrificing the interests of individual citizens,
or of any class of citizens, to what was supposed to tend to the political well-being of
the nation as a whole.   On these grounds, as has been
noted above, the taste of claret-drinkers was sacrificed, and
those who were fond of port were the gainers.   So, on a

*Individual
interests and
national pro-
sperity.*

larger scale, there was constant interference with the direction in which men employed their capital. The art of the statesman, as conceived by Sir James Steuart, the last of the mercantilists, was that of so playing upon the self-interest of individuals that they should devote their energies to those undertakings which fostered national power. It was for this reason that so much attention was directed to fisheries and to distant trades which employed shipping, and that premiums were offered for the encouragement of the Scotch and Irish linen trade. Bounties were also given on the importation of raw produce to be manufactured in this realm, as this seemed to be a real though a costly means of stimulating certain industries. With this same object, a revision of the tariffs was systematically undertaken by Walpole, who set himself to regulate the taxation of the country, so that manufactures might be directly encouraged Raw products were imported on easy terms, and foreign manufactures were heavily taxed. Attempts were made to foster English industry on many sides, and under the influence of this policy we became much more independent of foreign nations, and obtained a footing for our manufactures in all parts of the world. But though the result aimed at was attained, it is not certain how far the means employed really contributed to that end. Adam Smith's careful investigation has made it clear that the measures which favoured one industry or interest were very costly to others, and it seems quite possible that the industrial development of the country might have been as rapid, if it had gone on with less interference. Sir James Steuart had recognised that the practical difficulties were such as to render it almost impossible to legislate wisely for trade on behalf of the public; Adam Smith revolutionised the existing system by going one step further. He maintained that interference with trade

was so sure to entail some mischief that it was practically
better to leave it alone.

89.   The most disastrous results of this attempt to subordinate particular interests to the public good,
followed when it was applied not merely to   Colonial
individual industries, but was also used to dis-   interests and
criminate between areas.   None of the colonies   power.
contributed anything to the general revenue of the realm.
The greater number found it difficult to meet the expense
of their internal government.   Still, the colonists had their
trade protected by British fleets, and were dependent on
the mother country for assistance in the great struggle
with their French neighbours.   Their political interests were
bound up, though not very closely, with those of England,
while they took no direct part in contributing to the maintenance of these defensive powers.   Hence it came to be a
recognised principle of policy that the resources of the
colonies should be developed in such a fashion as to supplement the material prosperity of the mother country, but not
on lines which would enable them to compete either with
British industry or with British trade.   British land, British
industry and British trade provided the costs of common
defence.   It seemed fair to subordinate the economic
interests of the colonies to the interests of the mother
country, so that they might help to increase the fund of
wealth from which the expenses of the common defence
were defrayed.   This broad political principle was so applied as to enforce on the colonies that economic policy
which best suited the interest of the mother country, and
which thus contributed indirectly to the maintenance of
English power.

90.   The most favoured group of colonies consisted of
those in the West Indies which supplied products entirely

distinct from those of England. They thus supplemented
the resources of the mother country, and ren-

The West
Indian colo-
nies, and
Virginia.

dered her independent of the supplies which
must otherwise have been obtained from
French or Spanish possessions. The West
Indian colonies also furnished a depot for a profitable trade
with Spanish America, while they were conveniently situated
for the prosecution of the slave-trade, which employed much
English shipping. On these grounds they were specially
encouraged, and much pains were taken to develop their
resources and to foster their trade. So clearly was this felt
that the trade of the northern colonies on the American
mainland was somewhat restricted in the hope of giving
additional prosperity to the West Indian islands.

Virginia was also favoured to a certain extent. Tobacco
had not been grown in England or in Ireland in early times,
and when the first attempts at planting it occurred, in the
seventeenth century, considerable efforts were made to check
the new development. It was regarded as the staple product
of Virginia, and the British and Irish tobacco growers were
not suffered to compete with the colonists. In all probability this measure was, to some extent, dictated by fiscal
considerations, as it was far easier to collect duties on
imported tobacco than to levy an excise on any that might
be produced in England or Ireland. Still the fact remains
that in this one instance a British interest was sacrificed to
maintain the prosperity of a colony. Even though it was
an exceptional case, it yet seems to illustrate the attitude
taken by English statesmen and to set their whole policy in
a clearer light.

91. The northern colonies, from their physical and
climatic conditions, naturally came into direct competition
with the mother country. They had special advantages for

pursuing some trades, such as the manufacture of beaver hats or the smelting and manufacture of iron. The former of these industries was, however, discouraged by the home Government, and the latter was limited to those preliminary

The Northern colonies. Economic dependence.

processes which could not be so well conducted in the mother country owing to the increasing expense of fuel. Ship-building was another trade for which the northern colonies were naturally well adapted; but this received exceptional treatment. Colonial and English ships had equal opportunities for employment, and the colonies were also encouraged to export timber and naval stores to England. Even when there was no danger of competition with the industry of the mother country, the policy was pursued of confining the colonies to the raising of raw products. It was distinctly believed that by rendering the colonists economically dependent on the mother country for manufactures and other supplies, the political tie was strengthened. To some extent this may have been the case, but it might be argued that the general result of the policy was precisely the reverse of what had been intended. When the conquest of French Canada diminished the interest of the colonists in the political struggles and ambitions of the mother country, the restrictions upon their trade and manufactures proved a source of constant irritation and led directly to the breach by which these flourishing territories were lost to England for ever.

92. The policy already described receives abundant illustration nearer home, for it was in the case of Ireland that competition with the mother country was most possible, and that economic jealousy was consequently keenest. Ireland was well adapted for growing wool, and the

Irish competition in the woollen manufacture. The Irish linen trade.

peasants in some parts of the country had long been engaged
in the manufacture of a coarse cloth known as frieze.   There
is some reason to believe that in the fourteenth century there
had been a manufacture of finer cloth as well, while in the
seventeenth century repeated efforts were made to plant the
manufacture of broad-cloth—an important article of English
production.   As living was comparatively cheap, and as wool
could be obtained in plenty, it seemed as if Ireland would
have special advantages for this manufacture.   Strafford,
who saw that if the project succeeded it must be through
successful competition with England, opposed the scheme,
and tried to direct the industrial energies of the country
into the linen trade.   After the Civil War, however, renewed
attempts were made, although without much success, until
in the time of William III the West of England manufacturers awoke to the superior advantages which Ireland
had to offer, and migrated thither in considerable numbers.
But a change of this kind aroused great alarm.   England
was engaged in a struggle with Louis XIV, which strained
all her resources.   She had to depend chiefly on the land-tax
and the customs for her revenue.   In so far as the West
of England manufacturers migrated to Ireland the landowners would lose through a fall in the price of wool, and
the customs on the export of cloth would be diverted from
the English to the Irish revenue.   With the avowed object
of preventing this financial difficulty a tax was imposed on
Irish cloth, which was calculated to be a countervailing duty.
It was, as a matter of fact, so oppressive that, in conjunction
with the restrictions imposed by the Navigation Act, it
effectually ruined the prospects of an Irish woollen manufacture, and dispersed the artisans who were carrying it on
in Dublin and other Irish towns.   As these men emigrated
to the Continent, and practised their calling in Germany

and elsewhere, they set up rival manufactories which competed very seriously with those of England.

Even the linen trade, which had been fostered by Strafford and in which the Irish were encouraged to find compensation for the loss of the woollen manufacture, was not fairly dealt with. When, by the Union, England and Scotland came to have a common purse, the Scotch linen trade was encouraged, both directly and indirectly, while the Irish manufacture was not. There was even some jealousy of this trade on the part of English clothiers. It was said that towns in the Low Countries, which at that time offered a good market for cloth, would be practically closed against us, if we did not buy our linen from them; and thus English politicians were inclined to look askance at the development of this trade, even though it did not directly compete with any established English industry.

93. So far we have considered the effects of the economic jealousy of Ireland, that is, of successful hostile competition by Ireland with the mother country. But political jealousy was also an important factor. Both in the

Whig jealousy of Irish prosperity—Irish cattle.

time of Charles I and James II Irish armies had been formed and had been under the sole control of the Crown. They had served at least to threaten the English Parliament and to support schemes of policy which were regarded as unconstitutional. In this way the Whig jealousy of the royal power, from which William III suffered so much, came, indirectly, to be a jealousy of Ireland, as a source from which the king might draw independent resources of men and money without appealing to the English Parliament at all. This gave an additional importance to the hostile competition which has been already described. The migration of industry from the West of England to Ireland

meant the transference of resources from a region which
Parliament could control to a district where they lay directly
in the hands of the Crown.   This jealousy was expressed
in Charles II's reign on the occasion of an attack which was
made on the Duke of Ormond.   He was interested in the
development of cattle-breeding and grazing farms in Ireland.
The English landlords and graziers objected to what they
regarded as hostile competition, and Parliament imposed
restrictions on the exportation of Irish cattle, which effectually stopped the progress of cattle farms in that country.
That this was due to political jealousy is shown by the fact
that no similar measure was passed against Scotland, although
the economic competition of the two smaller kingdoms was
very similar in regard to this trade.

94.   Besides these repressive measures, which were
due partly to economic and partly to political
jealousy, the progress of Ireland was retarded
by some of the measures which gave encouragement to English interests.   This was
especially noticeable in the case of her agriculture.   Pococke,
in an account of his tour in 1752, gives a most instructive
picture of the backwardness of the country in this respect.
The Corn Bounty Act (1689), which did so much to
stimulate agriculture in England, rendered it convenient
for English farmers to grow so much corn that they had a
large surplus to export to Ireland.   Dublin and other towns
could obtain their food supply from England, and there was
far less demand for Irish grown wheat than would otherwise
have been the case.   As a consequence, in the eighteenth
century, while English tillage was advancing steadily, there
was little corn grown in Ireland, even in those parts which
were naturally well adapted for it.   It thus came about that
Parliament, in the interests of the power of the mother

English and Irish Protection. The Union.

country, felt justified in repressing the hostile competition
of the colonies and Ireland. While they welcomed such
development in the West Indies and America as supplemented the resources of the mother country, they gave no
free scope to any Irish industry, and the measures which
promoted the prosperity of England were positively injurious to its poorer neighbour.

When, after the Declaration of Independence by the
American colonies, greater freedom was given to the Irish
Parliament to manage the commercial affairs of that kingdom,
various efforts were made to adopt the various expedients for
promoting economic prosperity which had been carried out
successfully in England. Some of these—like the canals—
were not well adapted to the condition of the sister Island,
though useful in this country for the conveyance of mineral
wealth; others were of a costly character, and the dis-
ciples of Adam Smith denounced them as ruinous. Irish
patriots gave expression to a not unnatural hostility to
English manufactures; and the measures passed by the Irish
Parliament found few defenders on this side of the Channel,
while they were important elements in turning public
opinion against Irish commercial independence and in
favour of a closer union between the two countries.

CHAPTER VII.

MONEY, CREDIT, AND FINANCE.

95. FROM the very earliest times of which we have any
Barter. Money payment and competition. records the English appear to have been acquainted with the use of money. We cannot go back to any period and say that in it there was no exchange of commodities, or even that goods were only bartered for goods while money was not used at all. Still there has been very great progress made both in regard to the knowledge of the nature of money, and also in applying it to many transactions which were for centuries carried on without it. Some economists speak of the times, or the spheres of life, in which men procure their food and shelter without the intervention of money as instances of *natural economy*, and those in which money-bargains occur as cases of *money economy*. There has been a gradual substitution of money economy for natural economy in almost all the relations of life; some of the most difficult problems in economic history arise from our attempts to trace the steps of this change, and to show how it has reacted, for good or for evil, on social and political life.

It is easy to see that the introduction of money renders it much more easy to carry out an exchange. Barter is cumbrous, and it is also unlikely to be fair: it is difficult to estimate the quality of any goods quite precisely, or to pay for them accurately in cattle or other forms of wealth which are not easily divisible. Close bargaining is only possible when money is in ordinary use, as a means of defining clearly and paying accurately; and so it is a great assistance in rendering bargains fair as between man and man. When there can be such close bargaining, it is possible to readjust the terms of exchange more accurately with every little variation in the plenty and scarcity of goods. So long as barter prevails, there are likely to be customary payments of rent, wages and taxes; but as money is introduced, there may be frequent rearrangement of these payments and they come to be settled by competition. The *régime* of competition is almost impracticable among people to whom barter is the only method of exchange known. When money is first introduced in any sphere, there may be a long period of fixed or assessed money prices which perpetuate the old arrangements in a new form; but sooner or later competition, with its frequent and precise readjustments of prices, is likely to follow the introduction of the method of reckoning and of paying in money.

Competition is in these days a word of evil omen; its oppressive effects on some sections of society are very sad, and many of us are inclined to look back with regret to the more stable conditions of customary prices and assessed wages. But it is well to remember that competition has come into being as the result of the introduction of money economy; whatever incidental disadvantages there may have been in this change, there are also enormous advantages, which we are apt to overlook. These become very apparent when we trace the substitution of a money for a natural economy in connexion with the expenses of government. The intervention of the former renders it

possible for the demands of the Government to be much
more precise, and much more regular, and thus to be far
less onerous to those who have to defray them.   Money
can also be levied in smaller sums and from a much larger
circle, so as to be less burdensome to special localities ;
while it is possible to readjust the amounts and alter them
in detail, so that the necessary pressure shall fall on those
who can bear it best.   All these points come out in the
fiscal history of the country; but before dwelling on them
we must note the principal changes that have been made
in regard to money itself and the growth of experience in
the employment of silver and gold and other forms of
money.

96.   In the period before the Norman Conquest and
indeed long after it, silver was the standard
metal from which money was coined; and
though there were moneyers in different towns,
they exercised their calling under the control
and authority of the Crown.   There were, indeed, encroach-
ments on this, as on other Crown rights, from time to time;
but during periods of strong and vigorous government,
great attention was given to the maintenance of a definite
standard of purity and weight.   Henry I inflicted severe
punishment on dishonest moneyers, and Henry II busied
himself about the re-organisation of the Mint; from his
time onwards the excellence of the English coin came to be
a matter of just pride to the kings whose image and super-
scription it bore.

Some allusion has been made above (p. 127) to the difficulties which arose, during the time of the Edwards, when considerable quantities of debased foreign coin were brought into
this country by the alien merchants who came to purchase
wool.   Edward I tried to prevent the introduction of such

coin, so as to keep up the standard of the English currency;
but Edward III took the first step in a downward career,
by issuing coins from the Mint of less than the ancient
weight. It is almost impossible for good and bad coins
to circulate together at the same nominal value; people are
apt to pick out the best coins, either because they wish to
hoard them, or to melt them down and use the bullion for
export or for ornament. The effort to keep up the ancient
standard of the currency had not been successful; Edward III
probably tried to issue new coins that should be of about
the value of those in ordinary circulation. He also seems
to have tried to check the influx of debased silver, by
coining Rose Nobles of gold, which were to serve the
purpose of international trade with Flanders, and which
were emblematic of his claim to the sovereignty of the sea.
This left less excuse for the importation of corrupt foreign
silver, but he did not succeed in excluding it altogether. In
many continental countries, during the fourteenth century,
the debasement of the coinage was very rapid; there was a
slight temporary gain to the Crown, and the ulterior effects
were not fully understood, though expounded with great
clearness by a French bishop—Nicholas Oresme. Eventually
English kings betook themselves to this disastrous method
of tiding over temporary necessities. A wholesale debasement of the English coinage took place in the time of
Henry VIII and Edward VI, when the coins were not
merely reduced in size, but the metal was debased by a
very large admixture of alloy. The coins of one issue of
Edward VI contained only three parts of pure silver to
nine of alloy. The economists and moneyers of the time
did not fully realise the mischievous effects of this debasement, and much care was needed to reassert sound principles, and to give them effect in the earlier years of Queen

Elizabeth. In 1561 the silver coinage was restored to its original purity, but the new issues were smaller in size and weight than the statutory coins of Plantagenet times. A pound of silver was not minted into merely twenty but into sixty shillings. That recoinage marks a date when the responsible officers had learned from experience one useful lesson about the nature of money. As the *Discourse of the Common Weal* shows, public opinion in the time of Edward VI was not clear as to the evils of a debased currency, but, from the time of Elizabeth onwards, no English Government has ventured on the dangerous expedient of deliberately tampering with the standard.

97.   For alterations in the size or purity of coins neces-

The fall in the value of silver and rise of prices.

sarily bring about alterations in the number that must be paid for goods of any kind. If the quality of the money is worse, it is necessary to pay a greater quantity of coins than before, for any given article. In technical language, if the value of money falls, the prices of commodities of every kind must rise. Prices rose in the time of Edward VI; the coins were so bad, that the buyer had always to pay a greater number of shillings than before to induce the seller to part with his wares. But when the purity of the coins was restored to its ancient fineness, prices did not return to their old level, as people had expected. This was partly due to the fact that the coins were smaller than formerly, but it also arose from another cause that was not obvious until many years after the recoinage occurred. The silver of which the coins were made was much more plentiful, and therefore far cheaper, than it had ever been before. The first half of the sixteenth century was a time when silver was beginning to pour in from the New World, and there was a consequent fall in its value, which prevented prices from returning to their old level. In the reign of Elizabeth customers had to pay a larger number of pieces of cheap though pure silver for the purchase of commodities than they would have had to pay for the same goods at the beginning of the reign of Henry VII, when silver had been so much more scarce. This rise of prices, consequent on the increasing plenty of pure silver, went on steadily till about the time of Charles I; and it is generally calculated that during this period the nominal prices of commodities in England rose three or four hundred per cent.

98. These changes in the coins and in the value of silver render it exceedingly difficult to make any satisfactory comparison between money prices during the Middle Ages and at the present day. For a very long period the price of corn in England was nearly stable.

Difficulty in finding or applying a standard of value for long periods.

As, during this period, silver was getting scarcer and scarcer, and steadily rising in value throughout Europe, it appears probable that a deterioration of the coinage was going on slowly, or the rise in the value of silver would surely have been reflected by a fall in general prices. There appears, however, to have been one epoch at which the general range of prices was somewhat disturbed. The booty, procured by English soldiers from the town of Calais and the French campaigns of Edward III, appears to have got rapidly into circulation, and to have been sufficient to cause a slight rise in the general range of prices about 1347 and 1348. This seems to have given real ground for discontent with the attempt of the legislature, in the Statute of Labourers (1350–1), to force back the rates of payment to those which had been current in the year 1346. But on the whole it may be said that, from the earliest times when accounts are kept until the beginning of the Tudor period, the nominal prices of the necessaries of life were practically unaltered, except in so far as the variations of the seasons made corn plentiful or scarce. The changes which occur in the sixteenth and early part of the seventeenth century were owing to the reduction of the coins to less than a third of their former weight, and the reduction of the value of silver to one-fourth of what it had been. As a rough and ready method of comparison it may be said that a shilling of the later part of the seventeenth and succeeding centuries would not go quite so far as a penny in the fifteenth and preceding centuries. But this comparison of nominal prices, rough as it is, only takes us a very little way towards making any intelligent comparison of the standard of comfort. Partly from lack of information about the quality of goods, it is very difficult to compare medieval prices with those of the present day; even if such a comparison could be had, it must still be borne in mind that many of the comforts of modern life were entirely unknown, and wholly unattainable even by wealthy people in the Middle Ages.

99. From the time of Elizabeth until the Revolution there seems to have been comparatively little alteration in the coinage. The throes of the Civil War appear to have made but little difference in the issues of the currency. At the same time there can be little doubt that during this period the coinage was subjected to a very special strain. Money transactions were much more common than they had been in medieval times. The circulation of the coinage was more rapid, while there was less desire to hoard, and more encouragement for wealthy men to leave their gold with goldsmiths who lent it out to traders. The facilities which paper money gives were, if not wholly unknown, at least little developed. Exclusive

The recoinage of 1696.

reliance on bullion for payments exposed the coinage of the country to wear and tear, while it was also alleged that many of the money-dealers habitually enriched themselves by clipping it. In the time of William III, consequently, English coinage was again in a very unsatisfactory state. The chief practical difficulties which arose were felt in intercourse with other countries. William III had to maintain large armaments abroad; and to procure the necessary coin for payments in the Low Countries, he had to meet an adverse rate of exchange. One hundred and thirty-three nominal pounds of the clipped silver of this country had to be paid in order to secure a hundred pounds of current silver in Flanders. Hence the burden of taxation was immensely increased. As Professor Thorold Rogers has shown, the immediate effect of the recoinage of 1696 was to remedy the serious disadvantage under which England laboured. The adverse rate went gradually backwards, and within a few months the rates were so far equalised that nominal payments in this country exactly corresponded with the money obtained for military purposes from bankers in Flanders.

100. Eighteenth century difficulties about the coinage were of a somewhat different character. They *The gold* arose from the fact that gold and silver were *standard.* alike standard coins, and that it seemed impossible to fix and maintain the ratio of one metal to the other. In the time of Charles II guineas had been coined, which were intended to be of the same value as twenty shillings in silver. It was found, however, in practice that the gold was more valuable than had been supposed, and that twenty-one shillings were an approximate equivalent. But this was only approximate. Silver coins were, on the whole, rated somewhat too low, and there was a temptation to melt down silver coins and to sell the bullion for gold. The deficiency

of silver coins was, in consequence, a matter of frequent complaint, and the inconvenience, which resulted, served to give popularity and vitality to the mercantilist doctrine of legislating to secure a balance of trade. It was not until 1816 that a real attempt was made to get rid of the difficulty altogether by the demonetisation of silver. When gold became the sole recognised standard of value, silver could be coined with such an amount of alloy that it should never be profitable to melt it down ; while, when a limit was fixed beyond which payments in silver should not be legal tender, debtors were prevented from endeavouring to discharge their obligations in the less valuable of two standard metals. It may be possible, as bimetallists hope, to arrange by legislation and international agreement for a standard that shall be more stable and less fluctuating than gold. This, too, is liable to changes, such as occurred when Europe was flooded with the precious metals obtained in the New World, or there may be an exhaustion of the sources of supply such as was felt during the Middle Ages. It may be that a combined gold and silver standard—like a compensating pendulum— would serve better than either metal taken independently and by itself; but the experience of centuries seems to show that attempts to use one or other of two metals as a standard is sure to cause grave difficulties either within a realm or in the relations of international trade.

101. The foundation of the Bank of England (1694) had very important effects in popularising the use of paper money and other forms of credit. The Bank was a company which lent its capital of £1,200,000 to Government on condition of receiving £100,000 permanently as interest. This constant revenue gave it a strong position as a wealthy body, and the Bank was able to circulate its notes, or promises to pay, as if they had

The Bank of England and bank notes.

been actual coins. The public had confidence that these notes
could be exchanged for gold on demand, and were therefore
willing to take them as the equivalent of gold. The private
firms of goldsmiths, with whom the Bank competed, made
a serious attempt soon after its formation to discredit its
notes by causing a run on the Bank at a time when, owing
to the recoinage, there were special circumstances which
rendered it difficult to obtain the necessary bullion. The
Bank, however, defied this conspiracy; and as it was able to
meet the bona fide demands of its ordinary customers, the
incident does not appear to have done any serious harm.
This was, perhaps, the first instance of a problem which
has had to be faced again and again—namely, to determine
what reserve should be kept in a bank, so that it may be
able to meet its engagements and to pay gold for all the
notes that are presented. In Scotland where one Bank
was started in 1695, and another in 1727, banking was not
the monopoly of one great company, such as controlled
monetary transactions in London, and a large body of
experience on this point was soon formed. At one time an
attempt was made to render a sudden run upon the Bank
of Scotland impossible, by issuing notes which were convertible, not on demand, but only after a definite interval
had expired. Owing to this restriction, however, these notes
were *depreciated* and did not circulate on the same terms as
gold, or as notes which could be readily exchanged for gold.
In another case, that of the Bank of Ayr, there was a very
considerable over-issue of notes, and when the bank failed
through the dishonesty of a manager, there was very wide-
spread commercial disaster throughout Scotland. In the
case of these Scotch banks there were ready tests, if any
miscalculation was made; the notes either failed to circulate
at their nominal value, or they were repaid with great ra-

pidity, through the ordinary channels of trade, to the banks which had issued them, and the general range of prices was not greatly affected by their operations.

The Bank of England, however, was in a special position, as its notes were guaranteed by Government. When, at the close of the eighteenth century, Pitt made repeated demands for advances from the Bank, the governors were at last unable to meet their notes with gold, and they were forced to suspend cash payments (1797). When this occurred, the ordinary indications with regard to notes ceased to operate. The notes formed an inconvertible paper currency; their value merely depended upon their scarcity, and their scarcity depended upon the wisdom of the directors in not issuing too large a number. But the tests which had served, during the eighteenth century, for judging whether the issues were excessive or the reverse were no longer available (p. 152). There was a general rise of nominal prices, but it seemed as if this might be due to other causes, such as bad harvests or the exigencies of war. Though the Bullion Committee of the House of Commons (1810) detected the real cause, and showed that there had been a depreciation of the currency by an over-issue of inconvertible paper money, still Parliament and the nation were not convinced. It was not until 1819 that the evil was remedied, and that the gold standard was once more restored by the resumption of cash payments on the part of the Bank of England.

102. The development of banking, and especially the foundation of the Bank of England, led to some modification in the habits of traders. They became more and more accustomed to trade on borrowed capital. By means of their credit in the commercial world, they were able to obtain loans from bankers, and to carry on business on a

Loans; the Bank rate, and the Act of 1844.

far larger scale than would have been possible had they
been limited to their own capital.   Their credit enabled
them to procure capital; and the development of this credit
system gave great opportunities for the expansion of trade.
In the earlier part of the eighteenth century, when the
financial power of credit was generally recognised, people
were inclined to exaggerate its importance, and to regard it
as a substitute for capital.   But the credit of a trading company is not capital; and unless it is so used as to procure
the use of capital by borrowing, it does not really help to
expand a business largely.   The directors of the East India
Company and of the South Sea Company were guilty of
blunders in this matter.   They expended their capital in
procuring political advantages, and then got into difficulties
through want of sufficient means to carry on their commercial undertakings.

As time went on, however, larger masses of capital were
formed, and commercial men began to count on being able
to borrow money from the Bank in the ordinary course of
business.   When trade was going badly, the Bank was accustomed to raise the rate at which it granted accommodation
to traders; if this was done gradually, the Bank was able
to avoid making new loans and thus to strengthen its own
financial position, without giving any shock to credit in
commercial circles generally.   The raising of the rate tended
to make prices in England fall, and thus to encourage exports and diminish imports while it also tended to induce
foreigners to send money to this country for investment at
the higher rate of interest procurable.   Thus, in more ways
than one, the raising of the Bank rate tended to bring about
a favourable state of the exchanges, and a flow of gold to
this country which would, sooner or later, find its way to the
coffers of the Bank.   It could thus strengthen its position

and proceed to lend money on easier terms once more. The Bank was so well managed that in 1763, when the Hamburgh banks failed and there was widespread disaster on the Continent, the crisis did not extend to England. Similar good fortune attended their proceedings in 1782. In 1797, however, when Pitt borrowed so largely, the Bank rate was raised very suddenly, and was practically prohibitive to merchants who hoped to get the usual accommodation. The scare, caused by this action on the part of the Bank at a time of general commercial anxiety, augmented the evil, and very serious results followed in the City from a course which, at this distance of time, it is not easy to defend.

During the period when cash payments were suspended and the currency was partly depreciated, the Bank directors were unable to avail themselves of the indications given by the exchanges, and to control the state of credit in the City. But it was a disappointment that when cash payments were resumed, there was not the success which had been hoped for in avoiding financial trouble. There was a very bad crisis in 1825, and nearly twenty years later it was thought necessary to reconstitute the powers of the Bank of England, by what was known as the Bank Charter Act (1844). By this, the department of the Bank which issues notes was absolutely severed from that which makes advances and carries on ordinary banking business. In this way an attempt was made to separate the difficulties connected with the currency from those which arise through the fluctuations of commercial credit. The critics of the Act have complained less of what it has done than of what it has left undone. It has been held by many that the expedients requisite under the Act may sometimes lead to such precipitate action as to aggravate an impending crisis,

and to diminish the subsequent power of the Bank to grant
needed assistance. Other critics are doubtful whether, considering the scale on which business is now done, there is
anything like a sufficient reserve to render the Bank as safe
as it is habitually supposed to be. The impression that
the Government will somehow see it through any period of
disaster gives it a status which may enable it to maintain
the credit system of the country on a far smaller basis of
cash than would otherwise be possible.

103. All these facilities for currency and finance were
only gradually utilised by the Government for
public purposes. In the time of the Norman
kings the main support of the Crown came
in kind from the royal estates (§ 24); the
king lived 'of his own,' and much of his own
would be stored for the use of his household as he travelled
from one estate to another. Even the taxes which were paid
into the Exchequer seem to have been sometimes paid in
kind, as late as the time of Henry I; and when we remember that the king relied for his army on personal services
rather than on paid forces, we see that money entered to a
comparatively small extent into the finances of the realm.
The same holds true at first of other demands and of taxes
on trade. The king had a recognised right to obtain certain
commodities for his personal needs and those of his household, and to receive a share of the imports and exports.
It was a real protection to the subjects when these rights
ceased to be arbitrary and became definite. Thus the practice
of caption gave place to a recognised privilege of *pre-emption*
by the king's purveyors, though, even as late as the time of
the Long Parliament, there were many grievances resulting
from the manner in which they exercised their powers. It
was also a real boon when the customs came to be taken

Payment in kind and by service. Arbitrary and casual taxation.

at understood and definite rates, when the *prise* of wine
was limited, and excessive tolls (malæ toltæ) on wool were
given up. In the last case a rate defined in money set the
limit to arbitrary demands: this was a great boon to traders,
for the effect of arbitrary taxation on trade is most prejudicial.

With the growth of Parliament under Edward I and
Edward II the Commons obtained the power of stopping
that arbitrary taxation against which their forefathers had
protested in Magna Carta. In Norman and Plantagenet
times taxation on land and on personal possessions (1181)
was levied in money, and was casual in incidence rather
than arbitrary in amount. Different tenants held by different tenures, and the royal demands came upon them in
different forms and on different occasions. In some years
there might be demands of *aids* from tenants on the royal
demesne; sometimes there would be a *scutage;* sometimes
the towns were *tallaged*, while Henry III and Edward I
occasionally obtained the right to share in the spiritual taxa
tion which usually went to the Pope. Though taxation in
the time of Henry III was very frequent and very heavy
there were no two consecutive years in which similar payments were made by similar persons. The occasional and
haphazard nature of taxation must have rendered it very
inconvenient to many of those who were called upon to
pay; indeed, at this stage, it illustrates some of the evils of
a money economy, for these irregular demands gave great
opportunity for the operations of Jews and other money-
lenders. Hence it is not surprising that when the machinery
for collecting taxation came to be organised in Parliament,
special care was taken to render taxation regular so far as
might be. The taxes which were voted were still occasional,
but they were taken as far as possible at a regular rate, and

causes of dispute as to what each man ought to pay were
greatly reduced. The most striking inequalities in English
taxation in later times seem to have arisen from the instinct
of maintaining regularity at any cost and of clinging to the
fiscal arrangements once made, even when the circumstances
for which they were originally devised have wholly altered.

104. One striking illustration of this tendency to prefer
a fixed money payment to variable demands
may be found in the great financial agreement
of 1334. The taxation of moveables before
this time had been made by means of assessments of the actual possessions of the persons taxed. In
some cases these had granted exemption for the stock and
tools of the labourer ; in others the tax had been levied
more exhaustively. Sometimes taxation had been levied
at one fractional part and sometimes at another, but in 1334
it was determined that the king's commissioners should agree
on a composition which each town or village should pay, as
the equivalent of a tenth on moveables within the towns,
and a fifteenth on the counties. The terms *tenth and
fifteenth* henceforward meant a sum of about £39,000, and
when Parliament voted two or more tenths and fifteenths
there was an understood sum which each district was called
upon to pay.

This arrangement lasted until the reign of James I,
but long before that time difficulties had arisen. Some
parts of the country decayed and were unable to contribute
their quotas, while other districts prospered without having
to pay any additional charges. Towards the close of the
fifteenth century, in particular, we read of many towns
which obtained exemption. Sometimes a total of four
thousand pounds and sometimes no less than six thousand
were remitted. Still the expenses of government were apt

Margin note: Tenths and fifteenths. The Tudor subsidies.

to expand ; and, while these remissions were being made,
there was need of extra assistance in emergencies, such as
occasioned the celebrated poll-taxes of 1377 and 1381; while
the defence of land and sea imposed duties on the Crown
which it was not easy to fulfil.   Convoy money was taken
from certain ships, and attempts were made to organise
some defence for the coasts.   But these things hardly
affected the general taxation of the country, as the revenue
was levied, so far as possible, from those who benefited
directly by the new arrangements.   It is extraordinary, too,
to see how large a field, covered now-a-days by regular
government organisation, was then left to private munificence.   The maintenance of roads and bridges was but
little attended to except when it was undertaken by the
charitable and the pious.   Even the burden of defending
the realm against the Spanish Armada was largely borne by
loyal subjects, who voluntarily came to the aid of their
queen.   This personal sentiment of loyalty and willingness
to make voluntary sacrifices was shown for the last time
in the Civil War, when it was an important element in the
equipment of the army of Charles I.

Under Henry VIII a serious effort was made to readjust the fiscal system of the country to the condition of its
material prosperity.   The tenths and fifteenths were supplemented by a general subsidy of 4s. in the pound on the
yearly value of land and 2s. 8d. in the pound on personal
property.   Those who came under this denomination were
known as 'subsidy men'; after its imposition in 1514 there
was no real attempt at subsequent modification, although a
fresh assessment was made each time.   A subsidy came to
be a fixed expression for a sum of nearly £100,000, and
the proportions, which each had to pay, merely followed the
original levy of the tax.

105.   The fall in the value of silver during the sixteenth century had serious effects in a state which had so completely adopted a money economy.   The change affected all who lived on *Financial difficulties of the Stuarts.* fixed incomes, as many landowners did ; in so far as they were unable to raise their rents, they received the same money as before, while they had to purchase all that they required at much higher rates.   If ordinary landowners felt this severely, the difficulty fell with special force upon the Crown.   The revenues from Crown lands could not be increased rapidly, and there was difficulty in procuring additional resources from taxation.   It was becoming obvious that taxation must afford the regular source of national income not only in emergencies, as hitherto, but in ordinary times.   Elizabeth was ingenious and parsimonious enough to evade the difficulty, and the whole task of reconstituting national finance in accordance with the necessities of the times was still undone when the Stuarts succeeded to the Crown.   Their financial difficulties may have been increased through their own mistakes, and through the folly of some of their agents, but many of their difficulties were inevitable.   The Tudor kings and their courtiers had wasted much of the ancient heritage of the Crown, while the new conditions of European politics and the place which England was taking, as an important power in Europe, made it necessary that she should have a navy, and that the royal treasury should be replenished.   While there was a real plea of necessity for much that Charles aimed at, there was also an excuse for discontent.   The purchasing power of money had fallen, but the sums which Charles I obtained were nominally very large, and the non-success, for which lack of resources was partly to blame, appeared to show that he and his ministers were utterly incompetent.   Between the real

needs of the Government and the apparent mismanagement
of the Crown officers the financial position became more and
more strained, and was one of the most important elements
in the quarrel which gradually widened into a Civil War.
The most important financial expedient at which Charles I
aimed was that of somehow or other introducing an *excise*,
or tax on goods produced and consumed within the country.
It was easy to see that some such expedient as this would
be very profitable. Each consumer might pay very little,
but the total revenue to the Crown would be very large.
Strafford endeavoured to do something of the sort in Ireland
by means of a salt tax; and if the monopoly in soap had
been carried through, as it was designed, Charles would
have practically secured an excise on this commodity. But
the strength of public opinion was too great to allow
of his even attempting to procure a revenue by avowedly
imposing an excise, and he had no success in the
indirect efforts with which he attempted to attain this
object.

The attempt to impose an excise was due to a statesmanlike effort to distribute the burden of taxation over the
community generally, instead of allowing it to fall entirely
on certain classes. Throughout the Middle Ages, there
must have been large sections of the population who contributed little, if at all, to the national revenue. The tenths
and fifteenths, and the Tudor subsidies practically fell upon
landowners and upon householders in towns. Imported
commodities were of the nature of luxuries, and those who
did not consume them were unaffected by the rates at which
they were charged. Of the labouring classes generally it
would appear that the pressure of taxation hardly touched
them at all. The excise was approved as an expedient
for distributing the burden of taxation as widely as possible,

but Charles I failed to secure it, and it was left to those who defeated him to carry out this project.

106. The Parliamentary party were forced to raise money for the support of their army, and in this emergency adopted financial methods, *Parliamentary and Restoration finance.* which had been tried by the Dutch and approved by their experience. They levied monthly assessments from the landowners, or from tenants who could recover the amount from their landowners, and they also introduced an excise on beer. The measure was very unpopular, but it was very profitable; and, when once introduced, it became a permanent source of revenue. The successful organisation of the Post-Office as a money-making concern dates from the same period; and these two expedients were retained and perpetuated, when the whole financial system of the country was reconstituted at the Restoration. The new system followed the lines of the temporary methods of the Parliamentary party, and did not revert to the ancient methods which had continued in vogue until the fall of Charles I.

The Restoration Parliament was the first body which accepted the new order deliberately, and set about providing for the regular and ordinary expenses of the Crown by means of taxation. This would have been a difficult question at any time, but under the special circumstances of the moment, when the country was suffering from the effects of the war and from a famine of unexampled severity, it was no easy matter to devise expedients for raising a suitable revenue. They endeavoured to provide a regular income of £1,200,000; of this over £100,000 was raised by granting a hereditary excise, which was given in lieu of the money accruing to the Crown from feudal incidents like wardship and livery, while the claims from purveyance and pre-emption were also to be surrendered. All the advantages of this bargain lay with the landowners and especially with the tenants of ancient demesne, while the excise fell on the public at large, and the justice of an arrangement by which the burdens of the land were thrown upon the general consumer has been much criticised. It is probable that little was thought of it at the time. Public opinion had become accustomed to an excise, and there was less inconvenience in perpetuating the existing system than in trying to raise a much larger revenue by the direct taxation of the land. In levying taxes from the land, they were also careful to maintain the existing arrangements. The inequality with which the land-tax was levied in the home counties, as compared with the outlying counties, serves to reflect the difficulty felt by the Parliamentary party in collecting revenue from the royalist districts at the period when they imposed the tax. But curiously unfair as it was, it affords another illustration of the English preference for paying at a known rate, rather than for introducing a method which, by being more flexible, should be less regular and more fair. The Restoration Parliament had probably but little thought of abstract justice, and were chiefly concerned with the possibility of collecting a revenue at all. By maintaining the *de facto* system, however, they avoided the evil which arises from changes in the method of taxation, and by distributing the burden widely they were able to build on a firm basis a revenue system by which the ordinary expenses of government should be regularly defrayed out of taxation.

107. So far we have reviewed the changes in the fiscal system which followed the introduction of a money economy in matters of state. The development of credit was also important. Few English kings have been able to keep out of debt,

Public borrowing. The Bank.

and some, like Edward III, have broken faith with their creditors. When Charles I borrowed to pay the Scotch army in 1641, he was compelled to do so on the joint security of Parliament and himself, and thus incidentally forfeited the power of dissolving Parliament without its consent. In the post-Restoration period, public borrowing came to be part of the regular methods of finance and was no longer resorted to merely in emergencies. The Government was accustomed to borrow money from goldsmiths on the assignment of grants which were already voted, but had not been collected, and the goldsmiths could count on the early repayment of their loans, as soon as the taxes came in. In 1670, however, Charles II endeavoured to retain this money in his own hands, by stopping the payments out of the Exchequer which were due to the goldsmiths. By this breach of faith he caused much consternation in the City, and many of the public, whose deposits had been lent to the Crown, were also sufferers. A certain amount of interest was paid to these creditors, but the principal was never restored, and came in time to form the nucleus of the National Debt.

The National Debt, as a regular institution, may be said to date from the time of William III. He was engaged in a lifelong struggle with Louis XIV, and was ready to strain every nerve to carry it on. The Bank of England was a scheme which was hastily floated at the end of a session, when other financial projects had fallen through. It was not very favourably received in Parliament, but was eagerly taken up in the City, and the full amount required was soon subscribed. William III obtained £1,200,000 to use at once in the war, while he only had to raise £100,000 by taxation. He also obtained an immense political advantage by cementing the adhesion of the monied classes who subscribed to the Bank. The subscribers obtained regular interest in perpetuity for their money. This was secured to them on the credit of the Government, and by the assignment of the income from a tax on the tonnage of ships. They also had a monopoly in conducting banking business, and from the first they prospered greatly. But the success of this expedient was dangerous. The Government were tempted, again and again, to negociate large loans from companies to which special trading privileges were conceded. The conflict between the old and the new East India Company (p. 116) and the subsequent history of the South Sea Company have sufficiently put on record the wild character of much of the finance of this time.

108.   With the beginning of the Georgian era there was

The inci-
dence and
pressure of
taxation.

less immediate need for meeting special emergencies, and attention was chiefly directed to possible expedients for paying off the debt. The pressure of interest, along with the expenses of government, made it by no means easy to raise sufficient revenue, and Walpole's peace policy was probably dictated by a desire to improve financial conditions. There was a steady increase of national resources, but at the same time this was so slow that there was real difficulty in procuring the necessary revenue, and it seemed important to nurture the growing wealth of the country with extreme care. It was consequently under Walpole (1721—42) that the whole taxation of the country was recast in accordance with the principles of the mercantile system. By the introduction of bonded warehouses, he helped to make England a depot for the carrying trade, and by systematizing the duties levied on foreign manufactures and the bounties given on native products, he endeavoured to institute such tariff arrangements as should contribute to the general prosperity of the country.

The principles had been laid down long before, but it was only under Walpole that they were consistently put into practice. As has been pointed out above (p. 132), there are grave reasons for doubting the wisdom of the best intentioned methods for directing and fostering national industry. What with the industries that were hampered, the opportunities that were given for fraud, and the unsuitable trades that were galvanised into life, the benefit which was believed to accrue through Sir Robert Walpole's well-meant efforts must have been greatly frittered away. At the same time it must be remembered that, whether through his arrangements or in spite of them, the country steadily prospered on all sides of its economic life under the *régime* which he systematised. He was the first English statesman who took carefully into account the incidence of taxation with a view to obtaining a definite national object and not merely for the sake of revenue purposes.

This was a principle against which Adam Smith made an effective protest; he did not think taxation should be used to promote any commercial object. He had had opportunities in France of investigating the fiscal systems of different countries, and he applied economic doctrine to the problems of the incidence and methods of taxation much better than had been done by previous writers. Under his influence North introduced the succession duty, and the effect of the *Wealth of Nations*, published in 1776, was much more clearly seen when Pitt came into power (1783). This minister carefully followed Adam Smith's views as to the incidence of taxation, and endeavoured to distribute the burdens so that they should fall as lightly as possible on the poorer classes. This was apparent both in the remissions made in the earlier part of his career, and in the mode in which he imposed heavy taxation at the beginning of this century. His great

expedient was a *Triple Assessment*, which may be regarded as
the forerunner of the income-tax.   His borrowing was reckless in the extreme.   When Government credit was becoming exhausted he did not borrow at high rates, but accepted
sums of £80 or £90 as the equivalent of £100 of stock
borrowed at relatively low interest.   In this way he bur-
dened the nation with a large nominal debt which, just because it was running at low interest, could not be readily
extinguished by subsequent loans.   But though his action
was reckless he had considerable success in lightening the
burden of taxation for the community at large.

His work in this respect was carried on by Huskisson
and Peel.   They were interested in reducing the pressure of
taxation on the poor, while they also believed that by lightening the burden of taxation the general prosperity of the
country would be greatly increased.   The very motives,
which had led Walpole to construct a complicated system
of duties and bounties, weighed with financiers a century
later in their efforts to remove them.   It seemed to be a
risky experiment.   The country was suffering from depressed
trade, and it was difficult to make both ends meet, but, not-
withstanding, the tariff reforms were carried through.   Peel
was careful to impose some temporary tax, which might
serve as a source of revenue until his remissions had time
to stimulate trade, and to bring in a larger revenue at the
lower rates.   In his general scheme he was singularly successful.   There was a rapid expansion of industry, which
was felt all the more clearly when the free trade experiment
reached its culmination in the repeal of the Corn Laws
(1846).   Since his experiments have been thus completely
justified by success, it seems unnecessary to recall the
criticism to which they have been subjected; it must, however, be remembered that progress was already being made

towards very general free trade by means of commercial treaties, and that, though the sudden adoption of free trade gave us a great advantage for the time, we have lost the means of bargaining with other states, so as to prevent them from imposing hostile tariffs against ourselves.

109.   There is no serious proposal to return to a condition of barter in ordinary transactions, and there can be no doubt that the substitution of money finance for payments in kind to the Crown and personal service is advantageous in many ways. The burden of taxation is more precisely known, it is more regular, it is more widely distributed, and it is more adjustable ; there is a real benefit in many directions, especially where industry and trade are concerned.   To a very great extent these generally recognised advantages in national affairs are typical of benefits which have ensued in other departments of life from similar changes.   The man who works in definite hours for specified wages may have a hard life, but his obligations are more certain and his reward is better defined than in the case of the slave or the serf (§ 125).   Close bargaining and competition give opportunities to the man of energy and enterprise ; they appear under some conditions to be unfavourable to the well-being of the weak and the ignorant. But at least under a money system, we may have definite statements as to the condition and resources of those who are worst off, while under a more primitive economy the details cannot be clearly and precisely put forward.   To know the extent and the nature of evils is one step towards finding a remedy, and the substitution of a money for a natural economy gives us the means of acquiring such knowledge.

The advantages of a money economy.

CHAPTER VIII

AGRICULTURE.

110. In no single art is it more easy to trace the course of progress than in one which, like tillage, has been assiduously practised from the earliest times.

Extensive
cultivation.

The most primitive sort of agriculture is that known as *extensive* culture—a system which can only be practised by a people with a very large area at their disposal. Each year they clear and till a space sufficiently large to raise the necessary crops, or as much as may be possible with the stock and seed at their disposal. In some parts of the world, as for example in certain parts of India, where this method is still pursued, the ground is cleared by burning the coarse grass and brushwood which cumbers it, and the ashes supply a useful ingredient to the soil during the year it is under crop. When the harvest is over, the land is simply left idle. In the immediately succeeding years, other tracts are cropped in turn, until after an interval of several seasons necessity compels the use of a portion which has, at some earlier time, been under tillage. If eight or nine years elapse before it is necessary to revert to the same soil, the land has so much time to recover that the process may be carried on almost indefinitely without exhaustion.

This extensive system of cultivation is very adaptable. It may be used by nomads, who have no settled habitations, but who are able to linger at some point in their wanderings while a crop is being taken. It is possible even for a sea-faring people to linger for some months on shore and re-victual their ships from crops they have raised. This the Phœnicians did in their great voyage round Africa, and the Danes in Northumbria resorted to a similar expedient. It is the simplest and least laborious system, and may be retained for many generations by a people who have definitely settled down; while it may also be practised as a means of supplementing their resources by men who are acquainted with, and habitually use, more arduous methods of tillage. In this way it survived in Aberdeenshire at the end of the last century; there the *out-town lands* were cultivated extensively, while a much higher system of farming was adopted on the *in-town* fields.

If, however, the area at the disposal of a family, or group of families, is so restricted that they have to return to the same field within five or six years, Intensive cultivation. there is not sufficient time for the recuperative powers of nature to operate, and the soil becomes exhausted. We may speak of a time, when the whole capabilities of any land are brought into play for arable purposes, by using it all in turn and as frequently as it will bear, as a point of least exhaustion. When this point is past, it is necessary to resort to artificial means to stimulate and reinvigorate the soil, and with this we have the beginning of *intensive* culture. Intensive cultivation consists in replenishing the soil with manures or other fertilisers, so that it can be used more frequently, and yet not be exhausted. Progress in agricultural skill enables men to wring from the land six or seven times as much crop as they could by primitive methods.

They can get something from it every year, and yet the land is not worn out. It is always assumed that a tenant farmer will return the land to the landlord at the expiration of his lease in good condition. The problem for the agriculturist is to arrange his business so that he can regularly and habitually get as much as possible from the land, without exhausting it. If he is to get a great deal out of it, he will have to put a great deal into it. Much more labour must be expended in carrying and spreading manure and in deeper ploughing, on even the simplest system of intensive farming, than is needed when the land is tilled extensively.

111. When this is recognised, we can grasp more clearly
Diminishing the general course which agricultural improvereturns. ment has taken. When once intensive cultivation is adopted, if it is necessary to get more out of the soil, more must be put into it. More can always be got out of it, but only by increasingly arduous or expensive operations. Hence has been formulated a principle which is known as the law of diminishing returns. It holds true of any place at any time when intensive culture is in vogue. Each additional application of labour (and capital) to the land will give an additional amount of crop, but not at the same rate as before. Each new effort, be it a week's labour, or £10 capital, applied this year in addition to what was applied last, will be remunerated at a less rate than accrued to previous efforts. Double the labour will ensure greatly increased produce, but still it will be less than double the produce—a larger amount, but at a diminished rate.

This is a physical principle which is plainly true when
Agricultural we remember that labour is only one of the
improvements. necessary elements for the growth of a crop. By doubling the labour, we do not double the sunlight

or air ; we only improve some of the conditions on which growth depends. Other points must, however, be noticed to render this physical principle instructive in regard to social affairs, or the history of human progress. It only holds true, as stated, for any definite condition of knowledge. If there is such an advance in skill that men understand better how to avoid the exhaustion of the soil, its action is suspended for the time. The rotation of crops is an expedient by which land can be more constantly used without being unduly exhausted ; it does not involve any considerable addition to labour or capital. It serves to prevent exhaustion, and improvements of this type give a great increase to human powers of obtaining food from the soil. The improvement may be so great that it is possible to get enough food from a diminished area, and with less labour and capital than before. But if we take this new condition of skill as a starting-point, the law of diminishing returns will again begin to operate in farther efforts to procure additional subsistence. Agricultural progress has been of two kinds. There has been an advance of skill in avoiding the exhaustion of the soil, but, where no such improvement has occurred, there has been need for increased energy to make up for the exhaustion of the soil, and to replenish it. The improvement in preventing exhaustion has gone on so fast, that it may be doubted whether there is any increase in the drudgery of man and beast, employed in tillage at the present day, as compared with that required to procure the far inferior crops with which men had to be satisfied at the time of the Norman Conquest.

112. When intensive cultivation has once come into vogue, a farther condition follows. The good effects of most measures will last for more   Open fields. than one year. The improvement is not exhausted all at

once, and hence it becomes advisable to use the same land over and over again, and not to vary it, as it is natural to do on the extensive system. Instead of fields which change from year to year, the family or village which uses intensive culture will prefer to have permanent fields, constantly kept for tillage, even though there may be sufficient land to enable them to continue the old plan in a modified form. As a consequence, all through the Middle Ages, there were fields in each village, which were permanently set apart for tillage. They were laid out with marks which were never altered, and the divisions of the land, occupied by different people, consisted of narrow grass borders or balks, which divided each large field into a number of acre or of half-acre strips. These *balks* were common enough a century ago, but since that time they have been nearly all destroyed, and the few which remain here and there may be regarded as curious relics of a system which was once universal. The fields were known as *open* fields, because they had no fencing, except during those periods of the year when the crops were growing. At other times the cattle could range without restriction over the whole area of the village, and pick up what they could get, either from the herbage or the common waste, or from the stubble on the open fields.

The open fields were also spoken of as *common* fields, although they were not, in historical times, held in common. In the ordinary village, at the time of the Norman Conquest, the lord of the manor would have a considerable part of the fields cultivated for his own use by the villeins, and their holdings probably all lay intermixed with his own demesne farm. The tenant who held a virgate or yardland would occupy some sixty half-acre strips scattered in

Common rights.

different parts of the open fields ; but his virgate consisted
of a known number of known strips. Like the portions of
meadow land, the virgates in the fields were definitely
assigned, and no part of the open fields was common
property. The common rights to use the fields for grazing
purposes only began to operate when tillage was over for
the year, and when the fields lapsed for a time into the
rest of the waste. All the inhabitants who had land to
cultivate and cattle to do the work seem to have had
grazing rights on the common waste. But though the fields
were not held as common property, there was, in all probability, a great deal of work that was done together and in
the same fashion by the different holders of property in
each village. They combined to supply teams, at least for
the lord's land, and they may have arranged for a good deal
of collective work among themselves on the common plan
which must have been adopted, according as the lands
were laid out in two or in three fields.

This system of open field, with intermixed holdings, or
run-rig as it is termed in Scotland, seems to
be so very inconvenient, that it is difficult to   Survival of
understand how it could have been adopted,   open fields
and why it should have been retained   It possibly had some
advantage in the way of fairness, and the various pieces of
land could be distributed more equally, as regards quality
and exposure, according to this plan. There is little reason
to believe that all the inhabitants of a village were equal in
status or wealth at any known time ; but pains were taken
to maintain what was fair and equal among such of the
inhabitants as were on the same footing. But apart from
this, it seems possible that this curious arrangement was
first adopted from motives of practical convenience and
perpetuated later from the mere difficulty of substituting

anything else.   When the art of land surveying was unknown, and there were no definite measures of area, it was simplest to lay out land by merely breaking it up with the plough, and then to assign an acre—the portion ploughed in a day —to each villager in turn.   This was, undoubtedly, the method of assignment adopted while extensive culture was practised, and there was no necessity for any re-arrangement when intensive culture came into use.   When, during the last century, the disadvantages of the open field system became obvious, tenants were, with great difficulty, induced to accept any alteration (p. 187).   The process of enclosure meant the grouping of their scattered strips into separate and several holdings, but it was not an easy thing for the commissioners to re-assign the lands into holdings that would be considered fair equivalents for the old lands. The difficulty felt in discarding the system—even when its inconveniences were fully understood—may partly help us to understand how it came to be retained for so many centuries.

113.   The fullest information which we have as to the methods of cultivation during the Middle Ages is to be found in those writings on husbandry, compiled during the reign of Henry III, to which allusion has already been made (p. 37). Of these the most celebrated was due to Walter of Henley. The handbook, which he wrote for the guidance of landlords in the management of their estates, is most useful in helping us to picture agricultural conditions that have long since passed away.   He institutes a comparison as to the work which had to be done on the two field and three field system respectively.   These were two different methods of working the land, which, while involving precisely similar amounts of labour, yielded rather different results.

The two field and three field systems.

According to the two field system the following arrangements were carried out. One field (A) was sown with wheat or
rye in early winter.   This crop grew until the next summer,
was reaped at harvest time, and the stubble was left on the
land till the following summer. Thus, during the whole
year, the only work done on field A was that of reaping
the harvest. The second field (B) was the scene of much
more active operations.   In late spring or early summer the
stubble of the previous year was broken up and ploughed
twice ; the field then lay fallow for some weeks, after which
it was ploughed over again before being sown with wheat or
rye in the early winter. Thus while the one field was under
crop the whole year, the other was ploughed over three
times, enjoyed some weeks of fallow, and was eventually
sown with wheat or rye.

The three-field system was similar, save that an interme-
diate year was introduced. After each field had had a crop
of wheat or rye, it was usual in this plan to give it a second
crop of barley or oats. This crop was sown in the spring,
after the land had been ploughed over once, and was reaped
in the autumn. The barley year was brought in between
the wheat year and the fallow year of the two field system.
According to this scheme there were two years of crop,
wheat and barley, followed by one season when the field
was fallow, instead of alternate years of crop and fallow.
It is obvious that where the three field system could be
introduced, it gave a much greater return—two-thirds of the
land would be under crop each year, and not merely one
half.

Walter of Henley enables us to compare the two
systems more closely, as he gives an estimate
of the work which a team of eight oxen could   The work of
be expected to manage on one system or the   the teams.

other. Two hundred and forty acres of work was as much as they could accomplish in a year; and a team could either work 160 acres on the two field system, or 180 on the three. If the three field system was employed—three fields of sixty acres each—the team would plough up the wheat stubble before the barley was sown in spring (60 acres), and would also plough the fallow field three times in the course of the summer, making 240 acres in all. On the two field system the same team could manage two fields of 80 acres each. On one of those, where the crop was growing, no work would be done : the other was ploughed three times— giving 240 acres of work. Thus each team under the three field system could provide 120 acres of crop, as against 80 acres of crop, which were available on the two field system.

Both methods seem to have existed side by side at the time of the Domesday Survey, though it is probable that the three field system became increasingly common in subsequent times; but there was a modification of the two field system which is of some interest. This consisted in dividing the fields into half fields. Each was cropped every alternate year, but the half which bore wheat one year would be sown with barley when next it was cropped. Each half field thus underwent the following rotation,— wheat, fallow, barley, fallow, for four years. When in later times other crops came to be introduced, this four field system, as we may call it, was very easily modified into a four course husbandry of wheat, turnips, barley, clover. Not until the eighteenth century was there much systematic attempt to introduce these modifications and the scientific rotation of crops.

Hence we may say that the two field and three field systems seem to have held their own, from times preceding the Norman Conquest until the seventeenth or eighteenth century, as the ordinary and recognised methods of cultivation. During this long period there was apparently little, if any, progress in the art of agriculture, and Walter of Henley's *Husbandry*, written in the reign of Henry III, was not superseded by any better work until the time of Henry VIII, when Fitzherbert's treatises appeared.

114. The great plague which passed over England in 1349, when the Black Death swept away about half of the population, seems to have initiated a number of changes in rural life. When the numbers of the labourers were so much reduced, it was impossible to carry on tillage on the old scale, and the area under plough shrank very considerably. It could no longer, as we have already seen (p. 41), be profitably conducted on the old system of bailiff farming, and the re-arrangement of the social grouping and introduction of tenant farming was a gradual process. The scarcity of labour and the demand for wool combined to render it profitable for the landowner to give up tillage and to take to sheep-farming instead. This may be said to have been the first form of *capitalist* farming in England, when the land was turned from tillage to sheep-farming, and was used in the fashion that would afford wool for sale and bring in a good money return in the market. Till the Black Death, the procuring of subsistence had been the main object of the great lords in the management of their estates. Henceforward farming came to be regarded more and more as a business, and those who invested money in it looked for a return, like other traders, from the prices fetched in the market.

The general prevalence of subsistence farming in the early Middle Ages is clear from such treatises as that of Walter

of Henley, who in writing for large owners distinctly recom-
mends it. The estate was to supply the needs of the
household as far as possible, so that marketing might be
reduced to a minimum. The regular practice was to provide
for the household first, and when this was done the surplus
was taken to market. This is reflected in the accounts
which detail many of the outgoings and profits of the estate
in money, but allow for the corn in bushels, and only
reckon as much in money as was actually taken to market
and sold at the current rates. Since this was the custom
of the manorial lords, who could command facilities for the
conveyance of corn, it must also have been true of the
small farmers who would have more difficulty in regard to
carriage.

It seems, then, that subsistence farming was the usual
thing in the thirteenth and fourteenth centuries. Money economy was very partially
introduced in this department: the farmer
did not work with reference to a market, and only offered
for sale the surplus of his crop over and above what he
required for use. This state of affairs contrasts curiously
with what occurred at a later date. The quoted prices of
corn in the Middle Ages only represent the rate at which
the surplus was sold. The requirements of the rural population were, as we may say, a first charge on the harvest
before any of it was sold. Under these circumstances we
should expect greater and more rapid fluctuations in price
than we find in days when the whole crop is realised in
money, and the requisite food is subsequently purchased
by the farmer. Farther it may be said that since the farmer
worked for subsistence rather than for profit, fluctuations in
price did not directly affect him, and that in so far as he
was able to contract or expand his operations, he would be

Farming for the market.

led to do so by his own household requirements rather than by the price he could get for his surplus corn. The contrast becomes most curious when we notice that none of the conditions, which Ricardo assumed as the usual and regular thing, when he wrote his explanation of corn rent at the beginning of this century, had come into being in the fifteenth century. The crops were not thought of as taken to market at all, and the expansion or contraction of tillage did not directly depend on market price, but on the requirements and the industry of isolated households. There had, of course, been many great farming establishments before the time of the Black Death, where labour was carefully organised and much wealth was procured and housed in the granges. But these were not capitalist undertakings in the modern sense; the bailiff did not work with a view to income, but for the sake of the subsistence of the household. Capitalist tillage, as we know it, is very modern, for it is in connexion with sheep-farming that we first come across the rural enterprise of wealthy men, who invested their money in sheep or cattle and were guided in their operations by the state of the markets. They were able to take advantage of the conditions brought about by the Black Death. Land, which was left uninhabited or unoccupied, could easily be utilised for sheep-farming, and there was a marked tendency to turn it to account in this fashion. As the price of wool increased during the fifteenth and sixteenth centuries, the temptation to encroach on tillage and to develop pasture-farming became very strong. At various periods it was accompanied by rapid rural depopulation, and grave anxiety was felt as to the maintenance of our food supply, so that, as pointed out above (§ 50), deliberate efforts were made to check the movement.

C. & M. 12

115. About the beginning of the sixteenth century,
however, an improvement, known as con-

Convertible
husbandry.
Sixteenth
century
enclosing.

vertible husbandry, was introduced into tillage;
this rendered the diminished area much more
productive. It consisted of an alternation of
pasture and arable farming. A portion of arable land was
laid down in grass for a period of years, after which it
was then broken up again and used for tillage for a
time. This gave a far better chance for the land to recu-
perate than was possible with the fallowing every second or
third year, while it involved the breaking up of the permanent fields. The husbandman, instead of having scattered
strips in the open fields with meadow and pasture rights
over the common waste, henceforward occupied six *several*
or separate closes. Three of these were used for corn, so
that he could keep up the old alternation of wheat, barley
and fallow. One he used as pasture for his cows; another
as pasture for sheep or other stock, and another as meadow.
Then in winter, when he expected most difficulty in finding
provender, five out of the six closes were available for his
cattle—the remaining one would be sown with wheat. Land
which was enclosed with hedgerows gave far better shelter
for the cattle, and could be worked more carefully than when
all the stock of the village were allowed to wander over the
waste and eat it bare at once. It was a more prudent way
of using the common waste. It was also favourable to tillage,
as the cow pasture, when broken up after some years, was
greatly improved from the way in which cattle had been
constantly kept upon it. Not only had the land rest, but
it was also well manured.

When enclosure was carried out in the interests of tillage
and grazing alike, it was a general benefit. More corn
and food of every sort were produced for consumers. The

farmer had his land more conveniently placed for his operations, and even if, with the diminished area Enclosure
under tillage, there was less need for ploughing, and depopu-
there was an increased demand for labour in lation.
connexion with hedging and ditching. It was an enormous
saving in every way, though, possibly, it gave slightly diminished opportunities of employment. In many cases, however,
enclosing was carried out in the interest of grazing only.
The open fields and common waste were alike broken up
into closes for sheep and cattle, with the result that there
was little need for any labour but that of a shepherd and his
dog, while the country districts were depopulated. It is
not always easy to distinguish, at this distance of time, cases
of enclosure for the formation of parks and sheep-farms,
and cases of enclosure for the introduction of convertible
husbandry. Both were called by the same name, but one
was accompanied by depopulation, and the other was not.
Convertible husbandry did not involve any change in the size
of holdings or in the number of tenancies. This the large
sheep-farms did; and the pulling down of houses of husbandry was fixed upon as the special mark of the bad as
contrasted with the allowable and useful type of enclosing.

It is a little difficult to trace the course of the enclosures, good and bad, of the fifteenth and England.
sixteenth centuries. If we take Warwickshire,
we find that the greater part of the south-eastern half of
the county was enclosed in 1459. John Ross alleged that
depopulation had, in consequence, gone on very rapidly
and on a large scale. About a hundred years later,
in the time of Edward VI, we find fresh complaints of
enclosure in the same district, as if it were quite a new
thing. It is still more startling to discover that in the time
of Elizabeth and for two hundred years later, this particular

district was quite unenclosed, and remained in open fields. We are almost forced to suppose that the outcry against depopulation had proved successful once and again. Under the circumstances it is dangerous to specify any time when the change was going on with special rapidity. The fullest information we possess is for the thirty years preceding 1517. The greatest and most widespread dissatisfaction was shown in the time of Edward VI; and the last we hear of depopulation was under the stimulus of a high price of wool, in the last decade of the sixteenth century. Then it ended. The demand for corn had come to be such that it was not good management to prosecute grazing alone, to the exclusion of tillage; and enclosures, accompanied by depopulation, may be said to have ceased in England, in the reign of James I.

A similar movement, due to similar economic causes, Ireland and Scotland. has shown itself in later times, both in Ireland and Scotland. Soon after the Restoration, English capitalists found an excellent field for speculation in breeding and fattening cattle in Ireland. They were glad to form large ranches, which were cleared of the cottiers and left to the cattle. The profit from these herds was very considerable, and it was convenient to absorb the little cottier holdings which could be advantageously utilised as portions of these pasture farms. Though it was a very successful market speculation, the Irish disliked it, because it depopulated the country. As has been already indicated, the economic jealousy of English landowners combined with the political jealousy of English Whigs to check the movement (§ 93).

In more recent days, sheep-farms and deer forests have proved a remunerative speculation for proprietors in the Highlands, and crofters and small tradesmen have frequently been forced to make way for the one or the other. Capitalist farming, in all these cases, has taken the form of utilising the uncultivated land for feeding animals of some kind, and has pressed severely on the subsistence farming of badly equipped and impoverished peasants. There is much greater difficulty in organising capitalist arable farming; and this was in England, at least, a later growth.

116. One way in which capitalist pasture-farming tends to depress peasant subsistence farming is by the demand for increased rent. Under the conditions described, land used for pasturage has a high money value and yields a considerable rent. The landlord will naturally ask as large a payment for the use of land for arable purposes as he can obtain for its use as pasturage. The beginning of capitalist sheep-farming marks the beginning of competition rents. Medieval rents were practically fixed, and included the share of taxation which the peasant paid. They corresponded, too, with the value of the labour services of which the lord was deprived when the peasant became free to spend all his time on his own land. This would still be a natural basis for calculation, when yeomen with leasehold tenure were introduced by those landlords who ceased to work their domains with the help of a bailiff. But with capitalist farming a new element plainly enters into consideration. Rent comes to have the clear and obvious character of a payment for the use of the soil; its amount will be connected with the suitability of the soil for some special purpose. The landlord expects to receive a sum that represents the value of the land when employed in the most remunerative way, and those who like to use it for some less remunerative purpose may be called upon, so far as purely economic considerations go, to pay such a sum that the loss for their want of enterprise or skill shall not fall on the landlord. There was a great outcry in Tudor times against landlords who were guided by purely eco-

[sidenote: Capitalist pasture-farming and rents.]

nomic considerations in this matter, and political reasons were adduced for interfering to preserve for the peasant class the right to use land for a purpose which was not so remunerative as pasture-farming.

117. It is very difficult to estimate the precise progress of agriculture during the seventeenth century. There are some pieces of evidence which would seem to show that it was advancing here and there, though not very generally.

Seventeenth century husbandry.

For one thing, there was considerable interest in the subject, as is evidenced by the number of technical treatises which were issued. Fitzherbert and Tusser are practically alone in the sixteenth century, and their work is comparatively slight; but the treatises of Markham, Weston, Plat, Taylor, and other seventeenth century writers are conceived on a much larger scale. They were not content to record English experience, they also gave accounts of the crops and methods of cultivation employed in Flanders and Brabant, and indicated some points in which Englishmen might, with advantage, imitate their rivals. They discussed many details connected with the management of land, and gave much good practical advice. It was, probably, not entirely without effect, but at the same time it must be admitted that the descriptions, which we read of English farming in the eighteenth century, render it perfectly clear that the new expedients were not adopted at all generally when they were first set forth. Still these treatises serve to show that a certain number of men were studying the subject seriously; and the advances, which were made at a later time, were undoubtedly initiated by men of this type.

Brabant husbandry.

Another and a better indication of the prosperity of the landed interest may be drawn from the fact that efforts

were made at this time to extend the area of available land.
Here again, experience acquired in the Low   Drainage of
Countries was brought to bear for the im-   the fens.
provement of England.   There were two great districts
which were constantly flooded by the rivers which pass
through them.   The Cambridgeshire fens were intersected
by five rivers, and were liable to be flooded by surface
water.   A great scheme was proposed and gradually carried
out for constructing a new channel into which these rivers
might drain, and by which the water from the Midlands
might be passed to the sea.   It was worked out by a
Dutchman named Cornelius Vermuïden, and proved more
economical than any attempts to bank in each of the separate
rivers for the whole distance of their course through the fens.
Similar measures were taken at Hatfield Chase, near Don
caster.   In this case the difficulties between the old inhabit
ants and those who obtained possession of the land which
was recovered, led to open hostilities.   The draining of low
grounds involved the destruction of the fish, wild fowl, and
other products of the marshes.   The commoners, who had
adapted themselves to life in these districts, had no desire
that the land should be drained, as they did not wish to
betake themselves to pasture-farming or tillage, and they
showed their resentment by every means in their power.
Similar difficulties were felt in the Cambridgeshire fens,
but resistance to the change was neither so long continued
nor so violent there, as in the more northerly district.   When
we pass through the rich area of fertile corn-land which has
been gradually rescued from inundation, and see the harvests
it now bears, or remember how long chronic ague lingered
on the low lying lands, we cannot wish that this step of progress had been stayed, however much we may regret the
suffering which fell on one particular generation.

Besides the gain which accrued through the protection of the fens from inland inundation, there was also success in rescuing some districts from the sea. The salt marshes of Essex and the low lands of Norfolk were banked against the tide, and a large area of excellent pasturage was provided. In all this there was conscious imitation of the expedients employed by the Dutch. Owing to the political struggles of the seventeenth century, men, first of one party and then of another, took refuge in Holland. They were struck by the prosperity of the country, and advocated the adoption, in England, of plans which had been crowned with success elsewhere. Charles II was particularly impressed by the canal system, and was personally interested in proposals for improving the internal water-ways of England. This was urged, in his time, as a means of increasing the food supply of London and other large towns. Little, however, was done to give effect to these suggestions till a century later, when fuel, and not food, was the requirement which they were chiefly intended to supply (§ 18).

There is some incidental evidence which points to a condition of considerable rural prosperity. The era of depopulation had come to an end, and the competition for arable farms seems to show that tillage was a fairly prosperous business. There was a decided rise of rents in the seventeenth century, not merely from pasture-farms, but on ordinary agricultural land. This indicates that agriculture was developing on the whole. There was certainly greater approximation to modern conditions; market considerations were coming prominently into view, as well as provision for subsistence, in the management of land. Though the Civil War must have caused much disturbance, by affecting the rates of wages and exposing husbandmen to many risks and exac-

Farming fairly remunerative.

tions, and though the seasons at the close of the century were very unfavourable, farming seems to have been fairly remunerative, even though little general progress was made in the art of tillage.

118.   The eighteenth century, on the other hand, was a time of very rapid and much more general progress, which resulted in changes on every side of rural life.   The Stuart period was a time of promise so far as rural economy was concerned. The Hanoverian reigns, and especially the time of George III, were a period of performance.   The Corn Bounty Act of William III (1689) rendered farming less uncertain as an investment for capital than it had previously been (p. 84). In years of great plenty the farmer still got a remunerative price; and landlords and men of enterprise alike found it a profitable business.

The agricultural revolution.

Scientific agriculture was pushed on with great success.   The study did not merely consist of observations of practice elsewhere; it was pursued by careful experimental methods.

Improvements in farming and breeding.

Arthur Young's *Tours* give us a most interesting picture of the transition which was taking place in rural life.   On the one side he paints for us the wastefulness and ignorant methods of the yeoman farmers; the costliness and badness of their ploughing is a theme to which he frequently recurs. On the other hand we read of the spirited improver, who tried new crops, or new courses of rotation, and who kept accurate numerical returns of different experiments. The introduction of a suitable course of husbandry was the chief improvement he had at heart.   Turnips had been cultivated for some time, though carelessly, but artificial grasses and clover were little grown when he first began to write. Such crops could be used to take the place of the old fallowing, and, if properly managed, were a good preparation for wheat. In every way it was an enormous saving. In those counties where convertible husbandry had been already introduced, the rotation of crops could follow, as soon as any individual farmer recognised its advantages. Where the land still lay in open fields, and all the strips were cultivated according to a common custom, there were serious obstacles in making a change. Hence the enclosure of open fields was pushed on, during the eighteenth century, with a view to removing obstacles to the improved system of agriculture. There was a tendency also to replace the yeoman by more substantial and more enterprising men, and to throw two or three of the old forty acre farms into one larger one.

The improvement in tillage was very noticeable, but it extended to the breeding of stock as well. Mr Bakewell was successful in obtaining a type which was specially suit able for fattening, and ' the roast beef of old England ' began to approximate to the excellence it has since attained. The sheep-shearings at Holkham in Norfolk and on the Duke of Bedford's property at Woburn were great opportunities for improvers to meet and interchange ideas. Nor was royal patronage wanting, for George III, under the pseudonym of Ralph Robinson, took an active part in forwarding the movement.

The increase of the area under tillage at this time Progress of enclosure. is perhaps most easily traceable in the progress of enclosure. This meant not only the better utilisation of existing fields, but also the employment of additional land for corn growing. The open fields, consisting of strips of land separated by balks, could be better employed when the land was re-allotted and held in severalty, while the common waste could also be broken up

and used for tillage, with good economic results, though
with some social loss. It was not so much the change,
as the manner in which it was sometimes effected, that
made it a matter of regret. In any circumstances there
must have been grave difficulty in carrying it out satisfactorily. To allot to each of the small tenants in the village
a plot of ground, approximately equivalent in quality and
convenience to his bundle of scattered strips and including
compensation for the loss of meadow and grazing rights, was
no easy task. When it was done by commissioners from a
distance, it was apt to be very expensive. The cost of procuring a private Act of Parliament and the law charges were
extravagant ; while the expense of fencing the several holdings
was a heavy item. The whole affair was frightfully costly,
and brought a burden upon the poorer commoners which
they were not all able to bear. A more serious ground
for complaint arose from the fact that the proceedings were
not only expensive but unfair. Enclosure acts were obtained
at the instance of one or two wealthy or pushing men. No
enquiry was made on the spot as to the general feeling of
those who had common rights, and many of them were
unaware that any action had been taken until the time
arrived for carrying the new measure into effect. Protest
was then useless, and no real opportunity of expressing an
opinion, or of seeing that their rights were properly secured,
was given to the majority of those interested. These
high-handed proceedings were injurious to   Effect on
some of the yeoman farmers : much more   labourers.
serious evil was done to the labourers. They had often
been allowed, and in some cases had a right, to graze a cow
on the common waste. When enclosure took place, their
title to have any allotment was often disallowed ; or, if any
land was assigned them, it was so small an amount that they

could not utilise it.   Arthur Young instituted some careful
enquiries into the matter.   He was a decided advocate of
enclosure on economic grounds, though he deprecated the
extravagant fashion in which it was sometimes carried out.
He came to the conclusion that, when favourable consideration was shown to the labourers, they were all the better
for the change; but that in a very large number of instances
enclosure had been carried out in such a fashion as to do
them irreparable mischief.   This was one of the many tendencies which, towards the end of the last and the beginning
of this century, combined to depress the condition of the
agricultural labourer.   The system of allowances in aid of
wages sapped his independence (p. 94); the introduction
of the spinning-jenny diminished the family earnings (p. 222),
and the progress of enclosure prevented him from having a
cow's grass.   He was thus cut off from all the opportunities
hitherto available of increasing his means of subsistence,
and came to be wholly dependent on what he could earn
as wages, at a time when wages ranged specially low (p. 91),
and when, owing to the dearness of food (p. 85), his money
went but a very little way.   Attention was called to the
condition of the labourer by the Swing riots in 1812,
which were the direct outcome of this miserable state of
affairs.

The absolute dependence of the agricultural labourer
upon wages and the importance of maintaining as high a rate as possible were facts
so strongly impressed on the minds of some economists
of the day that they opposed measures advocated by practical men which would, in all probability, have proved beneficial.   Arthur Young urged the desirability of providing
labourers with allotments, especially in counties where it
was possible to provide a cow's grass for each cottager.

Allotments
and wages.

An allotment that would serve to support stock of any sort would be a great aid to the household without distracting the man from giving his full time to work for a master. Arthur Young suggested that such allotments should be granted on the distinct understanding that they would be forfeited by anyone who applied for parochial relief. In this way he thought they might be utilised so as to check the decline of independence. But his practical common sense was opposed by the leading economists; they argued that allotments would either tend to the decrease of wages, or that the additional comfort supplied by them would only result in an increase of population, and thus this beneficial project was delayed for many years.

In connexion with this subject it is worth while to point out that the disappearance of the small or yeoman farmers—a gradual process to which allusion will be made below, and which had advanced a long way by the end of the Napoleonic wars—reacted very unfavourably on the labourer. While there were small farms to be had, it was possible for the labourer, if he had real energy and skill, to rise in the world and to take a farm on his own account. But when small holdings were combined to form larger ones, which could only be profitably worked by men with a considerable amount of capital, the labourer was condemned to forfeit his best hope of rising in the world without deserting his old home. He was deprived, as we may say, of a legitimate object of ambition.

The character of agriculture during this period underwent a very remarkable change. Until the latter part of the last century England was able to produce with ease a sufficient amount of corn for home consumption, while under the influence of the Corn Bounty Act there was usually a surplus available for export to foreign markets. Even though manufacturing had advanced considerably and little wool was exported in a raw state in the eighteenth century, England still exported a large amount of raw products, both coal and corn. But during the years 1773–1793 a turning point was reached. England ceased to be a corn-exporting country (p. 85); her population was increasing, despite all the demands made upon it by wars abroad, and the check imposed by the war on cottages at home. With increased demand for food there was a higher price, which was sometimes very high. As an immediate result of this change, the system devised for keeping the price of corn steady ceased to act. The Corn Law was altered in 1773 in the hope that the price would fall. The result, however, was that the price of corn was no longer determined by the sum which could be got for it at the ports, but depended far more on the actual demands of English consumers. Hence fluctuations increased considerably in the last quarter of the eighteenth century, and were rendered more striking by the curious variation of the seasons. From the beginning of that century till about the Declaration of Independence (1776), prices had been re-munerative and stable, but from that time until the close of the Napoleonic wars they were very variable. Sometimes they were extraordinarily high and sometimes so low that the yield from the worst land in cultivation did not repay the expense of raising it. We can thus distinguish a time when agriculture was a steadily profitable pursuit, and one when it was a highly speculative business. The fate of the old-fashioned yeoman farmer was somewhat different during these two periods, as he was subject to entirely diverse economic influences.

119. These economic influences have hardly received sufficient consideration, as it has been the fashion to lay

a great deal of stress on some supposed political causes
for the disappearance of the yeomanry.   It is   The decay
said that the landowners were anxious to ob-   of the yeo-
tain political power, and bought out the small   manry.
freeholders.   This is hardly likely.   The landowner could
not obtain power in this way, as tenant farmers had no votes
till 1832 ; he only extinguished voting power by buying out
a freeholder, he did not bring it within the sphere of his own
influence.   The effects of this supposed cause were probably
quite unimportant, but on the other hand economic conditions were the chief factors in the change.   They have not
yet been examined in such detail that it is possible to speak
with much decision ; and the following explanation must
be regarded as somewhat tentative.

During the period of steady improvement it may be
said that the yeoman farmer was often an   Inability to
obstacle to changes, and that the best land-   compete.
lords were anxious to get him out of the way.   It was
the small farmer who worked his land badly ; whose strips
in the common fields were covered with weeds, and thus
served to undo the care exercised by neighbours in clear-
ing away the growth : he was the man who was impene-
trable to new ideas and kept up the expensive methods of
ploughing with large teams and heavy ploughs.   No wonder
that the owner of a well-managed estate was anxious to get
rid of such tenants, or that a wealthy improving landlord
was glad to buy out such neighbours if he could.   And the
opportunity occurred not infrequently.   Their ways of working
the land served for subsistence farming, but they were not
in a position to compete with the capitalist farmer in the
markets.   He could hold over and sell his corn at high
prices in the spring or summer, while the small farmer was
forced, for want of money, to realise his crop immediately

after harvest, when prices were very low. As he failed to take up the rotation of crops, and to cultivate roots or grasses successfully, he was at a still greater disadvantage in fattening his stock, and when any emergency occurred he was forced to give up the struggle and to make way for a more enterprising man. The agricultural struggles of the sixteenth century had been fought out over the extension of grazing, those of the eighteenth century concerned the progress of tillage. The sixteenth century had made little, if any, alteration in the size and character of the holdings which remained, but the eighteenth century saw a decided change in the way of uniting holdings wherever it could be managed. In the counties which had already been enclosed, we can hardly trace its course, but where there was much open field at the beginning of the eighteenth century, the progress of enclosure was doubtless accompanied by the gradual elimination of the less competent and energetic of the small farmers—whether tenants or owners.

The time of rapid fluctuation told against them even more seriously; the period of bad seasons at the close of the century must have been fatal to very many. Thus, in one Cambridgeshire parish, it is said that all the small farms were united in the hands of one man, who lent money to his neighbours and foreclosed when the continued bad harvests had ruined them. But those who were able to pull through this bad time enjoyed exceptional prosperity during the Napoleonic wars. The price of wheat was very high, and even though the burdens on the land—poor-rates, tithe and other taxation—were heavy, some agriculturists had a most prosperous time. The peasant farmers had their share of the large money returns, or, if they preferred to betake themselves to some other line of life, they were able to

Rapid changes of fortune.

obtain very high prices for their small farms. It is said
that many of them took this latter course, and so escaped
the reverses which came on the agricultural interest at the
close of the war. It was partly because some were bad at
their business, partly because some were ruined in bad times,
and also because others were able to take advantage of
good times, that the class of small farmers disappeared, and
gave place to the modern conditions with which we are
familiar.

In not a few cases their difficulties were aggravated by
the withdrawal of manufactures from rural places. There
was less employment for their households, and perhaps for
themselves, when spinning and weaving were concentrated
in factory districts. There was less local demand for such
products as eggs and milk when the weavers and their
families deserted the villages. All these tendencies were
concomitants in an agricultural revolution, the full importance of which has hardly been yet realised.

For whatever may have been the steps in the transition,
it seems certain that, with the disappearance   Ricardo's
of the small farmer, we have the disappear-   theory of rent.
ance, for the present at least, of subsistence farming in
England. During the nineteenth century—and generally
speaking during a great part of the eighteenth—farming has
been a trade, and the success of the farmer depends on the
money returns to his business. In the war period when
prices were high, it was worth while to extend the area of
tillage as much as possible, and to plough up land that was
badly suited for corn. When prices fell, this land, which
was on the margin of cultivation, was no longer used for
tillage. Ricardo was thus able to formulate his celebrated
explanation of the changes in rents for corn land. Land
which was on the margin and just repaid the expense of

C. & M.   13

cultivation would afford no rent for corn; but any land, better suited for growing corn, could do so; and the amount it afforded to the landlord would be the equivalent of the advantages it possessed over such land as was on the margin.   Ricardo's explanation of the differences and varia- tions in corn rent was instructive at the time, for it summed up and formulated a condition of affairs which, though familiar to us, was then somewhat of a novelty.   The ex- pansion and contraction of agriculture had come to depend on market prices, and the rise and fall of corn rents did not cause high prices, nor even follow them directly; but rents were affected by prices through the effect of the latter on the increase or decrease of tillage.

120.   Even before the close of the war, it was obvious

Permanent improve- ments.

that if peace were restored, and English ports were open to foreign corn, there must be a sudden drop in prices, and consequently a great diminution of the area under cultivation, with a subse- quent fall in rents.   It seemed as if ruin stared the whole agricultural interest in the face, and the Corn Law of 1815 was a deliberate effort to stave off imminent disaster by trying to keep the price of corn up to 80s. the quarter. The law of William III had been entirely different; it had aimed at making the price stable, whereas this measure was designed to keep it high.   The underlying political principle of rendering the country self-sufficing has been already discussed (§ 54), but the economic motive was certainly that of preserving the agricultural interest from ruin.   The con- demnation of the law lay in this, that it failed to accomplish its purpose.   In spite of the special protection which it re- ceived, agriculture went from bad to worse.   One committee after another examined into the condition of the country, and from 1815 to 1825 there were reiterated reports of the miserable plight into which the farmers had fallen. The Corn Law inflicted a great deal of suffering on the manufacturing interests, but it did not serve to avert very serious misfortune in the rural districts.

In so far as English agriculture was able to hold its own and rally, or to maintain itself when the full *Drainage* force of foreign competition was felt after *and high* 1846, it was because necessity was the *farming.* mother of invention. Every effort was made to secure greater efficiency—especially greater economy through the application of capital to land in permanent improvements. The experience of Mr Smith of Deanston had demonstrated the advantages of thorough draining. Land which was properly drained could be much more easily and more thoroughly worked, so that when this improvement was effected, better crops could be regularly produced. Large areas of bog and marshy ground have been reclaimed through this process, and made available for tillage, while other districts have been rendered far more productive. By the use of new manures and by high farming the general agriculture of the country has been raised to a degree of efficiency that has far outstripped the hopes of eighteenth century improvers. And this result has been chiefly attained by sinking capital in permanent improvements. Landlords and farmers have combined to use their capital to produce this result, and to raise English agriculture to the high degree of excellence and prosperity which it had attained in 1874.

121. The efforts of the agriculturist have been enterprising, but the greatly increased facilities for *Past and* communication with fertile regions in distant *future.* continents have seemed, during the last twenty years, to make it hopeless. Whatever fortune is in store for English agriculture in the future this may be insisted on; we cannot

hope to succeed by reverting to any method or system that has been already condemned. Extensive culture and the three field system could not compete successfully where the accumulated skill and enterprise of recent years have failed.

One hope may lie in saving some of the expense of superintendence. It is argued that on smaller farms the best methods of culture can be organised and carried on with less expense, and that a saving can be effected in this fashion. But to break up the land into smaller holdings is not necessarily to revert to an old condition. The small farms of earlier days were badly managed, and if small holdings are to succeed it will be because they can be better managed than the large ones; and because all the new methods, which have been introduced by wealthy farmers, can be adopted by men with less capital. While the land-lord can sink a good deal of capital, the peasant farmer may supply more efficient labour than he would give under supervision, and it is conceivable that there might thus be some saving in the payment for superintendence. Those who pin their faith to smaller holdings must mean that such farmers can take full advantage of modern improvements; we cannot go back to the small holding of the subsistence farmer or of the man who was half weaver and half grazier.

Still it may be doubted whether subsistence farming Gardens and allotments. could not be utilised as an adjunct to our modern system. There may be produce which it is hardly worth while to take to market, and which yet supplies excellent food. It is conceivable that the labourer might grow for his own use, in a garden or small allot-ment, produce for which he could hardly find a market, but which he would go without if he did not grow it himself. Poultry and pigs are possible adjuncts to a cottage with a garden; although they might not be remunerative as market speculations, they might be well worth having as aids to the subsistence of a family. A cottager can rarely compete with the capitalist or the foreign producer in the market, but if he has the means and ability to procure some important elements of subsistence, he may live in fair comfort even if he is not in constant receipt of wages. If the necessary work in his garden is compatible with his farm work, even at times of pressure, so that the two employments can be carried on alternately and justice be done to both, the cottager may possibly live in greater comfort, even if the farmer's payments for labour should be reduced.

Whether it is possible to turn attention to products which are not grown at present, and which would pay better than those already cultivated is a difficult speculation. Our temperate climate renders it possible for us to grow many things; but each of these various products will perhaps grow more readily in some other land, which is within easy reach by sea. The command of the sea has brought us into connexion with distant lands and climates unlike our own, and the very success of our commerce seems, year by year, to narrow the range of profitable occupations for the landed interest.

CHAPTER IX.

LABOUR AND CAPITAL.

122. ADAM Smith, in the opening chapter of the *Wealth*

The division of labour in industry and agriculture. *of Nations*, has drawn a contrast between the material well-being of a savage and of a civilised people. He ascribes the difference between the two, in their power of obtaining the necessaries and conveniences of life, to one main principle—the division of labour. It allows of a saving of time and a saving of skill in many directions, and by its means far more work can be accomplished with infinitely less drudgery. The effectiveness of the division of labour has been familiarised by the one classical illustration of the making of pins: but its general effects on society are worth a little consideration, especially when we remember that it is comparatively modern. Combination of employments has existed time out of mind, but the systematic division of labour was not very common before the eighteenth century.

In the first place it may be noticed that the principle cannot be applied equally well in all callings—for example, agriculture is not a favourable field for it. The processes of agriculture are dependent on the seasons of the year, and nothing that we can do will serve to hurry them on. Division of labour in industry enables men to do more in less time, but agriculture is dependent upon natural operations, and no exertion will make the harvest come prematurely. As a consequence, the agricultural labourer has to devote himself to different occupations during each season of the year. The old fashioned illustrations of the appropriate labours for each month—like the bronzes on the doors of S. Zeno at Verona—show that this has been the case from time immemorial. There has been great progress in agriculture since primitive times, but it is not nearly so striking as the revolution in our industrial powers: where division of labour is least possible, the change is least complete. From this it follows that the agricultural labourer has a greater variety of occupation than almost any other workman in our present society. If his life is monotonous and dull, this is not due to the deadening effects of mechanical work which are sometimes ascribed to the division of labour.

Division of employments, combined with the practical convenience of training a son to the occupation of his father, has served as the economic basis of the caste system ; and the pursuit of   Basis of class distinctions. hereditary callings seems to have led to the accumulation of inherited skill, so that each new generation has a special aptitude for the work it has to accomplish. In England there has never been such a hard and fast separation as in the East, but the social effects of the division of labour are very noticeable even here. For some kinds of work it is necessary that a man should have a long and careful training —as, for example, a surgeon ; while the employment of a bricklayer can be picked up easily. It is socially advantageous that each should keep to his line : the surgeon would spoil his hands as a bricklayer, while the bricklayer could hardly be trusted with a delicate operation. It is not advantageous that there should be frequent change on the part of adults from one occupation to another; and if there is division of employments at all, some persons will have higher or better work than falls to the lot of others. Apart from all questions of social importance or remuneration, it is best for anyone to take up such work as affords the widest scope for progress and improvement. The doctor or lawyer is likely to go on learning his business better all his life, while the artisan is at his best from twenty-five to thirty-five. And there is a very great difference in the whole status of those whose powers are constantly improving, and of men who have nothing more to learn in their work. This marks a real difference of social grade.

In all ranks of life the principle is generally adopted that the most highly skilled and responsible work should be the most highly paid. This is so obvious and natural that it seems unnecessary to dwell on it. There is, however, some slight indication of a feeling which views the matter from a personal rather than from a social stand-point. It is said that the professional man has pleasanter work to do, and that, therefore, he may be expected to work for less pay than the man who does more disagreeable work. This is a fair principle of adjustment within any social grade, and does take effect in the minor differences of remuneration within the same social class. But so far as society is concerned it is right that the man who, having the opportunity, does what is best worth doing, should get the greatest reward; and from this it follows that he has a better chance, if he desires it, of starting his children in a line of life similar to that which he has adopted, since he can pay for their longer training. However much we endeavour to break down any disabilities that may have hitherto prevented the boy of exceptional ability from

Differences
of opportunity.

rising in the world, there seems to be little prospect of a
time when all shall start with equal opportunities.   No very
satisfactory system of selection in tender years has been
devised, and so long as family ties are recognised at all, the
son of the successful man will have better opportunities in
beginning life than other people, since he has time to be
trained for difficult, responsible, and well-paid work.

The disabilities to which the medieval serf was exposed
have been done away, and obstacles to passing from one
social grade to another are far slighter than was formerly
the case.   The accident of favour from a patron had much
to do in the past with the promotion of individuals, even in
the most democratic of professions—the Church.   There has
been a conscious effort in our days to create a system which
shall offer an opportunity to the most energetic to rise out
of their class into a higher grade, by their merits and apart
from favour.   But the principle of division of employments
and division of labour has come into increasing operation
since medieval times ; and its tendency is to accentuate
and perpetuate the severance of classes, by introducing real
differences of thought and habit.   Class distinctions, if less
apparent than they were when marked by special kinds of
attire, are no less real.   In some respects they are deeper
than they used to be when a seven years' apprenticeship
was the similar mode of admission into a great variety of
different callings.

123.   While laying stress on the economic importance
of the division of employments and of labour,   Capital in
Adam Smith does not fail to allude to its   the cloth
necessary conditions.   "As the accumulation   trade and its
of stock," he says, "must, in the nature of   labour.
"things be previous to the division of labour, so labour can
"be more and more subdivided in proportion only as stock

" is previously more and more accumulated" (*Wealth of Nations*, Book II, introduction).   He thus fully recognises that division of labour cannot be introduced spontaneously. It is only under certain conditions that it is possible ; only under favourable conditions that it can be carried a step farther.   How far labour can be profitably divided, depends on the extent of the market, or, to put it otherwise, on the scale on which business can be organised.   It cannot be organised on a large scale without capital.   This is an essential condition for the minute division of labour in modern times; it is only through the existence of capital that labour obtains its greatest degree of skill and efficiency. Not only is this so, but in the progress of the industrial arts capital has come to take an ever increasing part in the work of production, and to interfere more and more with the unaided efforts of labour.   To some extent it has facilitated them, and to some extent it has superseded them; in fact these two things must go together—to render labour more easy is to leave less scope for the exertion of labourers in any given piece of work.

If we go back to the time of the Norman Conquest we find a marked contrast with our own day.   Industry was then practically altogether independent of capital.   The labourer possessed a few tools, as he does now, but this was his only stock in trade, and wealthy men did not use their money in industrial labour so as to procure a revenue.   Industrial capital, in the modern sense, was unknown—even after economic freedom had made some advance.   We may picture the medieval artisan to ourselves—in so far as a money economy had come in—as a man who had to spend much time in trying to dispose of his wares.   Hereward visited William's camp as a potter, and many craftsmen must have been, to some extent, pedlars or have visited fairs, in order that they might dispose of their goods. In other cases we may think of them as men who had to wander about in search of custom, as travelling tailors did in the early part of the present century. Under these circumstances there was no capitalist tailor, for the customer supplied the materials, and furnished food while the work was being done. There was no middleman and no employer, in the modern sense, for the artisan was in direct communication with the consumer. But whatever may have been the advantages of this system it certainly had its disadvantages—the craftsman who wanted to sell the product of his labour passed much of his time in seeking for custom. He could not devote all his strength to the execution of his work. This must have involved much anxiety and waste of time to individuals, and would be a considerable loss to society when there were still few suitable markets for labour and its products. Whatever the disadvantages of present conditions may be, it is at least an advantage that the craftsman can spend his time on the work at which he is really good, while he is not so constantly and habitually diverting his energies to the search for employment. Through the intervention of a middleman between the consumer and the producer, the craftsman is able to concentrate his energies on that for which he is really skilled.

The increasing intervention of capitalists in the staple industry of England—the manufacture of cloth—has been traced with great clearness by Professor Ashley. He shows that, in all

Capitalism in supplying employment.

probability, the different branches of labour requisite for turning out a properly finished piece of cloth were carried on as separate industries by independent workmen—with apprentices and journeymen in their houses—till the middle of the fourteenth century. The weaver bought wool or yarn, and made the cloth. He sold it to the fuller who worked it into a close fabric; it was then sold to the shearman, who smoothed the nap with his heavy shears and turned it out ready for the purchaser. The relations of these trades to one another are not quite clear, and it is probable that they varied, at different times, even in the same place. It is quite likely that the weaver sometimes employed shearmen and fullers for the work they did on the cloth he had made and which he proceeded to sell. But in the middle of the fourteenth century, we find traces of a class called *drapers*, who seem to have been merchants. They bought cloth from the weavers or fullers, and then supplied it to customers in distant markets. Their intervention was only natural when the English began to do a considerable export trade in cloth. The weavers and fullers had no direct access to foreign markets, nor even to those distant English towns to which the draper might send their wares.

This system, or something very closely resembling it, appears to have continued in Yorkshire till the present century. The weavers worked on their own account in the country round about the towns, and brought in the cloths to sell to merchants at the Hall in Halifax or the Bridge at Leeds. But in the Eastern Counties and other parts of England the trade had been organised in a different fashion as early as Tudor times. The clothier, in ordinary parlance[1], was an employer who arranged the whole trade in its various branches. He delivered wool to the weavers, and employed carders, spinners, dyers, fullers and other workmen. These master clothiers organised the whole

[1] According to Yorkshire usage the term clothier was used for a domestic weaver, who sold his goods to a merchant.

manufacture as a modern employer does. Some of them, like Stump of Malmesbury and John Winchcombe of Newbury, were the owners of establishments which closely resembled factories. They came more and more into prominence during the early part of the sixteenth century, and though an attempt was made to put them down in rural districts under Philip and Mary, there were numerous exemptions, and the measure was repealed under James I. From that time it appears that the clothing trade, throughout the greater part of England, was organised on capitalist lines, as the clothier furnished the materials, arranged for the various processes, and sold the finished product. The weaver had neither to busy himself about securing and preparing materials, nor about finding customers for his goods when they were woven; he might actually do his work at home, but, so far as economic relations were concerned, he was working for an employer.

From Yorkist and Tudor times there is evidence of difficulties between the weavers and the master clothiers. On the one hand there was often doubt as to the honesty of the weavers who were accused of embezzling materials, and on the other, there is a long series of acts against 'truck,' as the clothiers were apt to pay in goods and not in money. Still, though the domestic system held its ground in Yorkshire till the present century, we can see that it had grave disadvantages, and that the Yorkshiremen must have spent a good deal of their time—one day or more a week—in getting materials and frequenting the Cloth Hall, while all this was more likely to be saved by workmen elsewhere, who got employment from a master clothier.

124. The next form in which we find the intervention of capital is in supplying implements for doing the work.

The master-clothiers appear to have undertaken this function

Capital as
supplying im-
plements. in Tudor times, for they owned looms at which their employés worked, they possessed fulling mills, and they used gig mills; the latter were condemned under Edward VI as injurious, since they did the work badly. But the whole step becomes clearer in another trade which was, from the first, a machine industry. Knitting and lace work were carried on by means of frames invented by Mr Lee, in the time of Elizabeth. Like many inventors he derived little benefit from his ingenuity, but within half a century of his death the trade began to flourish greatly, both in London and Nottingham. The attempts of the Framework Knitters Company to regulate the industry in the interest of the journeymen were not very successful; early in the eighteenth century many abuses began to show themselves, and the workers were in a most distressed condition. One of the chief complaints arose from the large number of apprentices, so that trained workmen were deprived of opportunities of employment; they felt it a bitter grievance that, even while little work was given out to them, they should be charged regularly for frame rents. The frame was an implement worked by hand, and there were few attempts to introduce power, or to modify the organisation of the trade till after 1840. But at all periods of bad trade complaints of the same sort were heard. Dissatisfaction broke out in a violent form in 1816, at the time of the Luddite riots, when numbers of frames were broken; the disturbances were skilfully organised and seem to have been carefully directed against those frame owners who were specially unpopular.

125. In this particular instance of framework knitting, the implement, which the capitalists hired out to their

workers, did not supersede labour at all. It was an invention which called a new industry into being,   The depend-
and this may be noted as an early instance of   ence of labour
a trade that was completely organised on capi-   on capital.
talist lines. The employer not only found a market for the
goods, and supplied materials, but he furnished the necessary implements as well. Capital had intervened on every
side of the labourer's life and furnished the means by which
the workman could devote himself exclusively to his proper
calling. The division of labour was carried very far under
the master clothiers[1]. The steady progress, in favour of this
type of organisation, may be said to prove that it has had
distinct advantages, that the public are better served by its
means than they could ever be by the labour of isolated
workmen, each conducting his business, in all its sides, on
his own account. But if great advantages have accrued
through the intervention of capital, there are also risks of
serious danger. New facilities are given for the doing of
work, but the workman becomes dependent on his employer, for materials, for the opportunity of employment,
and for implements of labour. The period of the industrial
revolution showed, on the one hand, the ability of capitalists
to take advantage of new powers and new methods, but it
also brought into clear light the reality of the dangers which
are likely to arise under a system of capitalist production,
unless care is taken to guard against them.

There is a certain parallel between the changes which
have been described in connexion with agri-   Comparison
culture, and those which occurred through the   between agri-
                                                 culture and
capitalist organisation of industry. Medieval   industry.
tillage was subsistence farming; the modern agriculturist
is a trader who looks to the market for his returns. In

[1] Reports, &c., 1840, XXIV. 388.

somewhat similar fashion, the isolated workman may be said to have laboured with a direct view to subsistence. This work had direct relation to some customer's wants, and the price he charged was directly calculated from the food, &c. required during the time of labour. Subsistence was recognised as a first charge, and prices followed it. But the drapers, master clothiers and other employers were forced to look directly to the markets. The time of money economy had come in (§ 109). Prices settled themselves according to demand and supply. The market might be over-stocked, or owing to some unforeseen accident, buyers might be few. In either case the clothiers had to take what they could get, and the payment which could be afforded to the workmen necessarily depended on prices, and varied with them.

The two things must always have been closely con-

Reasonable and competition prices.

nected. Doubtless, in medieval times, there were many men who were unable to find customers, and who had to submit to forced sales; but the principle on which business was done is quite clear. Every effort was made to prevent the sale of English goods abroad, unless the price obtained was really remunerative. Every effort was made to fix the price of goods so that the artisan might get a 'reasonable' reward for his trouble. Prices were, so far as possible, adapted to the labourer's requirements, though doubtless the policy was not always successfully applied to practice. But with the intervention of capital, the old relations have necessarily been reversed. The effort, now, is to force a market and to secure a sale by producing cheaply. There is a constant tendency to cut prices down, and the reward of the labourer necessarily follows the operations of the capitalist. In old days when wages were practically fixed, the require-

ments of the labourer were a first charge, and this must
have tended to steady prices; but now that prices fluctuate
greatly, the condition of the labourer is directly affected by
them. While we may fully recognise all the advantages
that have come to the labourer through the introduction of
a money economy, we should also take note of the disadvantages as well. The modern labourer who is economically free (§ 66) has many advantages over the medieval
serf; he can go where he hopes to improve his position and
make his own bargain in definite terms for definite pay
(§ 109). His relations with his master are very precise—as
between man and man; but his opportunities of employment and his daily bread are dependent on the changing
conditions of trade in distant lands. He has gained in
independence, and in the precision of the terms of employment, but he has lost the comparative stability of his former
condition (§ 130).

These two views of the manner in which trade may be
most wisely conducted correspond with the   Good and
different conceptions of the meaning of pros-   bad trade.
perity in trade. We may have a period of slow and steady
development; this means stability in the employment and
remuneration of the labourer; and regular, though not
large, returns to capital. It is good for both. If, on the
other hand, we have, from any cause, a period of rapid
fluctuations when prices vary a great deal, the labourer
benefits very little, and many capitalists may suffer serious
loss: but the far-seeing and successful man, who is able to
take advantage of the change, may gain enormously. We
may mean by good trade, a time when there is steady and
slow development, or a time when the enterprising specu-
lator can make his fortune rapidly. The latter is, at all
events, a period of apparent prosperity. Sudden accumula-

tions of great wealth strike the public imagination, but they are not always symptoms of a really healthy condition of trade. The fortunes made by the East India Company's servants in India entirely misled the shareholders and the public at home, as to the real character of the trade of the Company. During the Napoleonic wars there were unexpected facilities and chances for the sale of English goods at monopoly prices all over the world, and this gave an unexampled opportunity for the making of fortunes. As we look back on that time we may see that it was really a period of unhealthy inflation, followed by a sudden reaction, that was very injurious to all persons engaged in trade.

126.   Men are never tired of repeating the truism that the interests of capital and labour are really one. It is obvious that both gain through the prosperity of trade, and that both lose when it declines. If ruin overtakes the capitalist, the labourer is thrown out of employment; if the workmen are ill-fed and incompetent, the capitalist cannot prosper. In the long run, or over a period of years, the interests of the two parties are similar; but at no point of time are they identical. They are always distinct and, at any given moment, the difference may come prominently into view. The immediate interest of the one is not the immediate interest of the other; and there is always danger of conflict when one of the two is called upon to sacrifice his immediate interest in favour of the prospective interest of both. When the element of time is properly introduced, it is a mere paradox to assert that the interests of capital and labour are the same; they are constantly distinct and frequently opposed to each other.

The immediate interest of the labourer tempts him to do as little as he can for the money he receives. If wages

The conflicting interests of Capital and Labour.

are good, he is able to enjoy the pleasures of pure idleness, and to obtain as much subsistence as he desires by working for half the week. Such a course of action may even appear to be unselfish and commendable; for if employment can be regarded as a constant quantity, and each man does very little, then there will be need for the services of a larger number, and work and pay will be distributed among a greater number of applicants. But irregular and inefficient work is very costly, and is almost certain to increase the expense of production; it is likely to lead to a contraction of trade and to a diminution in the amount of available employment. In a somewhat similar fashion, the immediate interest of labourers tempts them to demand a rise of wages in the expectation that prices can be raised without any diminution of demand, or of the field for employment. This may hold good when producers have a monopoly, either temporary or permanent, in an article of general demand; but under ordinary circumstances it cannot take place. A demand for higher wages will probably lead to a contraction of the demand and a diminution of employment, or to a reduction of wages. It is obvious that labourers may pursue their immediate interest so far as to damage a trade and to render a serious loss of wages and of employment inevitable.

Similarly the capitalist may pursue his immediate interest so as to damage trade. It is always his immediate interest to produce as inexpensively as possible, so as to command as large a market as may be. It is always possible to supply a low priced article, by producing an inferior quality, and it is sometimes possible to reduce the cost of production at the expense of the labourer—by sweating. Both expedients result in an immediate gain, and both are ultimately disastrous. When masters produce an inferior quality, the reputation of the trade suffers; and sweating tells, sooner or later, on the efficiency of the class who have to submit to it. Either labourer or capitalist may positively injure an industry by the short-sighted pursuit of their immediate interest.

Since the immediate interests of capital and labour are distinct and often opposed, it need not be a matter of surprise that men of one class or the other should, in all good faith, make different forecasts as to the best course to be pursued for the good of industry. By the latter part of the last century labour had become, as we have seen, largely dependent on capital. Capitalists were, generally speaking, in a position to give effect to their views of what was best for trade. They might well believe that the course they pursued was not a selfish one, but was really for the ultimate well-being of labour. If trade was bad they were inclined to reduce the rates of wages, in the hope that by cheaper production they would be able to secure increased sales. The alternative course, that of reducing the quantities produced in the hope that prices would rise again, meant that machinery would stand idle, and also that workmen would be thrown out of employment. There were immediate and obvious disasters to all parties in the trade; the hardship to the labourers of working at starvation rates might well appear to be a lesser evil than that which must ensue from throwing numbers out of employment altogether. The evil results of the depressed condition of the labourer seemed remote and uncertain, while the bad effects of reducing production were manifest and near at hand. It thus came about that during the uncertainties of the Napoleonic wars and in the terrible depression which followed, workmen, in one trade after another, were forced to submit to very considerable reductions of wages. So long as it was possible to provide employment, though at starvation rates, the masters believed it to be best to spread work among as many as they could, so that every family should earn something however small. Hence from another side the mistaken philanthropy of the masters resulted in a policy which resembled the short-sighted schemes of the men. The workers have sometimes wished to distribute a (supposed) fixed quantity of work among as many men as possible, so that the aggregate earnings of all might increase; the masters tried to distribute a diminishing quantity of work among a large number, so that no one should be absolutely destitute.

The period of depression, with all the poverty that accompanied it, continued for many years (p. 88). We are apt to rush to the conclusion that this was due to the introduction of machinery, but the more the facts are looked at in detail the less satisfactory does this explanation appear. The celebrated strike of the Bradford wool-combers (1825) occurred in a trade where starvation rates were being paid, but where there was no real competition with machinery till a later time. The framework knitters in 1845 were not suffering from any new reduction, but from conditions of trade brought on by reckless competition, and the same may be said of the starvation rates paid to cotton weavers in 1806. They suffered because it appeared from time to time to be necessary to cut down wages, and there was little, if any, subsequent recovery.

This line of policy had the approval of the leading economists of the day. They were all extreme   Doctrinaire
advocates of *laissez faire*; they saw that the   economists.
intervention of capital had been very beneficial to the public at large. And, having a firm belief in the power of

the capitalist to judge of the prospects of trade, they thought
it best that he should have a perfectly free hand.

At this juncture the working classes were in a position
which rendered it very difficult for them to state their views
as a class, or to offer any resistance to the demands made on
them.   The Combination Laws of 1799 and 1800 had been
passed under the influence of political panic.   They condemned as criminal the conduct of artisans who took action
which might strengthen their position in bargaining with
their employers.   The labourers were forced to submit, but
a sense of the disabilities to which they were exposed and
of the gross injustice which might be done them under this
one-sided law, made them very bitter, while the employers
were not unnaturally suspicious of the influence of illegal
associations.   The measure was, in all probability, quite
ineffective for checking real treason, but it bred an amount
of class jealousy and mutual suspicion which has wrought
infinite mischief.

Under the policy of the employers, approved by *doctrinaire* economists and unchecked by effective criticism
from the labourers, results came to light which roused
public indignation.   It became obvious that the course they
were pursuing, on *laissez faire* principles, was leading to the
moral and physical degradation of the English population ;
and it seemed necessary for Parliament to interfere and to
put an effective check on some of the deleterious tendencies
which were at work.

127.   The great development of machinery in the textile
trades gave opportunity for the employment
of children on a large scale ; numbers of them
were engaged in work in every factory.   Their
condition attracted public attention again and again, and
it was, in many ways, very bad.   At the same time it may

Moral and
physical
degradation.

be doubted how far it was really worse than that of other
children, who were employed by the domestic weaver at
home or as helpers in other trades. So far as it is possible
to compare the two in 1816, the factory child was in better
sanitary conditions and was better fed than the child employed at weavers' homes. The earnings were better; but
the life was rougher, and the regular strain was greater. The
worst cases of child suffering were not in factories of any
kind, but in connexion with chimney sweeping. The employment was dangerous to life and limb, and rendered the
young specially liable to very painful diseases. There must
have been an immense amount of cruelty at times in forcing
them to undertake such tasks. Still, without laying stress
on such comparisons, it is clear that the condition of factory children at the beginning of the century was so bad,
that it was wise for government to interfere, and, in the
interest of the future well-being of the population, to check
the tendencies at work under the influence of free competition. Even the most uncompromising advocates of *laissez
faire* were willing to recognise that this was a legitimate case
for intervention. The children did not and could not make
their own bargains. They were not free agents in entering
into any agreement; they were sent to the factories by their
parents, or by parochial authorities. Hence those who
argued that each adult ought to make his own bargain for
himself, were ready to legislate for the protection of children.

The first great measure on behalf of factory children
was brought in and carried by a mill owner; Factory
it was not the result of outside agitation. Sir apprentices.
Robert Peel, father of the great statesman, felt that the condition of the apprentice children in his own cotton mills was
not what he could desire, and he found himself unable to
exercise efficient supervision. He therefore introduced and

carried, apparently without difficulty, a bill for the regulation
of the status of apprentices in the cotton trade (1802).
The clothes they should receive, the meals they should have,
and the conditions of their dormitories were specified; the
bill limited the hours of work, and also insisted that
adequate opportunities should be given for their instruction.
The measure has reference to a state of society when apprenticeship was not only a time for learning a trade, but
also for training in regular habits of life under a master's
eye; and it was intended to secure that the colonies of
children attached to cotton mills should not be deprived of
similar advantages. This act had many beneficial results for
a time, but there were rapid changes in the condition of the
trade which rendered it inoperative before many years had
passed. The system of legal apprenticeship was abolished
in 1814, and as the children employed in factories were no
longer apprentices, the measure designed for their protection ceased to be applicable. In 1816 Sir Robert Peel
moved in the matter again; he succeeded in obtaining a
mass of interesting evidence on the condition of factories,
but no important legislation occurred till 1833.

In 1832 the case of the factory children was taken
up by Lord Ashley (afterwards Lord Shaftes-
bury) and others, and a Select Committee
took evidence as to their physical condition. The revela-
tions made were shocking in the extreme, and aroused a
storm of indignation among philanthropists and the public.
There was equal indignation among the mill-owners, who
had not had the opportunity of being heard, and who held
that the case brought before the Committee was not merely
one-sided, but grossly exaggerated. A Commission was
therefore appointed to take evidence on the spot, and
though it showed that the statements made before the

Official enquiries.

Select Committee were not trustworthy, it established a very serious need for interference. The physical mischief, resulting from the long hours during which children and women worked, was very noticeable, and there was every reason to fear a serious deterioration in the physique of a large portion of the population, if protection were not extended to the young and to the mothers of the next generation. The special evils differed in different trades. In the woollen trade the processes of sorting and preparing the wool were specially dirty and offensive. In the linen trade the mischief was of a different kind, as flax was spun when wet, and those who worked in the mills were apt to get their clothing thoroughly soaked; even if properly protected, they still had to work in a reeking atmosphere and on sloppy floors. There was a great deal of dust in some of the rooms in cotton mills, though, perhaps, they were hardly so objectionable as those devoted to similar processes in the linen trade. But, though some mills were well managed and others badly, there were certain points in which all showed room for improvement. Children were employed much too young, and the strain for women of standing and stooping for long hours was very injurious.

So far as the early age of employment was concerned, the mill-owners were not specially to blame; it was no advantage to them to take children very young. The pressure came from parents and poor law authorities, who wished to make the children earn something and to get them off their hands at the earliest possible age. As to the length of hours, the owners also protested that they were not altogether free agents. Competition with foreign countries was very keen; spinning was barely remunerative, and if the hours of labour were shortened, and the output reduced, they feared that it would be impossible for them to carry on business at all. The expectation of philanthropists that English spinners could raise prices, if they liked, was not justified, but on the other hand there has been such an increase of efficiency that the worst forebodings of the manufacturers have not been realised. The commissioners hoped it might be possible to organise double shifts, so that the machinery might continue to run for long hours, while the women and children were not overstrained. This system had been adopted in some mills, but there were grave difficulties in the way of carrying it into effect at all generally. The result of the investigation was the Factory Act of 1833, which only allowed the employment of children over nine years of age, and reduced their hours of work to forty-eight in the week. By far the most important work accomplished by this Act consisted of the new means of administration which it created. There had been difficulties in enforcing previous measures, and by calling into being a body of inspectors, who had authority to see that the act was carried out, an important step was taken towards putting down the worst abuses and for suggesting and securing gradual improvement.

These inspectors have, at least, been able to attend to one point on which the employers appear to have been careless—the proper fencing of machinery. The number of cripples who had been injured by accidents in mills was a matter which had specially roused public feeling; in this particular Bradford had an unenviable notoriety. Even though there seems to have been some exaggeration in the representations made on this point, there was a considerable foundation in fact. Wherever the blame may have rested, the effects of increased care in this respect have been very noticeable.

Carelessness about machinery.

The outcry which had been raised about children in factories was followed by an investigation into the conditions of child labour elsewhere. It Children in mines. was, indeed, high time, for the state of things in mines was far more serious than anything that had come out about the factories generally. The new limitations on employment in factories led to some increase of the evils in mines; for parents who had the opportunity of sending children, excluded from factories, to work in mines, were glad to do so. The long hours in the darkness and the heavy work in pushing trucks were very injurious, while the manner in which women were employed was brutalising. The regulation and inspection of mines was a necessary development of the regulation of factories, and could be justified on exactly similar grounds. In all these cases, it seemed to be necessary for the State to interfere to check the moral, physical and social evils which had arisen under the régime of free competition.

128. So far we have considered the capitalist system, and the evils which arose in connexion with it, when competition was unchecked. It is pleasanter to turn to the wonderful series of The course of the industrial revolution. inventions which were introduced with the aid of capital, and which so greatly increased human powers of catering for human needs. It may, perhaps, be most convenient to sketch the steps in the changes very rapidly, while the results of the introduction of machinery on the employment and remuneration of the labourer may be discussed when we are in a position to review the whole period of the industrial revolution.

The first remarkable invention which modified the condition of the textile trades was not so much a new machine as a better implement. The The flying shuttle.

flying shuttle did not do the work and was not, in any way, a substitute for skilled labour. It was distinctly sub-servient to the old forms of skill, and enabled the good workman to exercise his skill much more rapidly than before. It first came into use in weaving wide breadths of cloth. Hitherto the weavers had needed an assistant to throw the shuttle backwards and forwards across the loom, but with the help of the flying shuttle he could throw it backwards and forwards by himself. It enabled him to work faster, and just as well, while the work was done at less cost, since there was no need to pay for help. The effect upon the cloth trade was very curious. There was no increase in production, for there was no more wool available than before, and there was no fall in the price of goods. Nor was there any change in the rate at which the weaver was paid per piece. But the best men could work more rapidly than before; they had more to do and earned very high wages, while the inferior workers were hardly employed, and drifted into other occupations, especially into cotton weaving. The benefit from this improvement did not go to the public in the form of cheapness, but to the best workmen who were kept on in full employment. They, as a class, obtained a definite rise in the world, and in the subsequent hard times they seem to have looked back to the last decade of the eighteenth century as the halcyon period of their trade.

A whole series of important inventions revolutionised Cotton spinning. spinning; they were originally introduced into the cotton trade by Arkwright, Cromp-ton, and Hargreaves. Spinning is an art which is specially adapted for machinery, as the chief matter of importance is to obtain a regular and even thread. It is an operation in which a mechanical kind of perfection is specially re-

quired. In 1790 Mr Kelly of Lanark was able to apply
water as the motor power for this machinery, and in the
latter part of the eighteenth century the business of cotton
spinning increased with very great rapidity. It had been
a comparatively small affair before, centred chiefly round
Manchester. But with mechanical appliances, yarn was
produced in vast quantities, and mills were erected in all
sorts of places. Derbyshire, Nottingham, Worcestershire
and other counties were, for a time at least, centres for this
trade. The spinning business flourished exceedingly; and
English manufacturers who were unable to meet the foreign
demands for cotton cloth sent large quantities of English
yarn to the Continent. So rapid was the development
of the cotton industry that a new trade was practically
created by the machinery, and the employment, which
it afforded, attracted large populations to settle near the
mills. So long as water power was used, the employés
were more or less scattered, as the mills were not grouped
closely together, but at different points on the same stream
(§ 19). But when steam power was applied to machinery,
the mills were run up close together, and population was
attracted to form factory towns.

The condition of the children in this newly developed
industry has been already described (§ 127); it soon attracted the attention of the legislature; but adults also
were exposed to much suffering. In the villages which
grew up near water power there was often a difficulty about
getting supplies; everything was dear; wages went but a
little way, and the truck system was soon in full play. Dis-
comforts in the towns were chiefly due to the jerry builder;
cottages were run up, ill planned and ill built, with a disregard of the most elementary sanitary requirements. Not
until the visitation of the cholera in 1849 was public attention

fully aroused to the dangerous neglect which had hitherto attended the housing of factory operatives.

The introduction of machinery for cotton spinning brought about a new and sudden development. But there is more interest in tracing the steps by which machinery was introduced into the clothing trade, which had hitherto been the staple industry of the country, and which, in some form or other, continued to be widely diffused throughout a very large area.

Carding and spinning wool.

The machinery for carding wool, which was invented as early as 1748, appears to have been received with general approbation. The spinners were, apparently, glad to be saved the preliminary processes in the preparation of wool, and to rely on the slubbing engine. When attempts were made to adapt the spinning jenny from cotton to wool, there seems to have been wonderfully little interest in the matter. The invention spread but slowly; it was in use in Devonshire in 1791, but seems to have been regarded as quite a new thing in the West Riding, when Mr Gott introduced it some ten years later. Nor does it seem to have created much excitement in the villages. Spinning was very badly paid in the last decade of the eighteenth century, and very difficult to get even at the miserable rates of pay. When allowances were granted in addition to the labourer's wages, the family income was made up from another source, and the household did not feel the loss due to the cessation of spinning. Hence it seems that the allowance system (p. 94) tided over the change, which was made almost insensibly. It is only in 1816, when the transference of the industry was practically complete, that we hear of some destruction of machines for spinning wool; but this seems to have been a quite incidental act of violence in connexion with the bread riots in the Eastern Counties.

It is hardly possible to exaggerate the importance of the change which had thus come into effect. During the eighteenth century, at least, the art of spinning wool had been practised in many cottages throughout many districts of rural England. Spinning had afforded a very remunerative by-employment, and the earnings of the women and children had provided a most useful supplement to the wages of the labourer. When spinning was concentrated in factories and carried on as an independent employment, it was entirely diverted from the rural districts, and there has been no means of supplying its place in the domestic economy of the cottage home. Thus the decay of domestic spinning has had very grave effects on the comfort and prosperity of the rural population.

The inventions of Boulton and Watt and the application of steam power to textile machinery was another step in advance. The steam engine was first used in a cotton factory in *Water power and steam power.* 1785, and for thirty or forty years the contest between water and steam was carried on. Water was undoubtedly cheaper where a good supply could be had; but in many places the mills were liable to long stoppages for want of power. Steam power, though more expensive, was always available, and could be increased at will; and this superior convenience led at length to its general adoption. As has been already pointed out, factory towns arose in connexion with the use of steam power. In many ways it was a great boon to the operatives: the chief cases of overwork, through long hours, seem to have occurred in water mills, where the operatives were anxious to make up for time lost through the stoppage of the water. The stories of the harshness of slubbers towards the children who helped them, and who were worn out with working many hours at a stretch, all come from mills of this kind.   The disuse of water power has been accompanied by a cessation of any valid excuse for working excessive hours.   On the other hand it may be said that along with steam power has come the development of new machinery, carrying a very large number of spindles, and involving a far greater strain on the faculties of the worker than was requisite in the old mills.   Work goes on at higher speed, and there is increased tension and pressure on the powers of the operative.

The last of the great inventions, which it is necessary to note here, was the power loom which gradually displaced weaving by hand.   It was the invention of a singular man.   Dr Cartwright was a Kentish clergyman who, when visiting Matlock in 1784, entered into conversation with some Manchester men, and made a casual suggestion as to the possibility of a power loom which should follow up the spinning done by power.   His friends scouted the idea as impracticable, but he set himself to carry it into effect.   After some years he succeeded in producing a loom that was capable of being worked commercially; but the invention was hardly taken up during his life time.   He demonstrated that power weaving was possible, just as he also showed that wool-combing could be done by machinery; but hand loom weaving continued to be the ordinary practice till about 1840.   At that time a Commission investigated the condition of the hand loom weavers.   Power weaving had been introduced for the worsted trade of Bradford, but hand weaving was holding its ground in the woollen manufacture at Leeds.   In the cotton trade, power weaving had also come into vogue, but apparently it did not displace hand weaving.   The trade had been expanding, and the additional cotton cloth woven by power was sold without

interfering with the employment of those who worked on
the old system.

At the same time the rates of pay for weaving were miser-
ably low.   This may, conceivably, have been indirectly due
to the possibility of having recourse to power weaving, but
it was also a reason why the new invention was introduced
so slowly.   When wages were very low and the expense of
production by hand was small, it was not worth while to run
the risk of purchasing and setting up expensive machinery.
It was not advantageous to do this unless the margin of probable profit was considerable.   In 1840 there was reason to
doubt whether power weaving would be generally introduced
after all.   It did not seem likely to be less expensive than
poorly paid hand labour for low-class goods, and moreover
it had not been so far perfected that it could do the high-
class work of the best weavers.

The great advantage of machine production in the eyes
of the employers was similar to that which
led them to prefer steam to water power. For
all trade purposes it was desirable to have
the organisation of business under control.   Water power
could not be counted upon, and the hand loom weavers
could not always be trusted to work regularly.   They could
not be depended on to finish a job, so that orders could
not be executed for certain by a given day.   With power
weaving the whole was under the master's eye; he
knew both where he stood and what he could undertake.
Besides this the difficulties, which arose from time to
time from the embezzlement of materials, were far less
likely to occur in connexion with power weaving carried
on under supervision in a factory.

Some of these advantages could be secured by a system
which had been adopted before 1840 in the woollen trade

C. & M.   15

in Scotland, and which was beginning to come into vogue in the cotton trade also, though more slowly. The masters erected sheds in which looms were placed, and the weavers came and executed their work by hand loom but under supervision. Those who worked in this way got much higher wages than the men who preferred the greater free-dom of working at home: but after all, such hand loom sheds were only a transitional form. Weaving organised in this fashion had its advantages, and when thus managed the application of power was particularly easy, especially if it was already employed on the same premises in connexion with spinning.

The hand loom weaver was greatly attached to his calling and stuck to it when work was very intermittent and badly paid: but soon after the Commission of 1839 had reported, it became obvious that he was engaged in a useless struggle, and that power weaving must win the day. As it came more and more into use the transformation of the clothing trade became complete. It ceased to be a great industry which gave employment for great varieties of highly specialised skill, and was transformed throughout into a series of processes of production by machinery.

129. During the whole course of the industrial revolu-tion there was a decided feeling among many of the labourers that machinery was their enemy, diminishing their opportunities of employment and bringing about a reduction in their wages. This feeling found expression in many ways; sometimes in such riots as those in which the York-shire shearing frames were destroyed, and sometimes in proposals to impose legislative restrictions on the use of machines, so as to bring them to a level with hand work, and prevent them from doing the work more quickly or

Machinery, and the expansion of trade.

more cheaply than it could be done by hand. This latter suggestion rested on the old fallacy that employment is a limited quantity, and that efficiency of every kind is an evil, since it leaves less work to be done, and therefore less scope for employment at the old work on the old terms.

Under ordinary conditions this is a quite mistaken and, in any case, it would be a narrow-minded policy to pursue. Whatever the interest of a particular trade may be, the interest of the general public is best secured by efficiency. When goods are made more quickly and more cheaply, wants are supplied on easier terms. These are benefits which accrue to consumers generally, and in the case of articles of common consumption like clothing the working classes, collectively and individually, gain by increased efficiency and greater cheapness of production.

But this gain is sometimes so very slight and distant, that it is absurd to point it out as a consola-   Displace-
tion to a man who loses employment because   ment of work-
his work is done better and more cheaply by a   ers.
machine. The gain to the community at large may be very great and may be undoubted, but there is serious loss to the individual who is no longer required to do the only thing he can do thoroughly well. Despite its benefits, the introduction of machinery has meant the displacement of workers possessing special skill as spinners or weavers; and a mechanical invention, which renders their special attainments useless and valueless, causes them irreparable loss. It seems hard to weigh an infinitesimal gain to a large number of consumers, against the ruin of a skilled artisan whose whole employment is taken away from him by the introduction of a machine which has rendered him useless.

But, despite this real and immense loss to the workman whose skill is specialised, great gain has often resulted to labourers generally, and to the general demand for labour, from the introduction of the machine which supersedes him. By more efficient and less expensive methods, greater quantities can be produced at the same cost as before, with the result that the price can be lowered. The lowering of the price is almost certain to call forth an increased demand, and it is more than likely that, to meet this increased demand, a larger number of labourers will be employed to work the machinery than were previously required to do the work without the machine. So far as the effect on the labour market generally is concerned, there will possibly be more employment and a larger sum to distribute in wages, after the introduction of machinery than before. Increased efficiency, with consequent cheapness, is the one thing that can be counted on to stimulate demand permanently, and to give additional opportunities for employment.

This tendency may be illustrated by two simple cases. The cotton trade was a very small affair before the era of invention. The number of hands employed in spinning and weaving was quite inconsiderable. Good spinners were losers, when their special skill was superseded by machinery; but the expansion of the trade has given far more scope for employment in spinning and weaving than there was before. The factory towns are a conspicuous proof of the way in which the introduction of machinery has opened up additional employment for a large population. Again, the railway system of this country may be regarded as one huge machine for carrying on the internal traffic of Great Britain. Its introduction was opposed by many persons on the ground that it would supersede the work of and the need for horses, that coachmen, horse-breeders and others would suffer. Undoubtedly the special skill of the mail coach driver is no longer required and he has suffered; but railways, by rendering travelling very cheap, have created an unprecedented demand for means of conveyance, and the total field for employment, as servants, in connexion with railways, as clerks, porters, surfacemen, drivers, guards, &c., must be far greater than was available in coaching days. The invention of railways was prejudicial to one small class, but has, on the whole, opened up immensely increased opportunities of employment.

It may, perhaps, at first sight appear as if the destruction of some special kind of skill were an irreparable loss, for which the substitution of an increased number of less highly trained persons does not altogether atone. But it must be remembered that different, and perhaps higher kinds of skill are called forth in connexion with machinery. There may be less need for some one form of manual deftness, but more intelligence is required in working with a machine. It would be difficult to show that the present generation of workers are less intelligent, or more defective as human beings, because of the introduction of machinery, even though they may be destitute of some special form of manual dexterity.

On the whole, then, it may be said that labourers, generally speaking, have not suffered by the intro- Gain to consumers. duction of machinery, but only one class or another, which possessed a kind of highly specialised skill, that is superseded by some machine. This is a real loss; but it is a limited one which must be set off against the general gain—to the consumers in cheapness, and to labourers generally through the subsequent expansion of trade. It must be noted, however, that the advantage of increased employment does not arise, if, despite the introduction of machinery, there is no subsequent expansion of trade. In the case of an article that is not one of common consumption, it may be doubted if increased cheapness can ever greatly increase the demand. Top boots are but a small element in the cost of hunting, and if top boots were rather cheaper, they would possibly be very little more worn. In other cases no expansion in the trade may be possible because of the limited supply of the materials. Till Australian wool was brought in large quantities to the market, this was partially true of all departments of the clothing trade. It could not expand rapidly, as additional supplies of material were not forthcoming. As pointed out above, this limitation told in favour of the skilled weavers at the time when the flying shuttle was invented. But things worked out differently in the case of later inventions which were substitutes for, not subsidiary to, skilled labour in the clothing trade. When shearing was done by machinery, the shearmen, or croppers, were displaced. There was little, if any, expansion of trade consequent on these changes, and therefore there was a loss to this old-established craft, that was not recouped by labour generally. In the same way, wool-combing was a limited trade, and the introduction of combing machinery displaced skilled workers, without causing expansion, or opening up any new opportunities of employment. The stand that was taken against machinery by the shearmen of Yorkshire—an agitation which was closely connected with the Luddite riots—had more justification than can usually be alleged on behalf of such outbreaks. Skilled labour was displaced, and there was no further change by which other classes of labourers gained directly; their indirect gain, in so far as they were consumers who could obtain clothing cheaper, need not be taken into account here.

130. However interesting it might be, it is extremely difficult to attempt an estimate of the difference which the industrial revolution has made in the general social and moral conditions of the labouring class

The proletariat. Stability and progress.

Before the industrial revolution, the English woollen weaver was, generally speaking, resident in a rural district or had, in some way, an interest in land. He might have a garden, like the Sheffield Cutlers, or carry on pasture-farming, like the weavers near Leeds. He was not entirely dependent on his trade: in times of industrial depression he still had something to fall back on. He could, at least, tide over a few weeks of bad trade, and even though he might have to 'go short,' still it was possible for him to manage somehow. But with the aggregation of labour in large towns this was no longer feasible. The weaver was spared any waste of time in going for materials or in selling his cloth, but his house was cramped up in a crowded area, where neither he nor his neighbour could have any land. In this way his whole condition came to be directly dependent on the condition of trade. Wages were his sole means of support; if employment was difficult to get, or payment was low, he had no means of eking out his subsistence from any other source. Instead of having two strings to his bow he had only one; he was, consequently, in a far less independent position.

Industry divorced from land.

A similar loss fell on the agricultural labourer. While spinning was an occupation which was diffused throughout the country, the earnings of his wife and children came in as an additional source of income. He also had two strings to his bow—and if he had grazing rights also, he may be said to have had three. It was a position of great economic stability; but with the introduction of machine spinning, and the progress of enclosure, he was deprived first of one means of support and then of another. Like the factory operative, the agricultural labourer came to be wholly dependent on wages for the income of his household. His economic condition no longer rested on "the stable basis of land but on the fluctuating basis of trade," since he was merely a wage-earner, and his whole chance of employment and the rate of his pay had come to depend on the market price of the product.

Much is said at present about the desirability of rendering rural life more attractive, and of pre-venting the migration of labour to towns. The gist of the matter really lies in rendering the village household more prosperous. It may be possible to supply allotments, and re-create domestic subsistence farming; but the crucial difference between the past and the present lies in the fact that formerly there were many by-employments available, which have been concentrated, as it were, into distinct trades. The improvement of means of communication may make it possible to start works in villages—e.g. printing works, so that the artisan may once again enjoy the advantages of rural life, while still having regular employment at his trade, but it is not so easy to see any possibility of a revival of cottage industries, which might replace the peasant family in the stable position it occupied before the industrial revolution.

But, after all, the old condition of economic stability was inconsistent with progress. It passed away because the division of labour has rendered production more efficient, and because the enterprise of English merchants has brought us into commercial communication with all parts of the globe. Thanks to this progress, English artisans and labourers have gained in many ways. Tea drinking was

spoken of as a vicious extravagance in the eighteenth
century; it has come to be regarded as almost a necessary
in the most frugal households. Oranges and other fruit,
tobacco and newspapers, are luxuries which are much more
generally available than they were. These are distinct
additions to the comfort of life, which the labourer could
not previously enjoy at all. Besides this, clothing and
household utensils of every kind are far cheaper than they
were; the industrial revolution has done a great deal to
increase the purchasing power of wages. It is not easy to
balance the loss and gain in the labourer's material condition; the loss of stability is real, but the gain through
progress is also real. The problem which faces us is not
that of returning to the old circumstances and losing what
we have gained, but, if possible, of introducing some new
conditions of stability which shall yet be compatible with
farther progress.

If there is so much difficulty in estimating the precise change in the material well-being of   Factories
the labourer, it is far harder to trace the   and character.
effects on morals and character. There is a constant
tendency to idealise the past, and to represent each
generation as worse than its predecessors; it is easy to
make such assertions, and we rarely have the means of
testing them or of saying what elements of truth there may
be in this view. It is also easy to point out the demora-
lising and degrading elements in town life, and to regret
the wholesome influence of rural surroundings. But it is
true that rural surroundings do not always make for morality,
as the statistics of illegitimacy show. The dilatoriness and
dishonesty of the domestic worker were the chief reasons for
the progress of that factory system which brought him under
effective supervision. The life of the factory operative is

far more regular and disciplined; so that at first there was a
real indisposition to submit to the tyranny of the Factory
Act, and the better and more independent elements in the
population held out against it. But that is a thing of the
past, and it can scarcely be said that an influence which
has rendered the ordinary habits of artisan life more regular
and steady has been other than good.

The independent workman was also to a great extent
isolated: the aggregation of labourers in towns has had an
important socialising influence. It has prepared the way for
the formation of the great friendly societies, the co-operative
societies and other artisan organisations. The formation of
such societies and the management of their affairs are in themselves important educative influences, and have called forth
remarkable administrative powers. And even if the action
of Trades Unions has sometimes been open to criticism for
unwisdom, it should not be forgotten that the organisation
and disciplining of the army of labour is no mean achieve-
ment. The comparative self-restraint and freedom from
outrage which characterises recent labour struggles, as compared with those of 1812 or 1816, shows a remarkable progress in effective self-control on the part of the labourers.
Here, too, there is progress in morality.

Even when the disadvantages of town life are considered
Self-im-provement and amusement. —in high rentals, foggy air and other evils—
there can be no doubt as to the superior
attraction which it possesses. The opportunities for self-improvement and for amusement are far
greater in the town than in the country. It is impossible to
suppose that, with all the influence of education, the standard
of intelligence in rural districts has declined during the last
century; and the difference between the town bred artisan
and the agricultural labourer in the present day, in all

matters of intellectual capacity, is not an unfair measure by
which to gauge the progress in intelligence and culture that
has synchronised with the industrial revolution. There
are good and bad individuals in all classes and at all
times. The enumeration of single instances can never be
a satisfactory method of reaching a conclusion on this
difficult question. But the growth and development ot
social institutions is a far more satisfactory test, and this
seems to bear unimpeachable witness to the moral and
intellectual progress of the labourer during the last hundred
years.

131. The preceding sections may have served to bring
out the steadily increasing importance of   Individual
capital in the process of manufacture. It   and State ma-
has intervened to seek markets, to provide   nagement.
materials, to organise the different branches of a trade, and
to supply implements and tools. Those who are the owners
of wealth have gradually come to take an ever increasing
share in the work of production. The existence of industrial
capital, as a fund devoted to the production of more wealth,
has rendered it possible to carry out the division of labour,
and to render labour more efficient by supplying implements
and machines, while it undertakes the necessary purchase ot
materials and the sale of the product. The possessors ot
capital would not apply their wealth to these purposes, or
would not continue to do so, unless they saw their way to
gain, and this gain is termed profit. Besides the profit
which all capitalists expect to get when they undertake the
risks of business, the men who manage business and
arrange for purchases and sales are paid for their difficult
and responsible work, and obtain earnings of management
for their trouble. In a private firm, where a man owns
the capital and manages the business himself, he may

not be able to distinguish between the part of his income
which comes to him as profit on his capital and the earnings which are remuneration for his difficult work : but the
two elements are different, whether it is easy or not to
separate them, and it is by no means hard to distinguish
them in the case of a great limited liability company. The
capital of the London and North-Western Railway is owned
by the share-holders, and their profits come to them in the
form of dividends paid half-yearly. Very few of the share-
holders take any active part in the management, and those
who are called on to do so, as directors, receive fees for
their trouble. The greater part of the work of management
is done by salaried officers, who are paid for their trouble,
but who may not be share-holders at all. In such a case it
is very easy to distinguish the *profit* on capital from the
receipt of *wages of management.*

With the growing complexity and responsibility of
commercial organisation, the difficulty of
management has greatly increased, and there
has been a corresponding rise in the salaries paid to
efficient men for carrying on business of any kind. The
payments for ability of this kind, for showing enterprise and undertaking responsibility, have greatly increased,
and when we consider how much depends on such work
being done well, it is difficult to suppose that the great
companies, engaged in eager competition and keen to
make profits, allow themselves to be wasteful or extravagant
in this item. But while the earnings of management are
thus high, the payments to the capitalist, who by investing his
money in a business enables it to be carried on on modern
lines, are by no means so large as they used to be. The
profits of capital are steadily falling : the rate of interest, or
payment for capital borrowed, serves to indicate the direction

Wages of management. (margin note)

of changes in the ordinary rate of business profit. If men
see a reasonable probability of making high profits by the
investment of their capital they will be unwilling to lend it
at a very low rate of interest. The gradual fall in the rate
of interest to $2\frac{3}{4}$ per cent. since the time of Elizabeth, when
the crown had to pay 12 per cent., serves as an index,
which shows that there must have been a somewhat similar
decline in the rate of profit, and that capitalists now-a-days
are willing to invest their money in business for a far
smaller reward than they expected two centuries ago.
The functions of capital have increased enormously, but the
rate at which capital is remunerated has steadily declined.

There is, however, a very general impression in many
quarters that employers derive an undue share
of the results of production. When this is
said we ought to distinguish the two elements
in the employer's income, the profit on his capital, and his
earnings as a manager. Taking these two separately we
may consider whether there is any reason to think that this
important and necessary work can be done as well but at a
lower rate of pay.

The functions of employers.

Business cannot be carried on without capital, indeed
there is an ever increasing need for more and more, as
the part played by capital steadily increases. Many undertakings have been starved for want of capital, and the
difficulties of the Darien Company or the East India
Company at the beginning of the eighteenth century have
been a great object lesson as to the need of this factor in
carrying on business.

Capital is more easily obtainable and on lower terms at
the present day than was ever the case in England before. At
the same time it is conceivable that Government could
borrow money very cheaply and supply it to carry on the

business of the country at a still lower rate. To this extent it is possible that some kind of State Socialism might be cheaper than our existing system.

But when we come to consider the other item—wages of management—it is difficult to make out a plausible case for supposing that business would be done in a more thorough and enterprising fashion by Government departments than by private firms. Neither the management of the dockyards nor a comparison of the condition of railways in different countries gives any solid ground for supposing that State management would be less costly, or would in any way be better than that which is afforded by private enterprise. It is absurd to contend that employers are overpaid for the work of management, unless we can show some means of getting their duties done as well and at a cheaper rate. It is plain that they are highly paid, but this high pay is earned by responsible work; and we have no right to grudge high pay, as if it were overpay, unless we know that the work can be done as well and more cheaply.

There is also a certain jealousy of the action, rather than of the gains, of employers, which rests on the suspicion that business is often conducted on lines which do not favour the interests of labour. Hopes are entertained that under democratic government it may be possible to legislate so that industry shall be developed in those directions which suit the labourer, and not primarily in those which are advantageous to the capitalist.

Now this suspicion and expectation have some justification in the history of the past century. There have been times when capitalists, by reckless speculation or by spreading work at starvation rates, have injured labour. They have done more; they have injured trade, though

they may have succeeded in reaping a temporary gain.
But it is also true that if the labourers pursue, or have
power to obtain, their own immediate interest in disregard of
the future of their trade, loss must fall, not only on capital,
but on labour (p. **2**11). The only interests which the State
can be rightly called in to promote are the permanent, not
the immediate, interests of labour. In their permanent
interests and in the long run, capital and labour are not
antagonistic, since each is really interested in securing the
greatest possible efficiency.

The short-sighted pursuit of immediate interest, either
by labour or capital, is disastrous to both; a   Efficiency
short-sighted policy on one side or the other   and expansion.
has been the cause of keen antagonism. Sixty years
ago doctrinaire economists and capitalists alike denied the
impossibility of paying higher rates to the workers, since
they looked on the wages fund as a fixed quantity. They
had no expectation that trade would expand and argued
that starvation rates were inevitable; but an increase
of efficiency has increased the product to be divided and
wages have risen. The fund is fixed but only for a given
moment; it is always capable of expansion. The labourers,
too, have fallen into a similar error: they have acted at
times as if the field for employment were definitely fixed,
and incapable of expansion. They have spoken as if
scamping work, idling and 'making work,' were the only
modes of providing employment for additional hands. But
by so doing they were making business less remunerative,
and thus taking a course which tended to reduce the employment available. By increased efficiency work is better
done, and a demand is stimulated for more work. Increased efficiency is the one means by which farther
progress can be attained; it is the one security against

successful foreign competition. It has no immediate reward in deed; it can only be attained through fresh effort and more serious risks, but for all that it is the only expedient by which the permanent interests of capital and labour can be brought to be at one.

CHAPTER X.

132. In a preceding chapter attention has been called
to the importance of commerce as a support of International
the external power of the realm. It was in this rivalry and
competition
aspect that it has been specially favoured, and between
with this object that it has been fostered: but nations.
commerce has also played an important part in the internal
life of the country. It has reacted, in all sorts of ways, both
on agriculture and on industry. This influence has been taken
for granted, or alluded to throughout, but a few remarks on it
now may serve to bring these scattered hints together into
a brief summary.

The advantages of commercial intercourse are obvious
so far as raw products are concerned. There are differences
of climate and soil, so that each country gains by intercourse
with others. As Hales puts it in his *Discourse of the Common
Weal*, "Surely common reason would say that one region
"should help another when it lacketh. And therefore God
"hath ordained that no country should have all commo-
"dities; but that, that one lacketh another bringeth forth;
"and that, that one country lacketh this year, another hath

"plenty thereof the same year; to the intent that one may
"know they have need of another's help, and thereby love and
"society to grow amongst all the more" (p. 61).   Intercourse
with foreign lands has been obviously advantageous to consumers at home, and also advantageous to producers who
could find a vent for the surplus which was not required and
could not be profitably sold in England.   In the fourteenth
century there might be keen rivalry between traders, but
there was comparatively little room for economic jealousy
between different nations.

With the development of manufactures the case has
been somewhat altered.   For many kinds of manufacture
one country seems to have little, if any, physical advantage
over another.   Spinning and weaving are simple arts practised
in all parts of the globe among peoples who have made
but little progress in civilisation.   Governments realised
in the seventeenth century that by planting new manufactures, it was possible to do without the import of
some commodity, and to provide remunerative employment for labour at home.   When commerce came to be
concerned as subsidiary to industry, in providing materials
or in pushing commodities in foreign markets, there was far
more room for international jealousy and for the imposition
of hostile tariffs on foreigners, or of restrictions on the
natural development of colonies.

So long as specialised human skill was the main element
in successful manufacture, the possession of
a skilled population gave one country a
decided advantage over others in certain branches of trade.
This long inherited skill could not be easily fostered or
acquired.   The transference of skilled persons was the only
means by which a new trade could be effectively planted.
Hence the migration of artisans to England was of the

Special
advantages.

highest importance for her subsequent progress (§ 11). But, in an ordinary way in the eighteenth century, each country could hope to retain its special advantage for particular manufactures almost as completely as it retained its special advantage for particular products. With the introduction of machinery, however, there has been a change. Any country can acquire the means of producing ordinary commodities in the best way, and skill in manipulation is not so special, or so difficult to acquire as in the old days of manual labour. As a consequence, economic rivalry between nations is becoming keener in some ways, because there is a reasonable hope of successful competition in production of almost every kind.

There may, of course, be special conditions which give one country a physical advantage over another. The climate of Oldham is said to be specially favourable for fine spinning. Cheapness of materials gives an advantage to the Bombay mills, as the cotton has to be carried but a little way. Still the cost of carriage is comparatively small for such cargo ; on the other hand, abundant supplies of fuel and proximity to the natural centres of the engineering and hardware trades are real advantages so far as they go. In the early days of the free trade movement, they were probably regarded as the all-sufficient bulwarks of England's manufacturing supremacy. The increasing demands on our coal-beds, and the opening up of new fields in other continents, make it doubtful, however, how long this special advantage will continue to rest with us. On every side it is becoming obvious that special physical facilities are being more and more widely diffused : the industrial leadership of the future will lie with that people who shall attain to the greatest efficiency, by the combined excellence of their industrial organisation, and the high intelligence and character of their operatives.

16—2

133. In so far as any country has a special advantage for any kind of manufacture or product it is of course economically desirable for it to specialise in that direction, and to supply its neighbours with what they lack. By this means the consumers of such goods in all neighbouring lands will procure what they require on easier terms than would otherwise be the case. But when this course is considered as a matter of national policy, it becomes important to ask, who are the consumers of imported goods in any given land, and how far is this benefit widely distributed? This may be illustrated from two different periods of English history.

Edward III was anxious to encourage frequent and easy communication with the trading centres on the Continent. He was, as we may say, a free trader, who advocated a policy of ' plenty' or cheapness to the consumer. But the typical article of import at that time was wine, a luxury consumed at court and among the upper classes. The great mass of the population made very little use of any imported commodity, and the policy of cheap imports scarcely affected them. In the present day, on the other hand, our supplies of bread, eggs, cheese, meat and fruit are very largely brought from abroad. The very poorest are dependent on foreign commodities for the means of subsistence, and it is of the greatest importance for the population of England, as a whole, that goods imported from abroad should be plentiful and cheap. Frequent and easy intercourse are a necessity to us in our present condition ; we could not reverse the free trade policy, on which we have entered, without causing general and wide-spread suffering.

But this was not the case in former days : it may be said that in a country such as England, in the time of Edward III, the protection of home industries was the preferable policy in the interest of the public at large. If the rich paid more for fine cloths and wine, the poor were none the worse off. Protection served to create additional employment for English labourers. Where the mass of the people in any country make little or no use of foreign commodities, they do not feel the advantage which results from measures which render imports cheaper to the consumer; while they do benefit by having employment opened up or secured to them. Many of the colonies are in a condition somewhat similar to that of England under Edward III, and hence democratic governments are inclined, by hostile tariffs, to render foreign manufactures dearer, with a view to providing additional employment. Those who consume foreign luxuries are worse served and pay more, but a local industry can be planted and artificially fostered, so that employment may be provided for colonial producers. At the same time it is at least open to doubt whether any country is so well supplied with all the necessaries of life—including say clothes and boots— that it is economically wise, in the interests of its public, to adopt a line of policy which is unfavourable to the consumers of foreign goods.

In the case of England at the present day, when we are dependent on foreign sources for the necessaries of life, this economic considera- *Direct bearing of free* tion is paramount over all others. In other *trade.* countries, however, it may be an open question whether it is not wise to sacrifice some economic advantage for a political or social gain. The less developed countries of the world have their ambitions. They know that opportunities for culture of every kind and possibilities of importance in the world are precluded to a country with a very sparse population. They may prefer to secure an artisan or town population, as well as a rural one, and they may be prepared to make an economic sacrifice for this object. It is thus that the question of free trade raises issues which lie outside the scope of economics. There is no doubt where the economic advantage lies in the case of countries which are dependent on other lands for articles of common consumption; but the economic advantage of one course or the other is not so clear in the case of countries which only import luxuries from abroad. And when the economic question is decided, the political result from one course or the other must be weighed, before the matter can be settled. Under the circumstances it is difficult for Englishmen to hope that, though demonstrably the best for themselves, the policy of free trade will be very readily adopted by other countries.

At the same time, though the McKinley Bill and other hostile tariffs have raised, in recent times, many new barriers to complete freedom of commercial intercourse, there can be no doubt that it is, on the whole, increasing. The total volume of commerce is greater, and different countries are becoming more and more economically interdependent. Communication is now so easy that a very small amount of advantage renders it possible to drive a profitable trade. The progress that is continually going on, in opening up half-civilised or savage countries, brings about new developments of trade; and there is now regular and frequent intercourse with regions that were wholly unexplored a century ago.

134. If we turn to consider the internal condition of

Commercial intercourse as the solvent of social organisation.

England, there can be little doubt that the development of commerce, with its reaction on industry, has enormously promoted the material well-being of the country.

When we compare the present condition of England with
the state of affairs at the accession of Elizabeth we see how
greatly she has increased in material prosperity.   From
being an insignificant island realm she has come to take her
place as one of the great powers ; and her political importance has come through the wealth obtained by her commerce.   Population, too, is about six or seven times as
large as it was, and though the standard of comfort of
the lowest class in the community has not been raised, and
there is no preventive check to the undue multiplication of
the unfit, the great body of artisans have risen to a position
where they can command far better housing and clothing
than were available in the time of Elizabeth.   Commerce
gives them certain commodities at lower prices than they
can be produced in England.   Commerce has opened up
opportunities of employment that they could not otherwise
have had; it has contributed in every way to their material
prosperity.   On this point we need hardly be left in doubt
when we read the accounts of the frequent famines of the
Middle Ages, or of the almost chronic pestilences of the fifteenth and seventeenth centuries.   There is no need to fear
a recurrence of the former evil so long as we can draw our
food supplies from a large area; the disappearance of the
latter implies the removal of those insanitary conditions which
gave it such a firm hold.   The death rate, so far as we can
get at it, gives us a physical and, therefore, a definite means
of estimating the standard of comfort which was available
in past centuries.

But this improvement in material prosperity throughout
the country has gone on simultaneously with
other changes in internal conditions.   Commercial intercourse is a solvent which breaks
up industrial organisation.   Commerce brings different

*Self-suffi-
ciency and in-
terconnexion.*

groups or nations into economic interdependence, and is incompatible with the economic self-sufficiency which is favourable for the growth of long-lived institutions.

There was a time in England, before the Norman Conquest, when each manor or village was a self-sufficing group, as there are districts in India where the same thing holds good to-day. They possessed a good deal of collectivist organisation. The wants of the villages seem to have been supplied from its own resources, before anything was sold to outsiders. The swineherd and the beeherd may be regarded as village officials, who looked after one department and had a claim to support from their neighbours. Village artisans could meet the requirements of the place sufficiently. There was but little need for intercourse with the outside world, and there was no need for change in mutual relations within the group. But internal commerce soon broke all this down. The farmer now buys what he needs at the market town, and the village artisan is left unemployed, while each man utilises his land as he judges best, and all trace of collectivist organisation within the group disappears. The village, instead of being a small but self-sufficing economic whole, has sunk into being a mere rural element in the life of that larger economic whole—the country. Through commerce it comes to specialise in its production, and to buy those things which it has no advantage for making. It loses its economic self-sufficiency and the completeness of its economic organisation.

In a similar way, if we look back to the condition of England at the beginning of the reign of George III, we may say that it was, especially if its dependencies are taken into account, a self-sufficing country. At that time there was a curiously complete economic organisation of national affairs. Parliament expended an immense amount of care on the national direction of enterprise into certain channels which were regarded as advantageous, and which helped to build up the power of the country. Many measures were taken by the nation to plant, foster, and protect such industries as might afford remunerative employment for the population. Special attention was given to the national food supply, and such encouragement was bestowed on agriculture as might ensure a constant and regular supply of corn. The proper training of workmen was provided for, and there was, on paper at least, a machinery for ensuring him sufficient remuneration; while those who were unable or unwilling to work were kept alive, rather than cared for, by means of the Poor Law. There was a great system of commercial and industrial organisation, which took cognisance of every side of the industrial life of the nation. But the increased opportunities afforded by commerce, and the specialisation into a great manufacturing country, which is a very recent development, have broken down this great organisation. Enterprise is no longer controlled; it seeks its own channels. Industry has resented fostering care and asked to be let alone. Our food supply comes in the ordinary course of trade. The training of the workman is not systematic, and his wages are allowed to change in accordance with market fluctuations. The Poor Law, recast indeed, still remains as the sole surviving element in the great system of national economic organisation. Commerce has broken down that system, or has, at least, given free play to the special industrial developments which outgrew and superseded it altogether.

It would be easy to illustrate this action of commercial intercourse from the changes which are going on in India at the present time. It is enough to say that economic interdependence implies

Fluctuation and organisation.

fluctuation and changes, while thorough-going organisation
has grown most readily in the stable conditions furnished by
the self-sufficiency of a given group.   There were, of course,
institutions for carrying on commerce in the towns; in
these centres of commerce, there has been a strange faci-
lity in taking new departures and entering on new developments as the circumstances of trade have changed.   But
the systematic organisation of economic life is a different
matter.   There is an element of instability in the social
system wherever commercial intercourse comes in.   It has
served as a solvent in the past, and any attempts, made at
the complete economic organisation of society in the future,
must face the problem of how to take account of commerce
and the variations which it causes.   Can it be excluded and
a condition of primitive simplicity secured, or can it be controlled so that it will not react on the social fabric?   Is it
possible to devise a thorough-going economic organisation
of society in countries, which are very diverse in habit and
tradition, and are yet economically interdependent on one
another?   If such organisation is possible, would it rest on
a cosmopolitan or a national basis?   These are questions
suggested by the breakdown of social organisations in the
past.   The answers lie hidden in the future.

At any rate we may see, when we remember the gradual
process which has undermined the social life of the past,
that there is little hope of reproducing it successfully.   The
conditions under which medieval craft gilds or yeoman
farmers flourished are gone for ever.   We must look forward
and frame ideals for the future, which shall take account
of all the new powers which have come into man's hands
for subduing nature.   But we may also do well to turn at
times to the past.   The better we understand the circumstances under which economic life has flourished or has

succumbed, the better shall we be able to forecast the conditions, which will be most favourable for the realisation of
our aims in time to come.

135. The influence exerted by commercial intercourse
in breaking down old social institutions has
also reacted curiously on the economic re- Modern
lationships and responsibilities of individuals. complications
So long as each man was practically restricted and individual
duty.
to one neighbourhood, or confined within certain definite
limits of trade, there was little room for independent
action. Within each isolated group each individual stood in
known relationships to other persons. The harshness of a
lord to his serfs, or the negligence of a master in not *finding*
his apprentice properly, were definite acts which could be
easily brought home, and for which the blame could be
properly affixed. Similarly, the producer stood in very close
relations to the consumer for many purposes, and "fairness
as between man and man" could be made to cover ordinary
trading transactions, while conventional rules and a privileged position could be used to regulate the conditions of
foreign trade and to limit attempts at extortion. The sphere
for personal independent action was limited, and hence
the discharge of personal duty was comparatively easy.

To put it in the simplest way, if wrong were done, it was
comparatively easy to make restitution. Each group was
comparatively isolated, and economic relations were close and
direct. In modern times, on the other hand, when goods
go to market and are bought at market, there are many
intervening links between the producer and the consumer.
The man who does bad work may never know who is the
sufferer, nor is the person who buys goods as a great
bargain, at a price that must be unremunerative to the
producer, able to trace out the person by whose labour and

at whose expense he has gained.   If he pays more than he is asked, he has no reason to suppose that the person who has been sweated will be the better for it.   Hence an un-satisfactory state of affairs arises; economic wrong is done, and those whose action occasions it feel they can neither help it nor make up for it.   They have no direct personal responsibility.   The intervention of so many markets and so many intermediaries has removed it out of that range of personal action within which it fell in earlier times.

But while the break-down of the old social isolation has
Personal influence.
reduced the sense of personal responsibility, it has also given a far wider bearing to the economic action of individuals—both in time and place.   To give to a poor man in times when there was little freedom of movement was an isolated act.   Each case of hardship was an individual one about which there might be very full knowledge and which could be treated on its merits.   But since the Tudor period, when the vagrant class came into prominence, all this is changed: the indirect and ulterior effects have to be considered as more important than those that are immediate.   Open-handed beneficence may tend to create and perpetuate an idle and vagrant class: the very means which have been taken for the relief of the poor may aggravate the evil.   Wherever it is possible for a man to count on regular relief, or to obtain indiscriminate charity without working, the motives to shirk the ordinary routine of life are greatly strengthened, and the growth of pauperism is stimu-lated.   Thus it may easily happen that action, intended for the relief of the poor, will ultimately and indirectly increase the very evil it was meant to prevent.   This knowledge does not of course diminish the duty of trying to help the poor, it only imposes an additional duty of being circum-spect and considerate in our efforts to relieve them.

x.] *Results of Increased Commercial Intercourse.* **253**

But commercial intercourse also gives a new character to our relations with distant peoples. We are brought into contact with them and indirectly exercise an influence upon them. Cosmopoli-tan influence. So long as trade was confined to special points or to factories this was hardly the case, but the opening up of half-civilised countries to the traders of all nations has led to a sudden influx of European commodities and Western ideas. The sense of duty to native races and to dependent peoples is far stronger than it was a century ago, when national feeling was far more exclusive than it is now, and obscured the sense of humanitarian duties. It is strange to note the indignation expressed by Whitfield at the restrictions placed on the English in Georgia, which prevented them from supplying rum to the natives or from possessing slaves. The ordinary religious conscience is more enlightened now ; it has come to recognise that we, as a nation, have a real duty towards all those people whom we influence through our commercial relationships.

We are thus brought face to face with more than one economic influence which is so indirect and far-reaching that it cannot be effectively controlled by any single individual. There is need here for collective moral action : within the sphere of direct personal relation, the old moral duties of fair dealing remain. In the larger areas where markets intervene and individual action is powerless, there must be collective action through constituted authority to enforce duty in economic matters. It is easy to say that men cannot be made moral by Acts of Parliament, but it is true to reply that Acts of Parliament can enforce the performance of any duties to which the public conscience is really awake.

136. The differences, which separate the industrial life of the present from that of any earlier cen- Conclusion.

tury, are so complex as to render it exceedingly difficult
to apply the results of historical investigation directly to
the practical questions of our time. But though our
knowledge may not supply us with cut and dried formulae
for the regeneration of society to-day, it will help us
to understand our own age more truly. By tracing the
origin and growth of existing evils we may discover how
deep-seated they are, and how difficult to eradicate: we
may be able to make a more accurate diagnosis and to
state more clearly the problems which press for solution.
History may not repeat itself, but conditions, which are
more or less similar, do recur; and we can, at least, glean
suggestions from the past as to remedies which may be
tried with some prospect of success. We may receive
warnings and learn to detect some of the dangers that lurk
in many well-meant efforts for improvement; by so doing
we may reap a benefit from past disasters and profit by the
experience of bygone generations. It is, in some ways,
an admirable training to study some burning questions, as
they presented themselves to, and were worked out by,
former generations of men. Where our personal interests
are unaffected, and our private passions remain unroused,
we can, perhaps, more easily do justice to both sides of
a case; and those, who have learned to be fair in their
judgments on the dead, are more likely to be fair also in
controversies with the living. Enthusiasts who seek some
Utopian scheme, which will heal all disorders, may turn from
history in disgust; for them it may have no message. But
those, who patiently face the fresh difficulties which each
new age presents, will find that they can study them more
thoroughly and deal with them more wisely, if they do not
altogether disdain such help as may be gained from an
impartial study of the past.

CHRONOLOGICAL TABLE

	Immigrants to Britain. Physical Conditions (Chs. I., II.)	Manors. Agriculture (Chs. III., VIII.)
400 500 600 700	c. 449—600. **English Conquest.** 597. Roman Mission (Augustine). 635. Columban Mission (Aidan). 787—1042. Danish invasions, settlement, conquest and rule.	410. Romans leave Britain.
800 900		991. Etheldred II. levies Danegeld.
1000	1066—70. **Norman Conquest.** 1066. Devastation of North. Immigration of Norman artisans. Cistercian monasteries founded.	1051. Abolition of Danegeld. 1066—70. Norman Conquest. 1084. Revival of Danegeld. 1086. Compilation of *Domesday Book.*
1100		1130, 1156— *Pipe Rolls.*
1200		1175—1253. Grosseteste's *Rules.* Walter of Henley's *Husbandry.* 1236. Statute of Merton.
1300	1313—90. Regulation of Staple. 1331, 1336, &c. Influx of Flemings. Introduction of 'old' drapery. **c. 1350—c. 1600. Sheep-farming at expense of tillage.**	1327. *Extent of Borley.* 1348—50. Black Death. c. 1350—c. 1600. Sheep-farming, depopulation, and enclosures (for pasture). 1351. Statute of Labourers. 1381. Peasants' Revolt.
1400	Encouragement to English shipping.	1459. Complaints at Coventry *re* enclosures.
1500	1492. America discovered by Columbus.	Hen. **VII.** Convertible husbandry. 1517. Inquisition into enclosures. 1523. Fitzherbert's *Treatises.*
	1561—82. Immigration of Dutch, Flemish and French artisans. Eliz. Introduction of 'new' drapery.	1574. **Commission on villeinage.**

Towns. Labour and Capital (Chs. IV., IX.)	National Economic Life (Chs. V., VI.)	Money, Credit, and Finance (Ch. VII.)
597. Introduction of Christianity.		
	c. 790. Commercial treaty between Offa and Charles the Great.	
901—925 Edward the Elder fortifies Mercia.	918. Lewisham granted to Benedictine monastery at Ghent.	
1086. Domesday Survey taken.		
1095. First Crusade.		
Hen. I. Rise of Weavers' gilds.	Hen. I., Hen. II. Organisation of Exchequer.	1125. Punishment of dishonest moneyers.
Hen. II. Assize of Bread.	Hen. II. Connexion w. Gascony.	Hen. II. Re-organisation of Mint.
1190. Leicester Charter.	„ Assize of Bread.	
1197. Assize of Measures.	1197. Assize of Measures.	1181. Assize of Arms.
	Hen. III. Heavy papal taxation.	
Rise of Gilds Merchant.	Edw. I. Mint Regulations.	
1205. Coventry Bakers' Gild.	1277—83. Welsh Wars.	
1254. Riot at Reading.	1283. Statute of Acton Burnell.	1275. Antiqua Custuma.
c. 1266. Assize of Bread.	1285. Statute of Winchester.	1292. Statute de Moneta.
Edw. I. Migration from Northampton.	1290. Expulsion of Jews,	1297. Confirmation of Charters.
1270. Last Crusade.	1295. Model Parliament.	
1272. Riot at Norwich.	1296— Wars against Scotland.	1299. Statute de falsa Moneta.
1295. Model Parliament.		
1321. Submission of London Weavers.	Edw. III. Mint Regulations.	1303. Nova Custuma.
	1328. Complaints about aulnager.	1334. Financial agreement fixing tenths and fifteenths.
1327. Disturbance at Reading.	1313—90. Organisation of Staple.	
	1331, 1336. Immigration of Flemings.	
	1339—1453. Hundred Years War.	1335. Export of bullion without licence forbidden.
1345. Grocers' Company.	1351. Statute of Labourers.	
1348—50. Black Death.	1353. Statute of Staple.	
1381. Peasants' Revolt.	1360. Treaty of Bretigni.	1347, 1348. Rise in prices.
Edw. III. Craft Gilds.	1376. Good Parliament.	1351. Issue of lighter coins.
„ Drapers appear as dealers.	Ric. II. Attempts to restrict to one calling.	1377, 1381. Poll taxes.
„ Rise of Livery Companies.	1381. Encouragement to shipbuilding.	
	1381. Export of bullion prohibited.	
	1403. Treaty with Castile.	
	Hen. V., VI., VII. Encouragement of ship-building.	1412, 1464. Debasement of coinage.
Rural migration checked.	1429. 'Rovers of Sea.'	
	1465. Regulation of Cloth trade.	
	1474. Treaty with Hansards.	
	1480. Search for Brazil.	1472. Subsidy.
1455—85. Wars of Roses.	1485. Consul at Pisa.	
1465. Cloth trade regulated on capitalistic lines.	1490. Treaty with Iceland.	
Struggles between journeymen and weavers.	Treaty with Florence.	
	1492. Discovery of America by Columbus.	
Remissions of taxation.	1496. 'Magnus Intercursus.'	
	Rise of Merchant adventurers.	
	Hen. VIII., Edw. VI. Restrictions on possession of sheep.	
	1513. Arsenal at Deptford.	Hen. VIII. Debasement of coinage.
	1514. Incorporation of Brethren of Trinity House.	1514. General subsidy.
1517. 'Evil May Day.'	1517. Inquisition into enclosures.	
1519. Jurisdiction of Mayor asserted at York.	1548. Combination Law.	American mines.
Hen. VIII. Growth of new towns.	1555. Surveyors of highways.	
	1558. Migration from towns checked.	1551. Further debasement.
1552. Gig mills condemned.	1562. Almsgiving made compulsory.	1561. Coinage purified.
1555. Weavers' Act.	1563. Statute of Artificers.	
	1563. Act for encouragement of navy	
1563. Statute of Apprentices.	1565. Walloons at Norwich.	
	1570. Dutch Baymakers at Colchester.	
1589. Lee's knitting frame.	1581. Turkey Company incorporated.	

		Immigrants to Britain. Physical Conditions (Chs. I., II.)	Manors. Agriculture (Chs. III., VIII.)
1600		Newfoundland fishery.	Advance in theory. Markham, Weston, Plat, etc. write *Treatises*. Cultivation of root crops.
		1634, 1649— Draining of Fens. 1651, 1660. Navigation Acts.	1649— Vermuïden drains fens.
		1685. Immigration of French refugees.	1689. Corn Bounty Act.
1700			Improvements in practice, e.g. rotation of crops, cultivation of grasses.
		1709. Immigration from Palatinate. 1713. Treaty of Utrecht, Assiento contract.	1710— Enclosures (for tillage).
		1741. General Highway Act. 1760. Manchester and Worsley canal. 1760. Roebuck's blast furnace.	1759. Duke of Bridgewater employs Brindley
			1773—93. Exportation of corn ceases. 1773. Corn Law. 1776. Declaration of Independence.
		Water power and machinery.	1793—1815. Revolutionary and Napoleonic Wars. Decline of yeomanry. 1795. Allowances to labourers. Decline of domestic spinning.
1800			Fluctuation of prices.
		1815. Macadam appointed Surveyor.	1812. 'Swing' riots. 1815. Corn Law. 1815—46. Depression of Agriculture. 1832. Reform Bill. 1834. Thorough drainage advocated. 1846. Repeal of Corn Laws. 1846—74. Agricultural revival

Towns. Labour and Capital (Chs. IV., IX.)	National Economic Life (Chs. V., VI.)	Money, Credit, and Finance (Ch. VII.)
Town purchases of coal.	1600. East India Company.	
	1601. Poor Law.	
	1601. Saltpetre patent retained.	
	1612. E. I. Co. charter renewed.	
	1624. Sheffield Cutlers incorporated.	
	1624. Patents and monopolies limited.	
	1631. Baltimore destroyed by pirates.	
	1634. Ship money writs.	1634—39. Ship money.
	c. 1634. Linen manufacture in Ulster.	Commonwealth. Monthly assessments.
	1651, 1660. Navigation Acts.	
	1662. Parochial settlements.	„ Excise.
	1665. Aulnagers for Ireland.	1660. Commutation for Feudal dues.
	Ch. II. Negociations with pirates.	
	1665—97. Western clothiers in Ireland.	1666. Coinage of guineas.
	1666. Export of Irish cattle prohibited.	
	1670. Kidderminster Carpet Weavers.	1670. Closing of Exchequer.
	1684. Sandys v. E. I. Company.	
	1689. Bill of Rights.	
	1689. Corn Bounty Act.	
	1694. Bank of England founded.	1694. Bank of England founded.
	1697. Duties on Irish cloth.	1695. Bank of Scotland founded.
	1698. Eddystone lighthouse.	
	1698—1708. Struggle between London and General E. I. Co.	1696. Recoinage (Newton).
Abuses among Framework Knitters.	England v. France in India and America.	
	1703. Methuen Treaty.	
	1704. Importation of naval stores favoured.	1720. Failure of South Sea Scheme.
	1707. Act of Union with Scotland.	
	1709. Re-issue of Assize of Bread.	
	1721—42. Walpole's ministry.	
	1723. General Workhouse Act.	1721—42. Walpole. Reform of tariffs.
1733. Kay's flying shuttle.	1728, 1756. Wages assessed in Shropshire.	
1748. Paul's wool-carding machine.	1732. Export of American hats forbidden.	
1760. Flying shuttle in the cotton trade.	1741. General Highway Act.	
1767. Hargreaves' spinning jenny.	1763. Conquest of French Canada.	
1769. Arkwright's spinning roller.	1776. Declaration of Independence.	1776. A. Smith's *Wealth of Nations.*
1779. Crompton's mule.	1780. Irish commercial disabilities removed.	
1785. Cartwright's power loom.		
1785. Boulton and Watt's steam engine at Papplewick.	1782. Gilbert's Act.	1783—1806. Pitt. Simplification of Taxation.
1790. Cartwright's wool combing machine.	1793—1815. Revolutionary and Napoleonic Wars.	
Kelly utilises water power.	1795. 'Speenhamland' decision.	1797. Triple Assessment.
1793—1815. Revolutionary and Napoleonic Wars.	1795. 'Minimum' wage proposed.	1797. Suspension of cash payments.
	1796. Allowances further legalised.	
1799, 1800. Combination Laws.	1799, 1800. Combination Laws.	
1802, 1819, 1833, 1847. Factory Acts.	1800, 1808. 'Minimum' wage proposed.	
1803. Johnson's dressing machine.	1802, 1816, 1833, 1847. Factory Acts.	
1812, 1816. Luddite riots.	1809. Restrictions on Cloth trade removed.	
1816. Eastern Counties bread riots.		
1825. Bradford Wool combers' strike.	1813. Trade with India opened. Stat. of 1563 re wages repealed.	
1841. Regulation of Child labour in mines.	1814. „ „ „ apprentices „	
c. 1840. Power weaving supersedes hand work.	1815. Corn Law.	1816. Demonetisation of silver.
	1818. Piracy in Mediterranean ceases.	
1846. Incorporation of Manchester.	1824. Emigration permitted.	1819. Resumption of cash payments.
	1824, 1825. Repeal of Combination Laws.	1824—28. Huskisson's revision of tariffs.
1849. Cholera.	1846. Repeal of Corn Laws.	1842—46. Peel's financial reforms.
1856. Canongate, Broughton, Portsborow absorbed in Edinburgh.	1849. Repeal of Navigation Laws.	1844. Bank Charter Act.

BIBLIOGRAPHY.

IN reading generally upon the subject some confusion may arise from the divergent and sometimes conflicting views which are expressed by different writers. It should be the aim of the student, in all cases of apparently conflicting opinion, to follow out the matter so as to be able either to reconcile difficulties, or to form a judgment as to the reasons for differences. As a guide in this direction, a few notes have been added in regard to some of the books recommended below.

As already stated in the Preface, those who desire to study any part of the subject in greater detail are recommended to consult the corresponding portion of Dr Cunningham's *Growth of English Industry and Commerce* (Early and Middle Ages, 4th edit. 1905, and Modern Times, 4th edit. 1907). They will there find accurate references to a much larger number of authorities than can be included in this list.

Professor A. J. Ashley in his *Economic History* (vol. I. 1888) covers the ground from the Norman Conquest to the sixteenth century; he lays great stress on the arguments drawn from the analogy of Continental life.

Professor Thorold Rogers has treated agriculture, commerce and industry from the thirteenth century onwards in great detail, in his *History of Agriculture and Prices in England* (7 vols. 1866—1902), *Six Centuries of Work and Wages* (1886), *Economic Interpretation of History* (1891), *Industrial and Commercial Supremacy of England* (1892). He has for the most part fixed his attention on the records of prices, and has made little use of the help which may be obtained from other sources of evidence in interpreting them. Mr H. de B. Gibbins in his *Industrial England* (**1896**) has summarised Prof. Thorold Rogers' conclusions in a concise form.

Many useful articles will be found in *Social England*, edited by Mr H. D. Traill, in the *Dictionary of Political Economy*, edited by Mr R. H. Inglis Palgrave, and in the *Cambridge Modern History*.

I. IMMIGRANTS TO BRITAIN.

Cunningham, W. *Alien Immigrants to England* in the Social England Series (1898).

II. PHYSICAL CONDITIONS.

Articles *on the Distribution of Towns and Villages in England*, by G. C. Chisholm in *The Geographical Journal* (1897).

III. THE MANORS.

Davenport, F. G. *List of Printed Original Materials for English Manorial and Agrarian history &c.* (Radcliffe College Monographs, no. 6. 1894).

Gasquet, F. A. *The Great Pestilence* (1893).

Walter of Henley. *Husbandry* (edit. E. Lamond 1890).

Maitland, F. W. *Domesday Book and Beyond* (1897).

Page, T. W. *The end of villeinage in England* (1900).

Pollock, Sir F., and Maitland, F. W. *History of English Law* (1898).

Seebohm, F. *The English Village Community* (1883).

Trevelyan, G. M. *England in the Age of Wycliffe* ch. VI (1899).

Vinogradoff, P. *Villainage in England* (1892).

Vinogradoff, P. *The growth of the Manor* (1905).

Vinogradoff, P. *English Society in the eleventh century* (1908).

IV. THE TOWNS.

Bateson, Mary. *Borough Customs* (1904—).

Bateson, Mary. *Records of the Borough of Leicester* (1899—).

Clode, C. M. *The Early History of the Guild of Merchant Taylors* (1888).

Conder, E. *Records of the Hole Crafte and Fellowship of Masons* (1894).

Green, Alice S. *Town Life in the Fifteenth Century* (1894).
Archives of the Grocers' Company (edit. J. A. Kingdon 1886).
Gross, C. *The Gild Merchant* (1890).
Harris, M. Dormer. *Life in an Old English Town* (1898).
Hudson, W. *Leet Jurisdiction in the City of Norwich* (Selden Soc. 1892).
Madox, T. *Firma Burgi* (1726).
Maitland, F. W. *Pleas in the Court &c. in the Fair of St Ives* in *Select Pleas in Manorial and other Seignorial Courts* (Selden Soc. 1889).
Records of the Borough of Nottingham (1882—1889).
Smith, J. Toulmin. *English Gilds* (1870).
Stow, J. *Survey of the Cities of London and Westminster* (edit. J. Strype, 1720, or edit. C. L. Kingsford, 1908).
Unwin, G. *The Gilds and Companies of London* (1908).

V. NATIONAL ECONOMIC LIFE—ITS BEGINNINGS.

Gross, C. *Select cases concerning the Law Merchant* (1908).
Hall, H. *History of the Customs Revenue in England* (1885).
Hall, H. *Antiquities and Curiosities of the Exchequer* (1891).
Madox, T. *History and Antiquities of the Exchequer* (1711).
Pipe Roll Society's Publications.

VI. i. FOOD SUPPLY.

Cobden, R. *Political Writings* (1878).
Smith, Adam. *Inquiry into the Nature and Causes of the Wealth of Nations* (edit. J. S. Nicholson 1887).
Smith, C. *Three tracts on the Corn-Trade and Corn-Laws* (1766).
Cunningham, W. *Rise and decline of the Free Trade Movement* (1905).

ii. INDUSTRIAL LIFE.

Aschrott, P. F., and Preston-Thomas, H. *The English Poor Law System* &c. (1902).
Brentano, L. *On the History and development of gilds and the origin of Trade-Unions* (1870).

Eden, Sir F. M. *The State of the Poor* (1797).

Leonard, E. M. *The early history of English Poor Relief* (1900).

Mackay, T. *History of the English Poor Law*, being Vol. III. of Sir George Nicholls' work (1899).

Nicholls, Sir George. *History of English Poor Law* (edit. by H. G. Willink, 1898).

Report from His Majesty's Commissioners for inquiring into the administration and practical operation of the Poor Laws. Reports, 1834, XXVII (Reprinted 1905).

Unwin, G. *Industrial Organisation in the sixteenth and seventeenth centuries* (1904).

iii. COMMERCIAL DEVELOPMENT.

Egerton, H. E. *Short History of British colonial policy* (1905).

Hewins, W. A. S. *English Trade and Finance chiefly in the seventeenth century* (1892).

Levi, L. *History of British Commerce* &c. (1872).

Lindsay, W. S. *History of Merchant Shipping and Ancient Commerce* (1874).

Macpherson, D. *Annals of Commerce* (1805).

Records of the Merchant Adventurers of Newcastle (Surtees Soc. 1899).

Sellers, Maud. *Acts and Ordinances of the Eastland Company* (1906).

iv. ECONOMIC POLICY.

Levi, L. *History of British Commerce* &c. (1872).

Mun, Sir T. *England's Treasure by Forraign Trade* (1664) in Select Collections of Early English Tracts on Commerce (edit. J. R. Macculloch, 1856).

Smith, Adam. *Inquiry into the Nature and Causes of the Wealth of Nations* (edit. J. S. Nicholson 1887).

Wakefield, E. G. *A view of the Art of Colonization with present reference to the British Empire* (1849).

VII. MONEY, CREDIT, AND FINANCE.

Cannan, E.   *The History of Local Rates in England* (1896).
Dowell, S.   *A History of Taxation and Taxes in England* (1884).
Jevons.   *Money* (1875).
Rogers, J. E. Thorold.   *The first nine years of the Bank of England* (1887).
Shaw, W. A.   *The history of Currency* (1896).

VIII. AGRICULTURE.

Fitzherbert.   *Boke of Husbandry* (1523).
Hales, J.   *Brief discourse of the Common Weal* (edit. E. Lamond 1893).
Hasbach, W.   *History of the English Agricultural Labourer* (translated by Ruth Kenyon, 1908).
Leadam, J. S.   *The Domesday of Inclosures* 1517—1518 (1897)
Prothero, R. E.   *Pioneers and Progress of English Farming* (1888).
Report from the Select Committee on Agriculture.   Reports 1883, v.
Toynbee, A.   *Lectures on the Industrial Revolution in England* (1884).
Tusser, T.   *Five Hundred Points of Good Husbandry* (edit. W. Mayor 1812).
Young, A.   *A Six Months' Tour through the North of England* (1770).
Young, A.   *A Six Weeks' Tour through the Southern Counties of England and Wales* (1772).
Young, A.   *Farmer's Tour through the East of England* (1771).
Young, A.   *Tour in Ireland* (1780).
Report on the Employment of Women and Children in Agriculture.   Reports, 1843, XII.

IX. LABOUR AND CAPITAL.

Engels, F.   *The Condition of the Working Class in England in* 1844, transl. by Florence K. Wischnewetzky (1892).

Hutchins, B. L., and Harrison, A.   *A history of Factory Legislation* (1907).

Holyoake, G. J.   *The History of Co-operation* (1906).

Reports from Assistant Handloom Weavers' Commissioners. Reports 1840, XXIII, XXIV.

Reports of Commissioners as to the Employment of Children in Factories (Factories Inquiry Commission).   Reports 1833, XX, XXI.

Reports of Commissioners under the Children's Employment Commission (Mines).   Reports 1842, XV.

Toynbee, A.   *Lectures on the Industrial Revolution* (1884).

Wallas, G.   *Life of Francis Place* 1771—1854 (1898).

Webb, S. and B.   *History of Trade Unionism* (1902).

Webb, S. and B.   *Industrial Democracy* (1902).

X. INCREASED COMMERCIAL INTERCOURSE.

Gibbins, H. de B.   *Economic and Industrial progress of the century* (1903).

Levi, L.   *History of British Commerce* &c. (1872).

XI. BIBLIOGRAPHIES.

Cunningham, W.   *Growth of English Industry* &c.   Modern Times, Part II. pp. 942—998 (1907).

The Cambridge Modern History.   Bibliographies connected with sections on economic history.

The Dictionary of Political Economy (edited by R. H. Inglis Palgrave) contains bibliographies appended to articles.

INDEX.

Finance, Dutch 159
Financial policy, of Huskisson 164
,, ,, North 163
,, ,, Peel 164
,, ,, Pitt 163
,, ,, Walpole **162,**
163, 164
Fish, **21**
Fisheries, **21, 124, 125, 132**
,, Dutch 125
,, herring 21
Fitzherbert, Sir A. 175, 182
Flanders, 143, 147, 182
Flax, **15**, 126, 217
Flemings, immigration of **12, 14,**
97
Fluctuation, 249
Flying shuttle, 220, 230
Food, dearness of 188, 190
,, rents, 31
,, supply, 82, 118, 121, 138,
177, 184, 247, 249
Foreigners, **57**
Forest of Dean, **9**, 18
Forests, 19
Frame rents, 206
Framework Knitters, 206, **213**
France, 116, 124, 129, 130, 163
Francigenæ, 50
Freedom, economic 101, 108
,, of association 54, **101,**
104, 108
,, **of** employment 101, 103,
104
,, of movement 101, **102**
Freeholders, small **191**, 192
Free trade, 165, 243, 244, 245, 246
Friendly Societies, 234
Frieze, 136
Fruit, 244
Fuel, 19, 26, 126, **135,** 184, **243**
Fuller, 204
Fulling mills, 206
Furniture, 31

Galway, **123**
Gardens, 196
Genoese, 125
George III, 186, **248**
Georgia, **253**

Germany, **136**
Gig-mills, **206**
Gilbert's **Act,** 94
Gild merchant, **54, 60, 62, 63**
,, ,, at Preston 62
,, ,, at Shrewsbury 63
,, ,, privileges of 55, 56
Gilds, **105**
,, Bakers' 56
,, of journeymen 65
Glastonbury, 14
Gloucestershire, 23, 91
Gold, 127, 128, 129, 142, 147, **149**
Gold lace, 98
Goldsmiths, 146, 149, 161
Gott, Mr 222
Government, local 46
,, municipal 13, **16**
Granaries, **55**
Granborough, 40
Grasses, 185, 192
Graziers, 138
Grazing, **20**, 178, 180, 192
,, rights 187, 231
Grocers, 63, 113
Gross, Dr 54, 62
Grosseteste, Bp. 30
Guards, 229
Guineas, 147
Gunpowder, 98

Hadrian's wall, **18**
Hales, J. 241
Halifax, 204
Handloom weavers, 224, 225, **226**
Hand-work, 226
Hansards, 53, **111**
Hanse. *See* Gild merchant
Harbours, 25, 113
Hardware, 23, **243**
Hargreaves, J. **220**
Harvest, 39
Hatfield Chase, **183**
Hats, 135
Hayward, 38
Hedging, **179**
Hemp, 126
Henry I, **142, 153**
Henry II, 105, **142**
Henry III, **154, 175**

For EU product safety concerns, contact us at Calle de José Abascal, 56–1°,
28003 Madrid, Spain or eugpsr@cambridge.org.

www.ingramcontent.com/pod-product-compliance
Ingram Content Group UK Ltd.
Pitfield, Milton Keynes, MK11 3LW, UK
UKHW042209180425
457623UK00011B/109